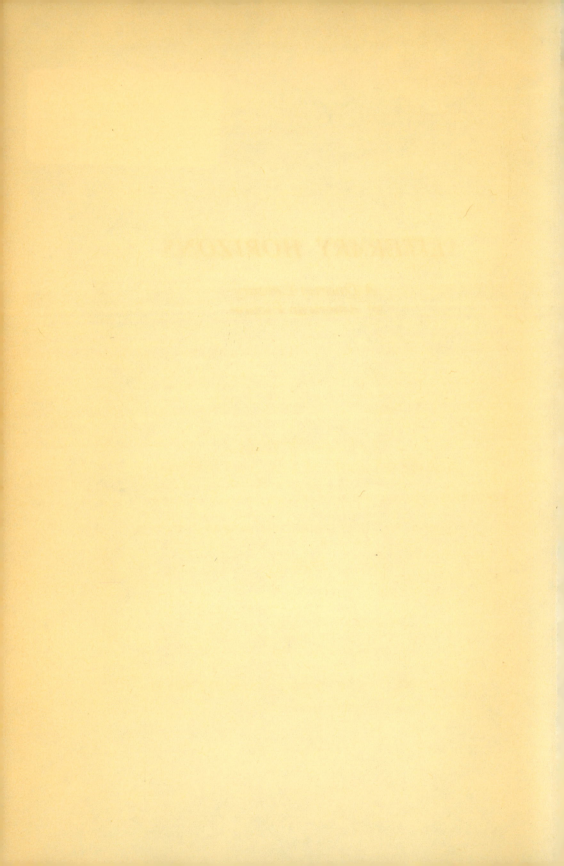

LITERARY HORIZONS

*A Quarter Century
of American Fiction*

LITERARY HORIZONS

A Quarter Century
of American Fiction

by Granville Hicks
with the assistance of Jack Alan Robbins

1970

NEW YORK: NEW YORK UNIVERSITY PRESS

© 1970 BY NEW YORK UNIVERSITY
LIBRARY OF CONGRESS CATALOG CARD NUMBER: 72-133011
ISBN: 0-8147-3354-9
MANUFACTURED IN THE UNITED STATES OF AMERICA

For Octavia

ACKNOWLEDGMENTS

For their permission to reprint the reviews mentioned below, thanks are due the following:

The Literary Guild Magazine for permission to reprint the review of Bernard Malamud's *Pictures of Fidelman,* June 1968.

The New York Times for permission to reprint the reviews of James Baldwin's *Giovanni's Room,* October 14, 1956; Kurt Vonnegut's *Player Piano,* August 17, 1952; and Vladimir Nabokov's *Pnin,* March 10, 1957. Copyright © 1952, 1956, 1957 by Granville Hicks.

The New Leader for permission to reprint the reviews of Wright Morris' *The Works of Love,* March 24, 1952; *The Deep Sleep,* September 21, 1953; *The Huge Season,* October 4, 1954; *The Field of Vision,* October 1, 1956; and *Love Among the Cannibals,* August 19, 1957; Saul Bellow's *The Adventures of Augie March,* September 21, 1953; and *Seize the Day,* November 26, 1956; Bernard Malamud's *The Assistant,* April 29, 1957; James Baldwin's *Go Tell It on the Mountain,* June 1, 1953; Flannery O'Connor's *A Good Man Is Hard to Find,* August 15, 1955; and Herbert Gold's *The Prospect Before Us,* March 1, 1954; and *The Man Who Was Not With It,* February 20, 1956. Copyright © 1952, 1953, 1954, 1955, 1956, 1957 American Labor Conference on International Affairs, Inc.

The Saturday Review for permission to reprint the reviews of: Wright Morris' *The Territory Ahead,* October 25, 1958; *Ceremony in Lone Tree,* July 9, 1960, *One Day,* February 20, 1965; *In Orbit,* February 18, 1967; and *A Bill of Rites, a Bill of Wrongs, a Bill of Goods,* March 16, 1968; Saul Bellow's *Henderson the Rain King,* February 21, 1959; and *Herzog,* September 19, 1964; Bernard Malamud's *The Magic Barrel,* May 17, 1958; *A New Life,* October 7, 1961; and *The Fixer,* September 10, 1966; James Baldwin's *Nobody Knows My Name,* July 1, 1961; *Blues for Mister Charlie,* May 2, 1964; *Another Country,* July 7, 1962; and *Tell Me How Long the Train's Been Gone,* June 1, 1968; John Updike's *The Poorhouse Fair,* January 17, 1959; *Rabbit, Run,* November 5, 1960; *Pigeon Feathers,* March 17, 1962; *The Centaur,* February 2, 1963; Assorted Prose, May 15, 1965; *Of the Farm,* November 13, 1965; *The Music School,* September 24, 1966; and *Couples,* April 6, 1968; Flannery O'Connor's *The Violent Bear It Away,* February 27, 1960; *Everything That Rises Must Converge,* May 29, 1965; and *Mystery and Manners* (collected by Sally and Robert Fitzgerald), May 10, 1969; Herbert Gold's *The Optimist,* April 25, 1959; *Therefore Be Bold,* October 11, 1960; and *Fathers,* March 25, 1967; Kurt Vonnegut's *God Bless You, Mister Rosewater,* April 3, 1965; and *Slaughterhouse Five,* March 29, 1969; Louis Auchincloss' *Venus in Sparta,* September 20, 1958; *Portrait in*

Brownstone, July 14, 1962; *Powers of Attorney,* August 17, 1963; *The Rector of Justin,* July 11, 1964; *Pioneers and Caretakers,* June 5, 1965; *The Embezzler,* February 5, 1966; and *Tales of Manhattan,* April 8, 1967; Vladimir Nabokov's *Lolita,* August 16, 1958; *The Gift,* June 1, 1963; and *Speak, Memory,* January 7, 1967; Joseph Heller's *Catch-22,* October 14, 1961; Reynolds Price's *A Long and Happy Life,* March 10, 1962; *The Names and Faces of Heroes,* June 29, 1963; *A Generous Man,* March 26, 1966; and *Love and Work,* May 25, 1968; Philip Roth's *Letting Go,* June 16, 1962; *When She Was Good,* June 17, 1967; and *Portnoy's Complaint,* February 22, 1969; John Barth's *The Floating Opera; The End of the Road; The Sot-Weed Factor,* July 3, 1965; *Giles Goat-Boy,* August 6, 1966; and *Lost in the Funhouse,* September 28, 1968; Norman Mailer's *Advertisements for Myself,* November 7, 1959; *An American Dream,* March 20, 1965; *Why Are We In Vietnam?,* September 16, 1967; and *Armies of the Night,* December 28, 1968.

Contents

LITERARY HORIZONS

A Quarter Century
of American Fiction

INTRODUCTION

I've been reviewing books for many years and, I'm afraid, have reviewed thousands of them. In college and for a time after I wrote reviews as a way of getting hold of books I wanted. Later they brought me a little pin money. In recent years reviewing has sometimes been my chief source of income.

Although I have reviewed books on a really shocking variety of subjects, fiction has always been my chosen field, and in the last couple of decades I have been able to devote myself largely to it. In the bi-weekly pieces I wrote for several years in the *New Leader* and in the "Literary Horizons" columns published weekly from 1958 to 1969 in *Saturday Review,* I looked for and, when I found them, kept an eye on promising young novelists. I also discussed books by and about some of the well-established novelists such as Faulkner and Hemingway and by such British figures as C. P. Snow, Iris Murdoch, Anthony Powell, and Anthony Burgess. But, in a manner of speaking, Young America has had first claim on my attention.

Therefore I can now compile a book such as this with the belief that it is not lacking in unity. With the assistance of Oscar Cargill and Jack Alan Robbins, I have selected fifteen novelists who seem to me both good writers and, in various ways, representative figures of the postwar period. Some I believe to have made substantial contributions to American literature; others are debatable but interesting.

I have reviewed most if not all of the fiction published by the fifteen writers in the past twenty-five years. The reviews of the novels by each of the sixteen are arranged, naturally, in chronological order, and one may follow, if he cares to, the shaping of an opinion. There are, of course, many contradictions, but there is also, unless I flatter myself, a substantial unity.

When I stopped writing for *Saturday Review*, some people wrote me to say that they were sorry. One of my correspondents, himself a book reviewer and the literary editor of a Western newspaper, said that he hoped I would prepare a text on how book reviews should be written. This is not my cup of tea, but it occurs to me that I might set forth some rules on which my own practice is, I hope, based.

1. Read the book. It should be unnecessary to say this, but, as anyone who reads reviews from a variety of newspapers and magazines knows, it isn't.

2. Read the book well. This is a more difficult admonition to obey. Even the most seasoned reviewer knows that he reads better under some circumstances than under others. It is not easy to devote your full attention to a novel when you have a toothache or have just received a hearty kick in the pants from the Internal Revenue Service, and yet many novels today demand nothing less. If possible, I like to wait a day or two after finishing a book before beginning my review, and I like to let the first draft wait for a day or two before I copy it and send it forever beyond the reach of second judgments.

3. Don't use the review as an opportunity for showing how much you know or how witty you can be. If a book doesn't deserve to be reviewed seriously, it probably doesn't deserve to be reviewed at all. A good wisecracking review can be very entertaining, but today TV offers a good market for wisecracks. I confess that sometimes I have been tempted by a book that was bad in pretentious ways to

poke fun at it. Readers often enjoy this sort of thing, and I've had fun myself, but as a general rule I suppress the urge.

4. Trust thyself, as Emerson said. At bottom all book reviewing is impressionistic. There are no set rules that can be relied on, no yardstick by which literary quality can be measured. Nevertheless an experienced reviewer develops general ideas about the nature of fiction that he more or less unconsciously applies to a novel as he reads it. When he sits down to review this particular novel, he may find that there is a conflict between the judgment he bases on these general ideas and his feeling about the book as a whole. Following the general ideas will make for a clear, orderly review, but it may seem to him wrong just the same. He may feel that he has missed the heart of the matter. Take, for instance, James Baldwin's *Another Country*: I couldn't deny that it violated the rules, and yet it seemed to me a powerful and memorable novel. As I look back, I believe that my impression was nearer right than my judgment, and I'm glad that I paid attention to the former. To be sure, there are educated tastes and ignorant tastes, tastes that are likely to coincide with the tastes of many well-informed people and tastes that are extravagantly eccentric, but a reviewer's taste is for better or worse his taste, and he does well to pay attention to it.

5. Tell what the book is about. There are circumstances in which this is unnecessary; for example in writing a critical article about a well-known author in a learned journal. But the average reviewer for a daily or weekly has to assume that his readers are not familiar with the book he is talking about. He owes it to them to tell them enough about the book so that they can decide whether they want to read it or not. He also has to tell enough about the book to make his criticisms comprehensible. Sometimes, in order to make what seems to him an important point, he has to tell how the book ends. This, I have discovered, is a practice to which many readers object: "You have spoiled this book for me; I shall never want to read it because you have told me how it comes out." I feel that this is a rather childish attitude unless what is involved is a mystery story. Be that as it may, one has to be careful not to tell either too much or too

little and not to be duller than necessary. Both a good deal of art
and a good deal of criticism can go into the summarizing of a novel
—or a play or a movie—and the reviewer ought to make the most
of his opportunities.

6. Take as large a view of the work in hand as it warrants. Almost any novel of merit is likely to suggest large thoughts about the
human condition, the destiny of man, the present state of society,
and so on. In so far as reflections on large topics of this sort are
really relevant to the book, they may add to the interest and value
of the review, but to use a book as text for a sermon or point of
departure for a polite essay seems to me unfair both to the author
of the book and to the reader of the review. Essay-reviews of the
far-ranging type have had a prominent place in English and American literature, especially in the nineteenth century, but any contemporary reviewer, it seems to me, had better think twice before
he undertakes one.

So much for the guiding lines that have been followed, I piously
hope, in the reviews reprinted here. For the rest, I want only to
repeat what I have said many times before: that the novel has
prospered in the years since World War II. Many people say that
the novel is dying. This may be true, just as it may be true that
Western Civilization is dying. But I believe that there is a good
deal of evidence in this book to show that the novel has not died yet.

WRIGHT MORRIS

Foreword

Of the American writers who developed after the beginning of World War II, the first to occupy my attention was Wright Morris, whose publisher sent me a copy of *My Uncle Dudley* in 1942. It was not until 1952, however, that I reviewed one of his books, *The Works of Love*. Although I hadn't reviewed the intervening volumes—three novels and two books made up of photographs and text —I had read them, and had something to say about them by way of preface to my remarks on *The Works of Love*.

As the review shows, I was not altogether at home with that novel, and it still puzzles me in some ways, though on the whole I admire it very much. When my not altogether sympathetic review was published, Morris wrote me that people born east of the Hudson, as I was, didn't seem to get the book. Perhaps that explains it; I don't know. At least Saul Bellow, who grew up in Chicago, told me at about the same time that he thought it was Wright's best book. Morris himself insisted on its being included in *The Wright Morris Reader* because he regarded it as the key to everything he has written. Reading it for the fourth time in 1969, when

I was preparing to write my introduction for the *Reader,* I felt that at last I was hearing everything Morris had tried to say, and in that introduction (pages xv–xvii) I sought to express my final judgment.

1 *The Works of Love*

Wright Morris is a novelist I have admired ever since I read his first novel, *My Uncle Dudley,* ten years ago. I wasn't perfectly sure what he was trying to do in that book, but I had no doubt that here was a writer with a style and a vision of his own, a man who knew a lot about American life and had a strong, individual feeling for people.

The people in *My Uncle Dudley* were, by conventional standards, failures and misfits, but Morris was neither condescending nor indignant. These people were all interesting and mysterious beings in whom good and bad were mixed in complex and astonishing ways. Morris revealed himself as a man of generous impulses, with a strong sense of justice, but he was simply not the kind of do-gooder whose idea of helping people is to try to make them more like himself. On the contrary, his great gift was his responsiveness to people as he found them.

All the books that have followed *My Uncle Dudley* have been interesting, including those in which Morris exhibits his dual skills —as a photographer and as a writer. Sometimes he has seemed too wayward, too self-consciously askew, even a little coy, but there has not been a book without its revelatory force. And in *Man and Boy,* published last year, it seemed to me that his various talents were all perfected and perfectly fused. It was a funnier book than anything else he had written, and at the same time it was more deeply serious. On the surface, it was a bizarre tale of a dominating wife and a henpecked husband, but more and more one found in it a wonderfully complex pattern of human relationships.

It would be a pleasure to report that *The Works of Love* is even better than *Man and Boy,* but I don't feel that it is. This is the life story of a man told in terms of the ways in which he is connected with and separated from other people. Fatherless and then motherless, Will Brady establishes his first significant human relationship with a prostitute. When she refuses to marry him, he offers to marry another prostitute, and to reward him she subsequently bestows upon him her baby, which is not his. For the sake of this child, he contracts a singularly unsuitable marriage. Nothing turns out well for Will Brady—not his egg business, though that prospers for a time, nor his big new house, nor his second marriage. He spends his last years in a Chicago slum, boasting to the neighbors of his son, who is not his son and nothing to boast of.

The novel is dedicated to the memory of Sherwood Anderson; and Anderson's influence is everywhere apparent in it, as it is to a lesser degree in other things Morris has written. Morris is writing about the mysteriousness of human personality and the tenuousness —the tenuousness and the importance—of the connections that can exist between human beings. These are important themes, and Morris always has something to say about them, but here his method is too abstract and too vague to be wholly effective. Anderson could make vagueness a virtue, but sometimes he fell into a trap of his own digging. Like Anderson, Morris wants us to see those qualities of character that are missed when analysis is sharp and definite, but what we see, not always but too often, is mere nothingness, a great blank. Much of the time, Will Brady is so mysterious that he doesn't exist.

Yet it remains certain that Wright Morris is one of our important novelists, a man who has taken his line and is resourcefully following it. Like several of the very young novelists, he is preoccupied with the grotesque, but, like Anderson and unlike most of these younger writers, he never seems to be interested in the bizarre for its own sake. For him, as for his master, the grotesque is a path to human truth, not away from it.

The New Leader
March 24, 1952

2 *The Deep Sleep*

In Wright Morris's novel, *The Deep Sleep,* one of the characters is a painter named Paul Webb. Early in the story we are told about Webb and his wife waiting in a railroad station along with a couple of elderly taxi drivers, to whose conversation about the bad old times Webb listens. It is a cold, stormy night, and one of the men clears a spot on the window so that he can look out. Webb joins him. "The painter Webb, the hack driver Steve." Morris writes, "gazed through the same hole at the same world, but it was clear that they did not see the same things. Webb had put his hand on the old man's shoulder—around his shoulder, as his wife said later —as he had felt their strange predicament as fellow mortals, each with two eyes in his head, each staring, but neither seeing the same thing."

That "strange predicament" has always been Morris's theme, and like Paul Webb he is moved by his sense of it to a great tenderness towards his fellow human beings. In *The Deep Sleep,* as in *Man and Boy,* he is particularly preoccupied with the mystery of marriage. That human beings can go on living together for year after year and still not see the same thing, or to put it the other way around, that people who don't see the same thing can go on living together for year after year, seems to him a phenomenon that can never be sufficiently marveled at. What astonishes him even more is that, in spite of the fact that the barriers to mutual understanding can never be surmounted, some indefinable but true and significant relationship between husband and wife may be established.

The action of *The Deep Sleep* takes place on the day after the death of Judge Porter, a distinguished lawyer. The principal characters are the judge's wife, his mother, who is nearly a hundred, his daughter Katherine, Katherine's husband, who is Paul Webb, the painter, and a hired man named Parsons. Each chapter except the first is presented from the point of view of one of these five persons. The action is made up of such commonplace matters as a shopping trip by the mother and daughter, in which Paul becomes unhappily involved, and a small gathering of friends, but out of these trivia Morris has shaped a moving and meaningful novel.

The novel Morris published last year, *The Works of Love,* was a book of grotesques, and it seemed to me that the characters were always on the verge of unreality. In *The Deep Sleep* every character is as real as your next-door neighbor, and yet each is seen, before the book is finished, as shrouded in mystery. In one aspect the novel is, like *Man and Boy,* the story of a domineering wife and a hen-pecked husband. Like Paul Webb, Morris is obviously fascinated by the kind of inner-directed woman, as David Riesman would say, who seems never to consider any point of view but her own and has no doubt that her standards are right and all others wrong. Webb studies, analyzes, marvels at, and rages against his mother-in-law: he indignantly exposes the subterfuges by which the judge, of whom he was fond, eluded his wife's discipline; yet he cannot get away from the fact that the marriage would have to be reckoned, from Judge Porter's point of view, as a happy one: and in the end Mrs. Porter reveals depths that he had not suspected.

Webb, the great analyst, is himself the subject of the contemplation of others. In the opinion of his wife "there was nothing in all the world so strange as the happy marriage of Paul Webb to Katherine Porter," but to that, she thinks impatiently, he has never given a thought. Nobody in the book is either what he thinks he is or what anybody else believes him to be. Parsons, who was the judge's confidante, but whose admiration is reserved for Mrs. Porter as a woman without human failings, is a many-sided and mysterious character. Even the grandmother, whose life has been simplified by her great age, asserts a self that is ultimately unfathomable.

Although death is central in the novel, and one of its themes is the strangeness of the ways in which grief finds expression, it is full of comic episodes, and Morris demonstrates once more that he is, when he wants to be, one of the funniest of American writers. He also reveals himself, not for the first time, as a master of dialogue, able to reproduce with overwhelming accuracy the banalities of everyday speech and to make them serve his purpose. And again, not to make too long a catalog of his virtues, he shows, as he has also done in his books of photographs, how loudly the impedimenta of daily living can speak of human character and the human condition. He is one of the most talented of contemporary novelists, and his talents are unique. No one else has so much curiosity about what we think of as ordinary American life, and no one else is so successful in showing how extraordinary it is.

The New Leader
September 21, 1953

3 *The Huge Season*

In 1942, I read Wright Morris's first novel, *My Uncle Dudley,* and was convinced that it was the work of an important new writer. Here was someone who could write about people who had had little or no formal education—so-called common men—without either condescension or an affectation of toughness. He had a penetrating eye, a dependable ear, an intimate knowledge of the country, and above all else a feeling for people—especially people like Uncle Dudley, who "did most of the things good souls should do but damn near all of them they shouldn't." Here, I had no doubt, was a man worth watching.

I have watched, missing only one of the eight books that have followed *My Uncle Dudley,* and I have seen Morris grow in wisdom and in skill. Especially in the last four years, with *Man and Boy, The Works of Love, The Deep Sleep* and now *The Huge Season,* he has demonstrated his right to be regarded as one of the major contemporary novelists. Not only is he highly gifted; he has that hallmark of the major writer, the ability to be always and unmistakably himself.

At the beginning of *The Huge Season,* one of the characters describes a picture of another character, Charles Lawrence, playing tennis. Peter Foley concludes: "On the other hand, the stranger might not notice it at all. It might strike him as not much more than a poor photograph. If you think that great champions can be made by eating Wheaties, that great songs can be written on commission, you will be inclined to feel that I am reading something into this photograph. In that sense you will be right, as I am reading into it most of my life." Morris is fond of talking about photographs, and one section of *The Man Who Was There* is built upon a series of pictures of the central character—Agee Ward. A picture is for Morris a challenge to the imagination, and his own photographs in *The Inhabitants* and *The Home Place* show how challenging an apparently quite literal kind of photography can be. But the passage I have quoted applies even more cogently to his fiction than it does to his photography. What he has invariably done is to invite the reader not merely to read but to read into.

Morris's passion for indirection may sometimes have led him astray, as, so far as I am concerned, it did in *The Man Who Was There* and *The Works of Love,* but it is the root of all his successes. In each of his books there is some element of obscurity, not because he doesn't know what he means but because he believes that the more important truths can only be hinted at, never stated. As the narrator says in *My Uncle Dudley*: "When you come right down to it, the last word is just a name, too. And if you can't throw your own light on it, it's still in the dark." When Morris is at his best, he achieves a co-operation between the reader and himself that is highly fruitful for the former.

In *The Huge Season,* Morris invites the reader to throw his light on some of the problems of growing up. Like Mark Schorer's *The Wars of Love* and Peter Matthiessen's *Race Rock,* the novel presents a group of characters—in each instance, curiously, there are several men and one woman—at two widely separated periods of their lives. Unlike Schorer, however, who describes the two periods in simple chronological order, and unlike Matthiessen, who relies on flashbacks, Morris has developed an ingenious form: chapters concerning the past, told in the first person by one of the characters, Peter Foley, alternate with chapters in the third person that describe the present. Thus, past and present constantly confront one another, but Morris handles his two narratives so skilfully that in each the suspense steadily heightens.

Morris is not merely examining two stages in the development of a group of human beings, as Schorer and Matthiessen are doing; he is also contrasting two specific periods, the 1920's and 1950's. The 20's are the huge season of the title, and to explain what he means Morris quotes from a book that Foley has never finished: "Young men are a corn dance, a rite of spring, and every generation must write its own music, and if these notes have a sequence the age has a style. . . . The great style, the habit of perfection, united George Herman Ruth and Charles A. Lindbergh, Albie Booth and Jack Dempsey, Juan Belmonte and Jay Gatsby, and every man, anywhere, who stood alone with his own symbolic bull. He had his gesture, his moment of truth, or his early death in the afternoon." This, as we shall see, may not be Morris's last word, but the book that he has written is in a sense the book that Foley could not complete.

The part of the story that is laid in the 20's begins in a California college, where Charles Lawrence exerts a powerful influence on the imaginations of his roommates—Peter Foley, Jesse Proctor, and Ed Lundgren. The scene is transferred to Paris; Dickie Livingston and Lou Baker are added to the cast; and the climax comes with Lawrence's suicide after he has been injured in a bullfight. Meanwhile, we are following Peter Foley on May 5, 1952, the day after he has read of Jesse Proctor's testimony before the McCarthy

Committee. He goes to New York—he teaches Latin in a college
near Philadelphia—and phones Lou Baker. After spending the day
in wandering about the city and thinking about the past, he joins
Lou and Proctor in the apartment they are sharing. Dickie Livingston and a stranger arrive. After moments that are hilarious
and others that are almost agonizingly intense, there is a partial
resolution, and then Foley returns to the Main Line, to resolve his
own problems and face his own future.

We are concerned here with the late 20's and with people young
enough to have been influenced by the Lost Generation. At least
Proctor, Foley and Lou Baker have faithfully read Hemingway,
Fitzgerald and T. S. Eliot, Lawrence, on the other hand, has read
nothing; he is simply what he is, a Hemingway character by
nature, and that is why he so impresses the others. Not only is he
an individual in the sense that Uncle Dudley and Agee Ward are
individuals; he is an individual in the heroic pattern of the period.

Through his portrayal of these people and what happened to
them, Morris seeks to pass judgment on the 20's. There is a very
natural nostalgia in the book, but there is more than nostalgia. In
the 20's, Morris seems to be saying, there were individuals—Lone
Eagles—who sought not merely to be themselves but to be themselves in a mode of perfection. By contrast, the world of 1952
seems to Foley—at moments, at any rate—ugly, colorless, ruled by
conformity and fear.

The figure of Charles Lawrence stands as the embodiment of
what Morris finds admirable in the 20's—and also, perhaps, of
what he deplores. "He can do whatever he has a mind to," Lawrence's mother says. "It doesn't seem to matter if he kills himself
trying." In his brilliant description of a tennis match Morris shows
what he means by the first part of that statement. But other incidents
make the second part seem rather too weak, for at times Lawrence
seems moved by a desire for death rather than a desire for perfection. (Foley, to be sure, puts it differently: "It was perfection, the
terror of it, that had killed Lawrence. The knowledge that he might
be caught with perfection on his hands and still be discontent.")

In any case, we know what Lawrence is for those who are close to him—that in him, as Foley says, their sun rises. But Lawrence died in 1929, while they went on living—as captives of the past. Dickie lives as if the 20's had never ended, and in 1952 he has "the still young-looking face of an aging juvenile delinquent." Proctor has been a Communist, has fought in the Spanish Civil War, has rescued Jews from Hitler's Europe, has defied Senator McCarthy, but he has never recovered from the shock of Lawrence's suicide. Lou Baker, "a raddled oracle," a not so very glamorous Lady Brett, has moved from country to country and from affair to affair, always working on the novel about the 20's that she knows she will never finish. And Peter Foley, living in quiet bachelordom and teaching a language "that is not merely dying, but dead," has his unfinished novel, significantly called *The Strange Captivity*.

Morris is saying that, even if the 20's were a huge season, to live in a past era is to destroy oneself, but he is not content merely to say something as obvious, as easy as that. Something happens to Peter Foley on this fifth of May to deliver him from his bondage. On the day he hears of Proctor's appearance before the McCarthy Committee, he feels that the jig is up: "What had taken more than twenty years to die was now dead. The Lone Eagles were now a covey of Sitting Ducks." He decides to burn his manuscript, for, though he now knows how to end it, it no longer has any meaning to him. ("You couldn't call a man a captive who had lost all interest in escape.") Yet, these are the closing lines of the novel: "A new day was breaking, the dawn like a sheet of clear ice on the pond. He took out his watch, started to wind it, and saw that time—the captive time—had stopped. At two o'clock in the morning, the first day of his escape from captivity."

Throughout the day, we get indications of what is happening to Foley. There is, for instance, the fine parable of the dancing chipmunk. There is his recollection of the day in 1943 when he appeared before his draft board and came to the conclusion that the trouble with him and men like him was their "gut-deep urge that in surrender was the moral victory, in death and defeat the

lasting possession of the lasting world." It seems clear, then, that
Foley is finally committed to involvement with the world. But there
is more meaning than that, for in his ultimate decision Foley is
sustained by some conviction, which one has to call mystical, that
he is himself the significance and justification of the experiences he
has described.

I am not sure what this means, nor, for that matter, am I sure
that my interpretation of Morris's judgments on the 20's and the
50's is right. What I do know is that we have here a deeply original
way of thinking and feeling, expressed both with great subtlety and
with a kind of textual richness that is a joy. One savors the variety
and suggestiveness of the figures of speech, the brilliance with
which the symbols are elaborated, the precision with which the
themes are sustained and interwoven. One can say of this novel, as
Morris says of a photograph he describes, that it embodies "the
mystery, the charm and the anxiety of life." On every conceivable
level, it is a pleasure to read.

The New Leader
October 4, 1954

4 *The Field of Vision*

The scene of Wright Morris's new novel, *The Field of Vision* is a
bullring in Mexico City, and the characters, seven of them, are lined
up on the shady side. Four are from Nebraska: Mr. and Mrs.
Walter McKee, their grandson Gordon, and Mrs. McKee's father,
an old timer called Scanlon. They are sitting with an oddly non-
descript trio—someone named Gordon Boyd who has written plays,

a psychiatrist friend of his, Dr. Lehmann, and Dr. Lehmann's friend and patient, Paula Kahler.

The novel lasts only as long as the bullfight lasts—a couple of hours at most. The bulls are brought in, and are dispatched with or without human casualties, but the novel is really concerned with what is going on in the minds of the seven visitors from the United States. We are taken from one mind to another, though never into the mind of Paula Kahler nor into that of young Gordon McKee. McKee, Mrs. McKee, Scanlon, Boyd, Dr. Lehmann, and so it goes, around and around again.

The relations among the seven soon reveal a clear pattern. At the center are Boyd and the McKees, who are bound together by a common past, a past that has been brought sharply back to their minds by the chance meeting in Mexico. Completely withdrawn both from them and from the bullfight are Paula Kahler and old Scanlon. Dr. Lehmann and young Gordon are less abstracted, but we know that the psychiatrist is as much occupied with his own thoughts as he is with the events in the ring, and we infer that the boy is also living a life of his own.

What happened in Polk, Nebraska, some decades earlier we piece together from the troubled thoughts of Mrs. McKee and the puzzled thoughts of her husband. As a boy and young man, Walter McKee had looked up to Gordon Boyd, a bold, imaginative youth, one who would try to walk on water or rip a pocket from the uniform of a baseball player. Lois Scanlon hadn't met Boyd until after she was engaged to Walter McKee, and on that first meeting he had kissed her in front of her fiancé. Although McKee seemed not to mind, and Boyd made nothing of the occurrence, it has never, we gathered, been long out of Mrs. McKee's mind, and it is very much in her thoughts this afternoon.

As for Boyd, his mind is characteristically leaping from subject to subject, but always coming back to the McKees, not so much to their relationship with him as to their relationship with one another; or perhaps I should say, to the lack of a relationship, for it is clear to Boyd, as it is to the reader, that the McKees, in spite of their three children, are unrelated. He thinks of himself, too, and of his strangely unsuccessful search for failure. He thinks of Dr. Lehmann and of the enigmatic case of Paula Kahler, and he never forgets the McKees' grandson, named for a father who was named for him. At the same time, unlike the others, he keeps a knowing eye on the bullfighters.

Scanlon, meanwhile, wearing a fake coonskin hat like the great-grandson beside him, is away on a wonderful, fantastic adventure of his own, reliving his father's hardships and triumphs as a pioneer. The Scanlon passages are perhaps the most impressive in the novel, a sort of surrealistic version of the pioneer experience, a bizarre but fundamentally accurate rendering of the essence of a thousand tales of the transcontinental crossing. As his wife once said, when the century turned Scanlon didn't. For fifty years and more, his physical, his external life has been the epitome of passivity. But the inner life that unfolds, never more than briefly interrupted by the coming of live bulls and the departure of dead ones, has a dazzling vitality.

Perhaps Paula Kahler, who calmly knits throughout the bull-fight, is also living a dramatic and colorful inner life, but we do not know, for "she" remains utterly inscrutable. I put the pronoun in quotation marks because Paula is really a man. Working as a chambermaid in a hotel, she strangled a man who attempted to assault her, and it was then that her sex was discovered. Dr. Lehmann, who has learned enough of the story to guess at some of the reasons for this transformation, is content to abide by what he regards as the decision of the personality. A sensitive, almost saintly youth, subjected to unbearable pressure, Paul Kahler has become Paula, and that is that.

Here is the cast of characters, and what Morris invites us—no, challenges us—to do is to look at them and to decide what we are seeing. It is not easy. "This crisp sabbath afternoon," Boyd reflects, "forty thousand pairs of eyes would gaze down on forty thousand separate bullfights, seeing it all very clearly, missing only the one that was said to take place. Forty thousand latent heroes, as many gorings, so many artful dodges it beggared description, two hundred thousand bulls, horses, mules and monsters, half man, half beast. In all this zoo, this bloody constellation, only two men and six bulls would be missing. Those in the bullring."

You see how difficult Morris makes it. If no two persons see the same bullfight, which is a comparatively simple thing, obviously we cannot expect any two human beings to have the same experience of another human being. And yet we see each character in the novel through the eyes of other characters. We see McKee's Gordon Boyd and Mrs. McKee's and Dr. Lehmann's. We also know some small part of what Boyd knows about himself. We have, in other words, four Gordon Boyds, and we must do with them whatever we can. The other characters, too, are given to us in multiple images that we can only try to reconcile.

In this ill-assorted congeries, most of the individuals are completely or almost completely passive. Scanlon resigned from life half a century earlier. Paula, having accomplished her great transformation, is at peace with herself and the world. Dr. Lehmann has learned to reduce his involvements to a minimum. McKee knows by instinct how to protect his passivity by a mask of conventional activity. Mrs. McKee, on the other hand, has a latent capacity for action, and young Gordon, of course, is unformed. The really active force is Boyd, who as a boy managed to unsettle McKee and, more seriously, Mrs. McKee, and who later on disrupted for a time the life of the son they named for him. Now, after many years of the blackest self-doubt, he is irresistibly impelled to exert his influence on the son's son, and his success is the climax of the novel.

For fifteen years now Morris has been writing his novels and building his world, and the reader of the earlier novels will recognize in *The Field of Vision* a number of themes that he has made peculiarly his. Gordon Boyd, for instance, is related to the uncle in *My Uncle Dudley,* to Agee Ward in *The Man Who Was There,* and to Charles Lawrence in *The Huge Season.* These are all persons who exert a great and not quite explicable influence on their associates. They have a kind of charismatic quality, a special grace that distinguishes them from and gives them power over other people. Usually they are failures, as Boyd is, but they are memorable failures.

The McKees, for their part, remind us of the Ormsbys in *Man and Boy* and the Porters in *The Deep Sleep*. Mrs. McKee is not so striking an example of the dominating female as either Mrs. Ormsby or Mrs. Porter, but the McKees seem to have even less in common than the other two couples. The moment McKee runs into Boyd in the hotel lobby, he says, "Mrs. McKee and me couldn't be happier." He is astute enough to realize that the remark is fatuous, but he never quite knows why. A sound, likable, by no means stupid man, he cannot imagine a relationship that is more than superficial. To Morris, for whom nothing is more important than profound and many-sided human relationships, there are both irony and mystery in the fact that a marriage can exist, endure, and even in appearance succeed without such a relationship.

As I have said, most of the characters in the novel are passive, and that is true of most of the characters in the other novels. Scanlon, however, is passive in a peculiar degree, and by that fact he reminds us of Will Brady in *The Works of Love*. It is the early Scanlon, however, the Scanlon who lives by himself in the deserted hotel in the deserted town of Lone Tree, who is like Brady. The later Scanlon, whose imagination has been released by contact with his great-grandson, seems to me both a more attractive and a more credible character than Brady. If he has withdrawn from life, at least we know what he has withdrawn into.

There is also in the book a new theme, though perhaps it was foreshadowed by the strange and wonderful story of the dancing chipmunk in *The Huge Season*. This is the theme of transformation. The extraordinary example of transformation, of course, is Paula Kahler, whose macabre story, with its puzzling overtones, at least demonstrates the power of the human being to make himself something different from what he is. There is also an element of transformation in the lives of others—witness three generations of McKees—but what Boyd seeks is a way of self-transformation, and at the end it is strongly suggested that he has found it.

To an even greater extent than Morris's earlier books, *The Field of Vision* demands the active participation of the reader. This is not an arbitrary demand on the author's part but the logical consequence of his conception of the imaginative process. As no two spectators see the same bullfight, so no two readers read the same book. Recognizing this, Morris feeds the reader's imagination instead of trying to impose upon it his own vision. He gives his insights as the material on which the reader must work. That is certainly not to say that the book is made up of raw material; on the contrary, everything in it has been processed to a degree almost unparalleled in contemporary American literature; but the aim of Morris's disciplined and devoted craftsmanship is to transform the reader into a participant in an adventure of the imagination. When the reader does participate, the book becomes a significant and enriching experience.

The New Leader
October 1, 1956

5 *Love Among the Cannibals*

My enthusiasm for Wright Morris goes back to 1942, when I read his first novel, *My Uncle Dudley*. As I have repeatedly said, Morris is a wonderfully sharp-eyed observer of the contemporary scene—his ears, too, are of the very best—as well as a devoted and subtle craftsman.

Keen observation and disciplined craftsmanship are apparent

enough in his new novel, *Love Among the Cannibals,* but in many ways this is a new departure. That it should be surprises the careful reader of Morris, for up to this point his work has been uncommonly homogeneous. The question he has always asked, and for that matter is still asking, is: "What does it mean to be an American?" Before this, however, that question has almost always resolved itself into another: "What has it meant to be an American?" He put this question to himself in *The Inhabitants* and *The Home Place,* two books in which his talents as a photographer were joined to his talents as a writer, and in *The World in the Attic* which is a sequel to *The Home Place* without the pictures. In these books and in *The Man Who Was There* and *The Works of Love,* the center of his inquiry is the Plains States, and in crucial episodes of *The Field of Vision* he returned to the region of which he is a native. "The books I have written, and hope to write," he said a couple of years ago, "are apt to bear, on close examination, the stamp of an object made on the plains." This is true in a general sense of all his books, but in a very specific sense of those I have just mentioned. *Man and Boy* and *The Deep Sleep* are full of echoes of a different sort, and *The Huge Season,* evoking the mood of the Twenties, is steeped in nostalgia.

Nostalgia is just what one doesn't find in *Love Among the Cannibals,* which exists wholly in the present. It is a story about a song-writing team, Macgregor and Horter, the latter being the narrator. We know nothing about them except that they met during the war and have been writing songs, with a moderate degree of success, ever since; and that is all we need to know.

"My story begins," Horter says, "like everything else, on the beach. Beaches are the same the world over, you peel down, then you peel off; they serve you up raw meat, dark meat, or flesh nicely basted in olive oil. A strip of sun and sand where the sex is alert, the mind is numb. The beach in question, one of the best, is near where Sunset Boulevard meets the sea."

It is on the beach that they meet "this little chick with her hair in a pony tail," Billie Harcum, who turns out to be very much to Mac's taste. Billie comes from Memphis, and that is all we have to be told about her. That same night the two men go to a party with Billie, and here Horter sees a girl—he calls her "the Greek" because of her statuesque appearance—with whom he falls in love on sight. And without much more preface than that, the four of them take off for Acapulco.

Thus we are rushed pell mell into two love stories and a romantic expedition. This is Morris's eleventh book, and it is the first in which sex plays an important part. He has not, of course, ignored the existence of sex, but its more urgent manifestations either have been ruled out by the nature of his material or have been disposed of offstage. It is as if he had decided at the outset that, in order to concentrate on the elements of experience that most interested him, he had to avoid the distractions of passion, as if, with so many novelists assuming that sex was the only subject worth writing about, he wanted to prove how much other kinds of experience could yield to a probing imagination. But in this book Morris deliberately turns that probing imagination toward the subject that he has hitherto avoided.

One of the stories, the story of Mac and Billie, he treats satirically, and he does it up brown. Billie, who speaks only in clichés, is herself a cliché from head to toe—the Memphis belle in the wilds of Hollywood. But she happens to be the kind Mac likes, "the million-dollar baby in the five-and-ten cent store," as Horter explains, and since she also happens to be, in her own mind at least, a singer, with a clear idea of what the team of Macgregor and Horter may be able to do for her, she is not indifferent to his attentions. Indeed, after the excursion to Acapulco, during which she displays many varieties of bitchiness, pretentiousness, and inanity, she succeeds in roping him into marriage.

The story of Eva—"the Greek"—and Horter is something else. We know that before the war Horter had serious literary ambitions, and his story could be full of soul-searching, bitter lamentations, and longings for the past. But as we see him, Horter has a good reason for living in the present, and he does so, up to the hilt. He is scornful of the entertainment industry of which he is part, and in general he has a grudge against the phoniness of contemporary culture, but he has retained an eagerness for what he can accept as reality, and for him Eva is real.

Of Eva we know that she is large, beautiful, young, and passionate, that she was married when she was 14 and nearly died in pregnancy, that she has been a student at the university, and that she earns her living as a nursemaid in a large family. She is not in love with Horter as he is with her, but she is attracted to him—she tells him that he is part of her development—and she goes to bed with him at once and without embarrassment. For Horter she is a dream woman, an incarnation of Robert Graves's White Goddess, a figure like Faulkner's Eula Varner. He sees her as "life without its clichés," and he is happy to make love to her, though he knows he cannot possess her. Jealous of the men she has had and the men he knows she will have, he realizes that he is letting himself in for heartbreak, but he is willing to pay the price.

The two men and their completely dissimilar girls—one tight, self-conscious and predatory, the other generous, careless of convention, impulsive—make the trip to Acapulco in a large and fancy car lent to Mac and Horter by the studio for which they are working. Just as they arrive within sight of the ocean, the car's front wheels drop into a ditch, and they proceed on foot to the villa they are to inhabit—a villa that turns out to be in a not very advanced stage of construction. And during the next few days, while they make the best of their primitive accommodations by spending most of their time on the beach, the car is systematically plundered and dismantled by the natives. It is a very funny business, close to the edge of fantasy but never incredible, and an effective symbol to boot.

In this stripped-down life Billie Harcum naturally fares badly, whereas Eva likes it, and Horter, as he tells her, likes it because he likes her. The trip is to end badly for both Horter and Mac, for

Horter because he loses his girl, for Mac because he gets his. The time comes, as Horter has known it must, when the Greek meets another man—this one a professor of marine biology—who is necessary for her development, and she leaves the party. With the same inevitability Billie manages to haul Mac in front of a parson. Yet Horter is not wholly unhappy, whatever may be true of Mac. The night after Eva has left he reflects: "Stripped down, like that car in its ditch, to what we referred to as the essentials, I possessed nothing under that moon but my past. That much I could take with me, if I cared to, and I did."

One finishes the book with the feeling that this is indeed a new Morris, but of course there is a lot of the old Morris, too. The humor, for instance, is no surprise to anyone who remembers *My Uncle Dudley, Man and Boy,* and the reunion scene in *The Huge Season.* There is satire, too, as there has been in most of the earlier books, for Morris's examination of American civilization is critical as well as careful. And the mastery of the vernacular—though the effect here is heightened by having Horter as narrator—is a quality Morris has displayed from the beginning.

But what is new is more impressive than what is old, not only because Morris has eliminated nostalgia and introduced sex but also because he has evolved a literary technique quite different from that which he has been perfecting in his recent work. There is only one of his novels to which *Love Among the Cannibals* can be compared, and that is his first, *My Uncle Dudley.* Here the action starts when Dudley and the boy-narrator, stranded in California during the depression, decide to get hold of a car somehow or other so that they can drive to Chicago. They get the car, and off they go, and everything follows. In *Cannibals* Mac and Horter are on the beach, and they meet a chick, and the next thing we know they are in Acapulco. In both books the movement seems perfectly casual and perfectly right, although *Cannibals,* of course, coming later by fifteen years of hard labor, is a richer and more rewarding book. In each of his books Morris has been extraordinarily successful in establishing the tone that he wanted. The point about *Canni-*

bals is that it is the first since *My Uncle Dudley* in which the tone he wanted is one of excitement, so that the reader is swept on from page to page.

It is primarily a book to be enjoyed, but, since Morris is a serious writer, one is bound to ask what it means. I suppose it's a book about what is real. When Mac says, "It's real," as he frequently does, you know that it, whatever it may be, is uncommonly phony. Horter writes: "What the hell, man. What else is there? The phony is. I mean it's here and now, and all that once was or is yet to be isn't. You've got to take what's phony, if it's all you've got, and make it real." Horter makes an exception of "her," meaning Eva; yet he knows that his dream of her is not free from clichés, and he knows that he must work through the clichés to reality. "You live your dream," he tells her, "which is to say you're a realist. Living with you has made me something of a realist myself. An essentialist, that is. The little inessentials have been stripped off." So Morris, I think, telling two love stories, one sordid, one romantic, has worked in and through clichés toward reality.

New Leader
August 19, 1957

6 *The Territory Ahead*

Beginning in 1942 with *My Uncle Dudley,* Wright Morris has published nine novels, as well as two books made up of photographs and text. Serious, talented, and versatile, he has produced more good work in the Fifties than any other writer I can think of.

Although he is anything but a dilettante, Morris has many interests, and whatever interests him interests him intensely. He has tried to be, in Henry James's phrase, "one on whom nothing is lost." Although one might not guess it from his novels, which are not in the least bookish, he has read much and read thoughtfully. *The Territory Ahead* is a report on some of that reading, with particular reference to the aims, possibilities, and perils of the writer in America.

Morris begins with the observation, frequently made, that American writers have a way of not fulfilling their promise, and he looks about for explanations. He finds two. In the first place, he maintains, American writers, with only a few exceptions, with only one really notable exception, have fled from the present. Flight may take any one of several directions, but in America the writer usually flees into the past.

Nostalgia is what our writers most often feel, and although it has given us great books, it is not the kind of emotion, the kind of attitude, on which literary careers are built. Then, in the second place, he argues that most writers share the general American preference for facts, for raw material, and are comparatively indifferent to the techniques by which raw material may be processed. Morris seems to recognize more exceptions to this generalization than to the other, but here again his great exception is Henry James.

As he proceeds with his examination of particular writers and their books, Morris sometimes bases his argument on one of his theories and sometimes on the other, and his analyses are not always easy to follow. I am not sure whether he holds that the two theories are related in some significant way, or are quite independent so that either fallacy or both may be operative. The truth is, indeed, that the book rests on a series of perceptions rather than on rigorous logic, but these perceptions are so acute that the reader doesn't worry much about the absence of a completely coherent esthetic theory.

What Morris does first is to look at four of the acknowledged masterpieces of the nineteenth century, books for which he himself has great admiration: *Walden, Leaves of Grass, Moby Dick,* and

Huckleberry Finn. Each of them he regards as both representative and exceptional. Thoreau fled to the woods, Whitman took to the open road, Melville sailed on the high seas, and Mark Twain embarked on the river. Furthermore, all four of these men, Morris insists, are preoccupied with facts, Thoreau and Whitman most obviously so but the others too. He makes the additional point that each of them was isolated, even Whitman, who wrote so much of comradeship but wrote best about himself. In spite of all this, each was able, for reasons Morris sets forth, to write a great book. None, however, was capable of growth. "Not knowing what he was doing," he writes, "never having truly known, Twain soon gave it up."

In a middle section Morris discusses Henry James as a writer who did know what he was doing, and then, surprisingly but aptly, talks about an illustrator, Norman Rockwell, as a master of the cliché. Now he is ready to turn to four contemporary writers: Hemingway, Wolfe, Fitzgerald, and Faulkner. Wolfe he despises, pities, and blames for a great deal of what is wrong with contemporary fiction; the other three he admires. But if he thinks that Hemingway has triumphed through his perfecting of a style, that Fitzgerald transformed nostalgia into a virtue, that Faulkner achieved greatness in the expression of rage, he sees in each qualities that have prevented growth.

Henry James has already emerged as the hero of the book. In addition to the chapter I have mentioned, there is a chapter on one book, *The American Scene,* and here Morris lets himself go. Writing some fifty years ago, he says, James saw more than the most perceptive observers see today: "The American novelist, midcentury, will read this book with fear and trembling, since it puts in question the very reason for his existence—his contemporaneity. Having climbed to some pinnacle, or dived to some depth, he turns to see that James, like Kilroy, was already there."

Morris quotes wonderful passages to support his argument, and he sums up: "It was James's distinction in *The American Scene* to have been the first to view that scene from the *present,* free from visions of the future and crippling commitments to the past. It is this *presentness* that resulted in impressions consistently prophetic."

Morris's enthusiasm for James is very great, and yet he has revealed in the earlier chapter that he does have misgivings. There is some validity, he grants, in "the charge that James lacked raw material." "His passion was his craft, but out of craft one cannot conjure up *the* grand passion. It is here that life exercises its precedence over art." And again: "In James we have the artist who apprehended much of life without the crippling effects of having lived it . . . He remains free to generalize; too free for the novelist."

It seems to me that Morris never quite comes to terms with these objections he has raised. But if he is not perfectly clear about James, he is clear about his own position. The concluding section of the book begins: "If I have emphasized technique, the primacy of technique, over such things as experience and raw material, it is because the primacy of life—in the American scene—is obvious . . . But there is no substitute for the material itself—the *life* in literature." Thereupon he transfers the argument overseas, preferring the life in D. H. Lawrence to the technique of the later Joyce and thus taking issue with T. S. Eliot.

Morris doesn't really make his point about Lawrence any more than he really solves the question of James. He is less than just to Melville, and perhaps to Hemingway and Faulkner as well. In part the disappointments I feel result from the brevity with which Morris has chosen to treat his subjects, but that isn't the heart of the matter. His mind lends itself to tangents, rather than, as he says James's did, to parentheses, and he can sometimes be led into outer space by a figure of speech. But he is not merely right in his general emphasis; his sensitivity is unfailing.

If its faults were ten times as great as I think they are, *The Territory Ahead* would still be a rich and rewarding book.

Saturday Review
October 25, 1958

7 *Ceremony in Lone Tree*

Of Wright Morris's many gifts as a novelist, perhaps the most conspicuous is his ability to create character. From the hero of *My Uncle Dudley* (1942) to Mac and Horter in *Love Among the Cannibals* (1957), he has brought to life a great variety of men and women. They live for us in all their strangeness and all their familiarity: Mrs. Ormsby in *Man and Boy*, Mrs. Porter in *The Deep Sleep*, Will Brady in *The Works of Love*, Lawrence, Proctor, Lou Baker, and Peter Foley in *The Huge Season*, and many others.

Ceremony in Lone Tree assembles the most remarkable collection of characters we have yet encountered in a Morris novel. Some of them were introduced in *The Field of Vision*: old Tom Scanlon; his daughter and her husband, Lois and Walter McKee; their grandson, Gordon McKee, and McKee's boyhood friend, Gordon Boyd. Others we meet for the first time: Lois's sister Edna, who is married to an Oklahoma millionaire; another sister, Maxine, married to Bud Momeyer, a postman; the Momeyers' daughter, Etoile (pronounced Ee-toal); the McKees' older grandson, Calvin, who is Etoile's boyfriend. Then, thrown in for good measure, there is Jennings, son of Will Brady of *The Works of Love*, and there is the girl Boyd picks up en route.

Except for Jennings, who just happens along at this time because he wants to talk to Scanlon about his father, these people come to Lone Tree to celebrate Tom Scanlon's ninetieth birthday. After the first section, which beautifully sets the stage, we see the characters as they converge on the deserted town. The second half of the novel describes the events of the night before the birthday. Scanlon dies, and, as the book ends, his corpse is being carried away in the covered wagon in which he was born.

Ceremony in Lone Tree is the most recent in a series of books—including two collections of photographs, *The Inhabitants* and *The Home Place*—in which Morris has sought to define the quality of life in the Plains States. In *Love and Death in the American Novel,* Leslie Fiedler says that Morris "has been trying to convince his readers that Nebraska is the absurd hell we all inhabit." This is a perceptive remark, although not free from Fiedleresque exaggeration. Certainly Morris's account is grim enough, and certainly he is commenting on more than a particular region. The Plains States offer him his key to the whole of America.

In *Ceremony,* as in the other books about the Plains, Morris is concerned with the role of nostalgia. Scanlon, as we know from *The Field of Vision,* lives wholly in an imagined past. Calvin McKee, when he runs away from home, goes looking for Scanlon's West and finds it, attaching himself to a gold prospector who scorns the searchers after uranium. Jennings writes adventure stories: "Although he had never mounted a horse, he wrote of men who lived in the saddle, their trigger fingers hairless from the heat of their shooting irons." Nor is it only the characters who feel the lure of the Old West who succumb to nostalgia: Gordon Boyd is still struggling to come to terms with his own past.

But the present is there to be reckoned with, and Morris does not think well of it. Clyde Ewing, the oilman, has the most modern of homes, but he spends most of his time in a luxurious trailer, and his only interest in life is his prize bulldog. McKee, comfortably well off, has his share of gadgets but does not enjoy them. Gadgets and violence are what the present seems to offer. There is the great violence of the atom bomb, of which Boyd is constantly aware, and then there is the violence that grows out of simple human frustration. Etoile's cousin, Lee Roy Momeyer, deliberately runs down and kills two classmates because "he just got tired of being pushed around." At the same time Nebraska is being terrorized by Charlie Munger, who shoots ten persons before he is caught. His comment is: "I want to be somebody." McKee feels that most of the young people he sees are capable of just such evil outbursts.

There is no one in the book who knows how to live in the present. Boyd's tough-talking girl, a kind of beatnik, goes along on a catch-as-catch-can basis; her most memorable act is to pop out her contact lenses. Etoile, who seems to know what she wants, is more likable, but in her heart she, too, is frightened and frightening. "Everybody hates everybody," she says apropos of Charlie Munger, "but nobody knows why anybody gets shot. You want to know somethin'? I'd like to shoot a few dozen people myself!"

As so often in Morris's books, the men have refused to grow up and their wives dominate them. Bud Momeyer, with his inventions and his bow and arrows, is a perpetual adolescent. His wife, Maxine, fully realizes this, but she is capable of a degree of compassion. Her sister Lois, on the other hand, is harder than nails, and one feels more strongly than in *The Field of Vision* the depth of her contempt for McKee. Lois's one weakness is her passion for her grandson Gordon, and this becomes a morbid sort of self-torture.

They are, when you get to know them as Morris makes you get to know them, a grim lot. At the end of *The Field of Vision* there was a tentative note of hope, a suggestion that Gordon Boyd, having touched bottom, might achieve some form of self-realization. Now we learn that not long afterwards he attempted suicide, and throughout *Ceremony* he is defeated and bitter. He turns on McKee with unexpected savagery, but he directs his sharpest sallies against himself. He is, he says, "the man who still had everything to live for, since everything worth living for had eluded him." He is the one of them, as Lois McKee, reflects, who might have done something, and by his own account he has done nothing.

They are a grim lot, but they cannot, as characters in Gothic novels so often can, be dismissed as grotesques. They are all, alas, people we know, people like us and our neighbors. This, Morris is saying, is what people are like, and he makes contradiction extremely difficult.

The skill with which Morris has achieved his effect can scarcely be exaggerated. Always a master of indirection, he has here developed his oblique approach into a brilliant strategy for the revelation of character. As always, he has his comic scenes, and they are very funny, but they are made to contribute to his fundamental purpose, which is deeply serious. He has never been more adroit in the use of the vernacular, and his style is an important element in his achievement. All his resources are brought into action, and the result is his best novel, the novel in which his vision of life is most fully rendered. For a long time there has been no doubt in my mind of the importance of Wright Morris; I hope that *Ceremony in Lone Tree* will serve to convince many other persons.

Saturday Review
July 9, 1960

8 *One Day*

There are certain writers to whose new work one eagerly looks forward, and for me, as for a goodly number of other persons, one such writer is Wright Morris. Ever since his first novel, *My Uncle Dudley,* was published in 1942, I have read each book of his, and though I have liked some better than others there has not been one lacking in the special qualities that give him his distinction. Often and justly praised as a brilliant observer of the American scene, he is more than that. It is the human condition that he writes about, with humor, with compassion, and sometimes with a kind of fury.

One Day belongs with his best work. The day to which the title refers is November 22, 1963, the day President Kennedy was assassinated. The scene, however, is neither Dallas nor Washington but a small California community known as Escondido, and the characters are not the major actors in a national tragedy but a few out of the millions of common people for whom that was a day like no other. For that matter, the novel does not devote much space to what these people think and feel about the President's death. They have been busy living their own lives for just about half the book before the news of the assassination reaches them, and, one way or another, they go on with these lives. *One Day* is a novel about people, not a study of national trauma; but, having come to know the people, the reader can measure the intensity of the shock.

There is a kind of prefatory chapter describing Escondido late in the evening of November 22. We see the town, meet some of the characters who are to occupy our attention, hear echoes of some of the events with which the novel is to deal. There is no reference to the assassination, but even the reader who had no previous knowledge of Morris's theme would feel something portentous in the atmosphere. As the hour passes, we find ourselves in a diner:

"Well," says the cook, "I guess that ends it." He lifts his eyes to the clock as he pulls out the cash drawer.
"Ends what?" Cowie mutters.
The cook makes no comment. He knows better than Cowie that this day had a beginning, but who could say that it would ever end? The question hangs in the air as the finger on the clock's face returns to that point where the day began.

Now we go back to the early morning. Escondido has a pound, built by Evelina Cartwright, a widow, proprietress of a gift shop, and the town's great lady. Ignacio Chavez, a Mexican man of all work, comes to open the pound, looks into a kind of night depository with a trap door, and finds there not a dog nor a cat but a baby in a basket.

Morris proceeds by bringing the main characters onto the stage. Wendell Horlick, assistant at the pound, makes his appearance, a sad sort of man who strongly prefers animals to human beings. He has an unpredictable wife, who finds vegetables more beautiful than people, and a fat-bottomed son whose greed is matched only by his shrewdness in getting hold of money. His superior is Dr.

Cowie, another sad man, with strange sleeping habits. Like Chavez before them, Horlick and Cowie are nonplussed by the baby. Finally Evelina Cartwright arrives, and immediately suspects that the mother of the child is her daughter Alec, who returned the night before from Paris and various other points. She is right.

With this revelation Morris has reached his first climax. Alec, we have realized, is a rebel and something of a beatnik, and her leaving the baby was a gesture of protest. "What had she hoped would change the world? A child left in a pound. The enormity of it, the profundity of it, the desperate and touching pathos of it, could not help but jolt the world awake." But the scene before her eyes seems closer to farce. "Would anything disturb the tenor of this world? The pillars of Hercules were but lampposts. The sky was upheld by indifference, by the simple assurance that it would not fall." First she breaks into hysterical laughter, but then, as she looks about her in Escondido, she asks herself sobering questions: "Had Alec Cartwright believed that *she* could undo something like this? Stranger yet, had she truly imagined there was a *better* way to arrange it? People being, as Horlick said, really no damn good? . . . The system *worked*. Wasn't that all one could reasonably ask?"

Approaching this climax, Morris has drawn full portraits of his characters. As he has often demonstrated before, he has an extraordinary kind of comic inventiveness. For instance, the story of Horlick's trip across the continent with the dog that had to wear dark glasses is wonderfully funny. Episodes in Cowie's saga, especially his recovery of his marble box, are amusing in a grim way. Evelina Cartwright is a perfect subject for the kind of affectionate caricature Morris can do so well. Luigi Boni, barber and, by the grace of Evelina, successful painter, is a clown of whom Alec is understandably fond. It is a remarkable gallery. I have spoken of the characters as common people, and so, in the newspaper sense of the term, they are; but Morris takes pains to show us just how uncommon each of them is.

So here these people are when the word from Dallas arrives.

Most of them, to begin with, scarcely take it in; only Dora Boni, wife of the barber, is capable of a great emotional outburst. Alec, as might be expected, reacts hysterically. "We all killed him," she cries. "If *any*body did it, we did it." Later she tells Dr. Cowie: "I'm *not* crazy. I just wish to Christ I *was* crazy. We did it just as much as he did it. Right when he did it I was trying to think what the hell would crack it, and he cracked it. I helped will him to do it. I wanted to make a noise heard round the world and *he* made it. It's too horrible to think but we all did it, we've all got a hand in it." "All of us make me sick," she says, "sick."

Meanwhile, as the news spreads through Escondido, Morris has a short interlude, a radio speech by the town's mortician. Beginning as a parody of the apologies offered by spokesmen for the burial business when under attack, it becomes a sardonic comment on the tastes and desires of the American people. Holmes can be witty: "The kiss of death being the last kiss we are apt to get, a man should look his best." And at the end he observes, "As your mortician I am obliged to advise you that fear of death shows signs of slipping; the upswing is definitely toward fear of life."

Although more or less dazed by the word from Dallas, the characters live their lives in the present and contemplate the past. Luigi Boni thinks of his boyhood in Italy, while Ignacio Chavez thinks of Mexico, remembering how he carried his dead baby to the mountains for burial and was followed by scavenging dogs. There is also the account of the strange death of Adele Skoje, Evelina Cartwright's enigmatic companion. But Alec is the central figure, and at last we come to her story—her life in Paris, her affair with a young Negro civil rights worker, Lyle P. (for Protest) Jackson, and her disillusionment with him when she sees him again in the South. ("I believe in segregation," she says, "and I want a black face so I can't be integrated. I don't want to be in. I want to be out.") Her baby is born, and she returns to Escondido, and makes her gesture on the eve of that Friday. Thus the book, which begins with the ending of the day, ends with its beginning.

It is a rich book, full of those extraordinary common people to whom Morris has dedicated his literary career. Although each

character is a newly created individual, some have had their pred-
ecessors. Evelina Cartwright, for example, reminds us of other
domineering women, especially Mrs. Ormsby in *Man and Boy*. Dr.
Cowie is related to all the Morris characters who "cannot bear
connection," the prototype being Will Brady in *The Works of Love*.
Alec is a little like the girl called Daughter in *Ceremony in Lone
Tree*, a little like Cynthia in *What a Way to Go*, a little like Lou
Baker in *The Huge Season*.

This is simply to say that there are certain kinds of people that
perennially interest Morris, but in a larger sense all people interest
him. During her pregnancy Alec has a spell of going to bad movies.
"An indescribably bad movie, with the horses shyly nuzzling one
another, what was it but the waxworks museum of life *brought* to
life. All crazy. All indescribably marvelous. There it all was, the
loony bin of life, so desperately sad, so intolerably touching, that
her eyes filmed over."

"So desperately sad, so intolerably touching"—that is how
Morris sees his people. But he also sees them as infinitely comic.
He finds them terribly exasperating in their muddleheadedness and
their refusals to make the most of the gift of life, but astonishingly
heroic in their moments of courage and dedication. In the mass
their conduct seems dismally predictable, but, looked at carefully,
each individual is a surprise. "Except among those creatures referred to as beasts it seemed to Cowie that life showed two eternal
aspects, an infinite capacity for corruption, a finite capacity for
perfection. For this libretto love provided the music, some good,
some bad."

There are no great men in Morris's books, no generals or geniuses,
but housewives and teachers and here and there a failed poet—
morticians, veterinarians, barbers. In *One Day* we do have the
shadow of a great man, but Morris is concerned with what happens
when this shadow falls across the lives of common-uncommon
people. It would have been easy to have written a sentimental story
on this theme, but Morris's book has the ring of truth, which is
sometimes a harsh sound.

Morris has written sixteen books, one a critical study of American literature, two made up of photographs and text, the others novels. These novels constitute a body of work for which I find no parallel in contemporary American fiction. A thoroughly disciplined, highly sensitive craftsman, Morris strives constantly for perfection and sometimes comes close to achieving it. He has written mostly about the United States, but he has laid parts of novels in Mexico, Italy, Austria, and Greece. He has written about both the past and the present, but particularly about the past in the present. *One Day* may convince many people of what I have believed for a decade or more—that Wright Morris is a major figure in modern American literature.

Saturday Review
February 20, 1965

9 *In Orbit*

Wright Morris published his first novel, *My Uncle Dudley,* in 1942. Since then he has published sixteen books, most of them novels, and I have read them all, and liked them all—some, of course, more than others. His seventeenth book, *In Orbit* is one that I like very much, though perhaps not quite so much as its immediate predecessor, *One Day*.

My Uncle Dudley is an uncommonly funny book, although, as a picture of a group of victims of the Depression backtrailing from California, it is also a serious one. All Morris's books are both funny and serious, the proportions variously compounded. There are not many books that have made me laugh out loud as often as *Man and Boy* did, and yet it is a thoughtful commentary on American life. *The Field of Vision,* Morris's best-known novel, addresses itself to questions about the nature of man and the nature of art, but a dozen passages are high-spirited and amusing. The participants in the University of Chicago conference on "The Arts and the Public" discovered that Morris was like that himself: usually laughing and making others laugh, not only witty but irresistibly comic, and yet contributing more than most to the discussion of the weighty matters with which the conference was concerned.

Like many of the characters Morris has created, the people of *In Orbit* are ridiculous, even to the point of being grotesque. The central figure is a high-school drop-out, Jubal Gainer, who is responsible for a one-man, one-day crime wave in an Indiana town: a fist fight, a theft, a rape, an assault, a stabbing. Also in the cast are simple-minded Holly Stohrmeyer, alleged victim of the alleged rape; Curt Hodler, hard-working editor of the local newspaper; Felix Haffner, a teacher of languages at a nearby college, strange in appearance, strange in speech, endowed with a great gift for doing the wrong thing; Oscar Kashperl, a preposterously fat, by no means stupid dealer in secondhand wares; Pauline Bergdahl, who runs a diner, supplies Hodler with news, and finds rape puzzling; Charlotte Hatfield, a faculty wife with many surprising traits, including a passion for solo dancing to the music of Kid Ory; and Charlotte's husband, Alan, teacher and poet, who spends a good deal of time trying to understand her.

As always, Morris has an eye for the vivid detail and an ear for the telling phrase. The novel begins: "The boy comes riding with his arms high and wide, his ass light in the saddle, as if about to be shot into orbit from a forked sling." Sanford Avery, who after a fashion takes care of Holly Stohrmeyer, reports to Hodler: "I was gone a little better than forty minutes. In the time I was gone she peeled a couple dozen apples and got herself raped." When Haffner picks up the young criminal, Morris writes: "The man behind the wheel is no larger than a child, and looks to Jubal like a clever Hollywood chimp, trained to drive a car." This is Kashperl: "In spite of the temperature, and the season, he wears a topcoat that hangs within inches of his shoes. The material is chinchilla, it was tailored in Odessa, home of Kashperl's dreams and the Moldavanka gangsters whose blood—and it drained them to do it—now flows in his veins. He wears the coat draped on his shoulders, the cuffs of the empty sleeves tucked into his pockets. The effect is that of a giant who stands at slightly parted folding doors." When Kashperl first sees Jubal he knows by his outfit, which might have come out of Kashperl's store, what sort of boy he is dealing with: "Everything is familiar, in stock, and selling—except the face. The spattered visor conceals it, but Kashperl knows the type. Lumpy pimples on the shoulders, bad teeth, advanced athlete's feet." Of Pauline Bergdahl: "She was born in the woods that stretch behind the diner, had a good education up through spelling and fractions, fries all of her eggs hard on both sides and serves them with ketchup poured on the French fries. Her coffee comes with the spoon in it, a film of grease on the top."

When Pauline first sees Jubal on the stolen motorcycle, he looks as if he were about to take off into orbit; and poor Holly is under the impression that she has been visited by a man from outer space. Hodler meditates on what has been happening: "Hodler is a sober man, but for this boy on the loose, free to indulge in his whims, he feels a twinge of envy. There is something to be said for impulsive behavior, although Hodler is perhaps not the man to say it. Visiting spacemen are free to act in a way he is not." After the stabbing of Kashperl, Hodler listens to the unhelpful replies that bystanders give to the sheriff: "Did they all dream of being a man on the loose? Envied by inhibited red-blooded men, pursued by comical galoots like the Sheriff. He went that-a-way. With the thoughts, fantasies, and envious good wishes of them all."

The boy is in orbit, on the loose, free. Like many other Morris characters, from Uncle Dudley on, he does the things that other people dream of doing. His flight, one can see, is not going to be greatly prolonged, but he has swept in and out of Pickett with all the unpredictable and unreasonable violence of the twister that visits the town on that same memorable day. The one character who really understands him is Charlotte Hatfield, though her contacts with him are slight. As her husband observes, Kid Ory's horn is enough to send her into orbit. "You're going to think I'm peculiar when you know me," she once said to her husband. "That," Morris tells us, "was more than a year *after* they were married."

It is a short novel, full of action, and the seriousness can mostly be found between the lines. In his address at the Chicago conference Morris spent forty-five minutes in vividly and wittily and unhappily describing the absurdities of contemporary culture. "The lower depths," he said at one point, "so long pastured in hell, have come up for air." "Properly defined," he remarked, "the absurd is what is commonplace." Regarding the young rebels, he said he was struck "by how remarkably sane their daydreams are." "They don't want stupid wars, they don't want to live stupid lives." If one does read between the lines of *In Orbit,* one can see against what Jubal Gainer's rebellion, thoughtless and aimless as it seems, is directed. One might say that he is, like millions of his contemporaries, a Huck Finn without a Mississippi.

Saturday Review
February 18, 1967

10 *A Bill of Rites, a Bill of Wrongs, a Bill of Goods*

In Wright Morris's fiction anger and compassion are delicately balanced. The compassion is for people, "so desperately sad, so intolerably touching." The anger is for the conditions in which these sad, touching people live today, for the so-called "civilization" that, for the most part, they accept uncritically. In his nonfiction, anger is likely to take over. *A Bill of Rites, a Bill of Wrongs, a Bill of Goods* is written out of almost pure indignation. Morris has a gift for finding the exactly right epigraphs for his works, and in *A Bill* there are two beauties. One is from Henry James: "What was the case but magnificent for pitiless ferocity?" The other is from T. S. Eliot's *Little Gidding*:

> Second, the conscious impotence of rage
> At human folly, the laceration
> Of laughter at what ceases to amuse.

What is he angry at? Among other things, the triumph of raw material over imagination. This is a subject that he discussed in literary terms in *The Territory Ahead*; here his scope is wider. If Emerson could say more than a century ago that "things are in the saddle, and ride mankind," it is not surprising that Morris now finds humanity crushed to earth by its burden. He quotes Keats: "I am certain of nothing but the holiness of the heart's affections and the truth of Imagination." Now that the heart is, as Morris puts it, "an interchangeable part," it is hard to know what its affections are, and why should we trust the imagination when we have computers?

Emerson saw the predominance of "things" as a moral problem; Morris deprecates our love of facts as a possibly fatal distraction from the business of being human. He cites the Masters-Johnson report on sexual behavior as an example of the transformation of values in contemporary society. Why did several hundred couples accept—no, welcome—"what we call scientific observation" of their sexual activities? "What good is it? It makes news. The liquidation of privacy is a personal contribution to the expanding empire of communications: their motto might be, They also serve who publicly copulate."

He discusses other aspects of contemporary culture that illustrate and support his thesis: pop art, the behavior of the affluent elderly, the decline of the individual, the problem of the image. (" 'We're not ashamed of being scavengers,' said the executive of the Golden Gate Disposal Company, 'but we do want a better image.' It will be supplied.")

One of the most amusing and depressing essays is called "Reflections on the Death of the Reader." Morris describes a program on educational TV. The first book the critic mentions has disappointed him, and he is afraid the author is slipping. The second he praises, and then asks ominously where the author, having reached his peak, will go next. "All the reviewer risks," Morris comments, "is an opinion. The author, the more celebrated the better, is fair game for one and all to shoot down. The public listens with relief to the assurance that one more author they have not read will soon be among those it is already too late to read." Then there is the teacher of literature. "The idea that books are safes with secret combinations, and poems are ingenious double crostics, is not new, but only recently has achieved the status of a doctrine." The doctrine is a boon to professors, who, as Archibald MacLeish put it, find it easier to teach difficulties than poetry. "What *study* does to what used to be reading" is a disaster, Morris says.

So Morris goes his witty, savage way, hurling epigrams and aphorisms against the bastions of stupidity. "People are made by fools like you and me," he observes, "but only prime time can make an image." He is often funny but always serious. "We accept war, which we know at first hand, rather than a peace that passeth understanding. As it does: it passeth such understanding as we have." "What it takes to live *with* madness we have: what it takes to live without it we have not." Speaking of last summer's "fire season," he writes, "The black child-woman, eight months pregnant, says what she wants for her child is more *things,* that's all, *more things.* Her brain has been washed of the horror of her condition. Her nature has been drained of its human nature. She is not quite human. Being human is an effort that she lacks the strength, or the motive, to make."

Does he see no cause for hope? He is sometimes cautiously

hopeful about the young. "Behind the frequently theatrical facade of rebels who are now preoccupied with causes, I am struck by how remarkably sane their daydreams are. Far-fetched, it's true, but appallingly sane. They don't want stupid wars, they don't want to live stupid lives. The sheer novelty of it is not overwhelming, but the concept is still revolutionary. Not to wantonly kill, not to blight or destroy, not to live stupid lives." He sees the shortcomings of the beats and the hippies clearly enough: "The Haight-Ashbury scene has commitment and style, an ethic of love, freedom, and fraternity, but on the evidence it is sadly lacking in brains." He knows that most youth leaders—like most other Americans—have no capacity for growing up. Yet he believes that something important and just possibly encouraging is happening in what he calls "Campus City."

The people who lash out against the times in which they live are liable to make two mistakes. They may blame on the contemporary situation evils that have been fairly constant throughout history and perhaps are inherent in the human condition. And they may see personal inconveniences as universal calamities, regarding offenses to their peculiar tastes as blemishes on civilization. In small ways, I think, Morris is guilty of both faults, but most of his blows hit the mark. One of the wisest things he says is, "This is not a happy time to be an artist, but it is even worse not to be one." Too many people blind themselves to the present crisis, which is principally cultural though it is also economic and political. Too many who do see the crisis console themselves by saying there is nothing they can do about it and in the meantime, before the collapse, affluence is pleasant. Most artists, however, feel the crisis in their bones, and one way or another their uneasiness is expressed in their art. Morris has found explicit and powerful words for his uneasiness, and we had better listen to him.

Saturday Review
March 16, 1968

Afterword

In 1968 Morris published the third of his books made up of photographs and text, *God's Country and My People*. I have discussed this and its companions, *The Inhabitants* and *The Home Place* in my introduction to *The Wright Morris Reader*.

By the time he reached his sixtieth birthday, Morris had published fourteen novels, three books with photographs, two collections of essays, and the *Reader*. He has always been disciplined and industrious, and I expect him to continue to be. As I wrote in concluding my essay, "He is still going strong, full of energy, full of plans, and, to play his game with clichés, full of promise."

Afterword

SAUL BELLOW

Foreword

Although I found *Dangling Man* interesting when I first read it, I had no sense that this was the beginning of an uncommonly distinguished career. (Re-reading it in the light of Bellow's subsequent writing, one sees how much of the later Bellow it foreshadows.) *The Victim* was a different matter, a tightly constructed novel, built on fresh insights into the problem of responsibility. But it was *Augie March* that caught me, as it caught a large section of the reading public. Here was a man who had created a style for himself and unleashed an energy such as I had felt in only a few contemporary writers—the early Faulkner, for example. It happened that I reviewed the book along with Wright Morris's *The Deep Sleep,* and I have allowed some allusions to the latter to remain in the text, for the comparison still has some value.

1 *The Adventures of Augie March*

In most respects Saul Bellow's *The Adventures of Augie March* is different from *The Deep Sleep*. It is a big, loosely put together novel, covering many years and many miles, and introducing a large number of spectacularly unusual characters. Its nervous, aggressive, individualized style is as far from Morris's quiet colloquialism as the Chicago slums, in which some of its scenes are laid, are from Philadelphia's Main Line. Yet this, too, can only be described as a book about the mystery and the grandeur of the human personality.

Augie March's story, which he tells himself, is to a great extent the story of a series of persons who tried to shape his life. The first of these was the woman he and his brothers called Grandma Lausch, though she was not related to them but was a paying guest in the home their mother precariously maintained. She was a woman of standards and ideas, and she did her best for Augie. Next came William Einhorn, a cripple but in his way a man of affairs—"the first superior man I knew." After Einhorn and the Renlings, who wanted to adopt him, Augie followed the lead of his older brother, Simon, who was on the make. But he and Simon quarreled, and he was at loose ends until Thea Fenchel took him to Mexico to hunt giant lizards with an eagle. Later on he married a girl named Stella, and after the war his way of life was largely determined by her and by a wise and wealthy Armenian named Mintouchian.

If Wright Morris's Mrs. Porter is an example of inner-directed character, Augie might be thought to exemplify Dr. Riesman's second type, the other-directed character. Yet, though he seems so susceptible as always to offer a temptation to those people who like to change other people's lives, he always resists the influences that he appears to invite. His central quality, in fact, is his determination to be himself, and the only difficulty is that, unlike Mrs. Porter, he doesn't know what he is. Whether he has found out by the end of the book is a question, but along the way at least he has learned a lot about what he isn't.

In the course of telling Augie's story, Mr. Bellow, as I have said, covers a great deal of ground, for this is a picaresque novel set in an age of rapid transportation and great social mobility. Poor, illegitimate, Jewish, Augie starts with plenty of handicaps, but before he is out of his teens he has had a taste of the life of the well-to-do, thanks to Mrs. Renling, as well as some experience with both business and crime. He associates simultaneously with penniless students and the very rich Jews of Simon's acquaintance. Thea takes him to Mexico; the war introduces him, along with millions of other Americans, to Europe; when the book ends, he is living in Paris.

There is no limit to the number of amazing people Augie meets in the course of his adventures. Chicago is full of them: Padilla, the sockless young Mexican with a flair for mathematics; Frazer, the erudite radical; Mimi, Frazer's mistress, who has her own brand of feminism; and a dozen others. As if Thea and her eagle weren't enough to keep anybody busy. Augie encounters a large group of eccentrics in Mexico. As a merchant mariner, he becomes the confidant of his shipmates, and it is his luck to find himself in a lifeboat with a monomaniac.

Why does Augie meet so many remarkable people? Because, Mr. Bellow is surely saying, people are remarkable, and not in any quiet way either but in a highly assertive one. Augie says of Mimi: "The thing I began to learn from her was of the utmost importance: namely, that everyone sees to it his fate is shared. Or tries to see to it. You may say that I should have known this before. I should have, and in a way I did, or else Grandma Lausch or Einhorn or the Renlings would have had more success with me." He recurs to that theme in a variety of forms; for example, "That's the real struggle of humanity, to recruit others to your version of what's real." In the end he comes to be "good and tired of all these big personalities, destiny molders and heavy-water brains. Machiavellis and wizard evil-doers, big-wheels and imposers-upon, absolutists." But he realizes that human assertiveness is not only a peril but also the secret of survival, and the book closes with a tribute to the power of hope.

Augie is alert and perceptive, and whatever else may be said of the men and women who share his adventures, they are not boring. On the contrary, Mr. Bellow convinces us that we live in exciting times, and that is not the least of his achievements. Any reader of *Dangling Man* and *The Victim* knew that Saul Bellow was one of our able young writers, but there was nothing in the earlier books to prepare us for the abounding energy of *Augie March*. In its language and its ideas, as well as the fantastic variety of its cast of characters, it is a prodigal book, a breathtaking exhibition of sustained creativity.

The New Leader
September 21, 1953

2 *Seize the Day*

Saul Bellow's new book, *Seize the Day*, contains a novella, three excellent short stories, and a one-act play. The novella, whose title the volume bears, is not much more than a hundred pages, but it makes as solid an impression as *The Adventures of Augie March*, which must have ten times as many words. This isn't said to disparage the longer novel, which is right as rain, but to commend the economy and strength of the novella.

Seize the Day gives a harrowing picture of a man at the end of his rope. It is the story of the day in which Tommy Wilhelm is forced to confront the emptiness of his life. In his middle forties, Wilhelm is out of a job, separated from his wife, almost penniless. We see him with the utmost clarity—a man who has been getting by, who hasn't had to pay for his mistakes, who has convinced himself that he won't ever have to pay for them. "Haven't I always done my best?" he asks his wife. He pleads with her: "Margaret, go easy on me." But he knows that he has not done anywhere near his best, and he is beginning to discover that no one will go easy on him.

Having left his wife and their two sons, Wilhelm is living in the same Manhattan hotel as his father, a retired doctor. The day begins as he goes down to breakfast, and we get our first sense of his anguish in his random talk with the man at the newsstand. At breakfast he appeals to his father both for financial help and for sympathy, and is given neither. He has allowed himself to be persuaded by a Dr. Tamkin to gamble in the commodity market, and, after vacillating for a time between hope and despair, he learns that he has made a terrible mistake. Meanwhile, he has meditated on his other mistakes—leaving college with the idea of becoming a movie actor, changing his name, marrying Margaret, throwing up his job as a salesman out of vanity. Desperately he appeals to his wife for mercy and again to his father for help, but both are implacable. And then, when he is in the greatest need, and because he is in the greatest need, he finds deliverance.

Much of the novella portrays Wilhelm's relations with Dr. Tamkin. The doctor talks the glibbest kind of psychological theory, boasts of his adventures in many parts of the world, describes his astounding inventions, and offers instructions in the rapid accumulation of wealth. Although Wilhelm believes that Tamkin is a liar and may be a fraud, he is fascinated by him. If the doctor is a liar, at least he succeeds in impressing people. If he is a fraud, he is getting away with his fraudulence. And Wilhelm has a persistent hope that Tamkin isn't a fraud, because, if he isn't, Wilhelm may not be a failure. If Tamkin has had the adventurous life he pretends,

Wilhelm can hope that the emptiness of his own life may yet be filled. If Tamkin is as wise as he claims, Wilhelm's questions may yet be answered. If Tamkin has found an easy way to make money, Wilhelm's most pressing problems are not insoluble. In short, Wilhelm wants to believe in Tamkin because he wants to believe in his own past and his own future. Against his better judgment, he entrusts his last $700 to Tamkin and is cleaned out.

Tamkin is an extraordinary character, one of the finest Bellow has created, completely convincing and yet at the same time, like Melville's confidence man, deliberately ambiguous. But Tamkin exists in the book rather for the sake of Wilhelm than for his own sake. He exemplifies the way of life Wilhelm has drifted into. He claims to have all the answers, the easy answers Wilhelm has always wanted to believe in. Only when his falseness has been catastrophically exposed can Wilhelm be forced to recognize the falseness of his own character.

If Wilhelm is anything but an admirable person, he is not an unsympathetic one. On the contrary, Bellow rouses in us a deep compassion for him, not merely because he is in such a wretched plight but also because we can so easily see how he got there. His moments of contrition are completely genuine. "Oh, God," he prays. "Let me out of my trouble. Let me out of my thoughts, and let me do something better with myself. For all the time I have wasted I am very sorry. Let me out of this clutch and into a different life. For I am all balled up. Have mercy." Equally genuine are the moments in which he excuses himself: "He believed that he must, that he could and would recover the good things, the happy things, the easy tranquil things of life. He had made mistakes, but he could overlook these. He had been a fool, but that could be forgiven. The time wasted—must be relinquished. What else could one do about it? Things were too complex, but they might be reduced to simplicity again. Recovery was possible." Always he speaks in a familiar vein; he is like people we have known; indeed, he is like us.

Because we sympathize with Wilhelm, we are shocked that he

finds no sympathy in those around him. Tamkin, of course, we
could not expect to have mercy, and we know too little of the wife
to be surprised at her ruthlessness, but the father's harshness is
distressing, particularly so because it is put on selfish grounds: Dr.
Adler is old and tired, and he cannot be bothered any more with a
son for whom he has neither liking nor respect. Yet this distressing
harshness is perfectly sound. Dr. Adler would be a more attractive
person if he forgave Wilhelm for the seventy-seventh time, but in
fact such patience is not a common virtue. All his life Wilhelm has
been repudiating his father, and neither he nor we ought to be
astonished when his father repudiates him. What Wilhelm has to
learn is that he cannot go on counting on the virtues of others.

It is because of the compassion we feel for Wilhelm that we can
believe in the possibility of his redemption. I shall not describe the
manner of that redemption because a summary of the incident could
only make it seem ridiculous. That it does not seem ridiculous in
the novella—but, on the contrary, completely credible—is, of
course, a measure of Bellow's achievement.

The New Leader
November 26, 1956

3 *Henderson the Rain King*

Saul Bellow's *Henderson the Rain King* is an adventure story with
large and important implications. Like almost everything else
Bellow has written, it is an account of a man's struggles to find and
to transcend himself, but Henderson's quest takes him into strange
and romantic places. It is as if Bellow were inventing for his hero
physical perils commensurate with the inner hazards of his search.

However one reads it, this is as exciting a novel as has appeared in a long time.

Bellow has created many bizarre characters, but Henderson is the most extravagant figure of them all. Fifty-five years old when he introduces himself to us, he is a giant of a man, six feet four inches tall and correspondingly heavy and strong. Rich and of good family, he has by his own account wasted his life. When he thinks of that life, he says, "A disorderly rush begins—my parents, my wives, my girls, my children, my farm, my animals, my habits, my money, my music lessons, my drunkenness, my prejudices, my brutality, my teeth, my face, my soul!" He is a man who is driven, but by what and towards what he does not know.

Henderson at this moment of his life has to go somewhere, and by chance he goes to Africa. Leaving his companions and striking off on his own with a faithful guide, he comes upon an isolated tribe, the Arnewi, gentle people, whom he likes. Eager to do them a great service, he brings disaster upon them, and, as so often before, is crushed with remorse.

He proceeds, this modern Gulliver, to visit the Wariri, a sterner tribe. But though his welcome is not cordial, he eventually finds himself on intimate terms with the king, Dahfu, who has studied medicine in missionary schools and who speaks English. This time Henderson's impulses lead him to expend his great strength in carrying a huge statue, and his success gives him an important role in rain-making ceremonies. And since rain does fall, he becomes the Sungo, the Rain King.

All this is strange enough, but the strangest is yet to come. Dahfu has a kind of private lion cult into which he tries to initiate the reluctant Henderson, the two meanwhile engaging in intense discussions of the nature and destiny of man. Then comes the climax— a hair-raising lion hunt conducted according to the risky precepts of Wariri ritual. Dahfu is killed, probably as the result of a plot against him, and Henderson has to flee to avoid becoming Dahfu's successor. He returns to America with a lion cub and the conviction that he has found what he was looking for.

No one has ever conveyed so well as Saul Bellow the anguish of a man who is capable of honestly contemplating his nature but incapable of changing it. This agony is to be found in his first book, *Dangling Man,* and in his recent novelette, *Seize the Day.* The hero of the latter, Tommy Wilhelm, might in some ways be regarded as a preliminary study for Henderson, but there are great differences between them. Tommy is a slob, and the best one can say for him is that he knows he is, and wishes he weren't, and this makes him pitiful. Henderson has acted like a slob again and again, as he insists on reminding himself and us, but one never doubts that he has good and even great qualities. Often enough, as with the Arnewi, it is his good intentions that lead him into disaster, and he is so genuine a seeker for salvation that his predicament seems tragic rather than merely sad.

Because he has qualities of greatness, Henderson can have heroic adventures as well as comic misadventures, and Bellow's uninhibited inventiveness has given his virtues and vices full scope. I suspect that resemblances between the Arnewi and the Wariri and existing African tribes are purely coincidental, but whether this is true or not makes little difference, for the main thing is that Henderson has a world in which he can find himself. Bellow has also given him a style of his own. Augie March expressed himself in colloquial language with rich literary overtones. Henderson's style is more purely colloquial, and what gives it its special quality is its headlong energy. The style is the man, and Henderson is revealed to us not only by what he says but also by the way in which he says it.

There was, I recall, a reviewer of *The Adventures of Augie March* who spent much space in expounding the symbolism of that novel, making everything stand for something else. (He then turned around and scolded Bellow for the symbolism that he, the reviewer, had dreamt up.) *Henderson* is likely to be misinterpreted in the same way, although Bellow has been quite specific. The lions are lions, the pigs are pigs, the bear is a bear. That the lions have a special significance for Dahfu, and that he hopes they can have a similar significance for Henderson, he says flatly enough. In the same way Henderson knows there was a reason why he raised pigs. But whatever meanings the animals have, they have as animals, and they have these meanings to particular individuals. Lion does not equal this; pig does not equal that.

Although Bellow is dealing with deep mysteries, he does not indulge in mystification of any sort, but brings to his difficult theme as much clarity as possible. "Don't you believe in regeneration?" Henderson asks. He does, and so, with greater reason, does Dahfu. "Well, Henderson," Dahfu challenges, "what are the generations for, please explain to me? Only to repeat fear and desire without a change? This cannot be what the thing is for, over and over and over. Any good man will try to break the cycle." Earlier Dahfu has explained how the cycle can be broken: "Imagination is a force of nature. Is this not enough to make a person full of ecstasy? Imagination, imagination, imagination! It converts to actual, it sustains, it alters, it redeems!"

Henderson differs from *Augie March* in many interesting ways. In the earlier novel Bellow uses a loose structure to illustrate, through a long series of essentially realistic episodes, the vast possibilities of contemporary life. Beginning in poverty and illegitimacy, Augie ranges far, horizontally and vertically, to end in uncertainty. Henderson, on the other hand, born to every advantage, has lived fifty-five years of unquiet desperation. Of Augie's kind of patient pilgrimage he has never been capable. He is driven by the voice that cries, "I want, I want," and the story of his search is both romantic and dramatic. I cannot say that *Henderson the Rain King* is a better book than *Augie March*; the denseness of experience in the earlier novel is something almost unparalleled in contemporary literature. But *Henderson* is a wonderful book for Bellow to have written after writing *Augie March*. It is a book that should be read again and again, and each reading, I believe, will yield further evidence of Bellow's wisdom and power.

Saturday Review
February 21, 1959

4 *Herzog*

Saul Bellow begins his new novel, *Herzog,* with this sentence: "If I am out of my mind, it's all right with me, thought Moses Herzog." The book continues:

Some people thought he was cracked and for a time he himself had doubted that he was all there. But now, though he still behaved oddly, he felt confident, cheerful, clairvoyant, and strong. He had fallen under a spell and was writing letters to everyone under the sun. He was so stirred by these letters that from the end of June he moved from place to place with a valise full of papers. He had carried this valise from New York to Martha's Vineyard but returned from the Vineyard immediately; two days later he flew to Chicago, and from Chicago he went to a village in western Massachusetts. Hidden in the country, he wrote endlessly, fanatically, to the newspapers, to people in public life, to friends and relatives and at last to the dead, his own obscure dead, and finally the famous dead.

Herzog, now in his late forties, has been a student and teacher and has written two scholarly and well-received books, but has come to an impasse. He has been twice married, and both marriages have collapsed, the first through his fault, the second, he believes, through his wife's. When we meet him, he is, as Bellow's characters are likely to be, at the end of his rope. "Late in spring Herzog had been overcome by the need to explain, to have it out, to justify, to put in perspective, to clarify, to make amends."

Through the writing of letters, most of which are never sent, he carries on the process of self-analysis that seems to him so important. His letters reveal the operations of a brilliant and well-stocked but at the moment erratic mind. Herzog knows the answers that the great thinkers have given to the problems of man and the universe, and he knows that he has to find his own answers. The letters are a device that could have been abysmally dull, but, as Bellow has handled them, they are lively, sometimes profound, and always revelatory. We know with remarkable clarity what is going on in Herzog's psyche.

Herzog is often reminded of events in his past, and in flashbacks the reader gets an account of the recent weeks, the weeks of crisis, and sees something of the earlier years. Herzog deserted his first wife, Daisy, to marry Madeleine, and it was at the latter's urging that he bought an old mansion in the Berkshires and spent in renovating it a small fortune inherited from his father. The marriage was a mess, and Madeleine left him, taking their child. Since the divorce he has been having an affair with a young woman in New York City but has avoided matrimony.

Although the story comes out in fragments, which are not always in chronological order, so that we have to piece it together, we come to know what Herzog's life has been like and what has led to the present crisis. We see something of his family, and we have a detailed account of his miserable life with Madeleine. After each glimpse of the past, Herzog returns to the letters, in which he expresses the constant turmoil of his mind.

Herzog goes to Chicago to see his daughter, and it is arranged for him to have an afternoon with her. Everything seems to be going well when he has a minor automobile accident. Because he is carrying a revolver—this is carefully explained—he is held by the police. Madeleine, more vicious than usual, comes for the child. On the way to the police station, he continues his meditations: "But what is the philosophy of this generation? Not God is dead, that point was passed long ago. Perhaps it should be stated Death is God. This generation thinks—and this is its thought of thought— that nothing faithful, vulnerable, fragile can be durable or have any true power." He continues: "Perhaps what had made him faint was not the accident but the premonition of such thought. Nausea was only apprehension, excitement, the unbearable intensity of these ideas."

He returns to the Berkshires and settles into his long-abandoned mansion. He repeats the book's first line. "But if I am out of my mind, it's all right with me." Now, however, we know that he is not out of his mind, and we also understand why he is in a state of crisis. During the next few days he writes letters more furiously than ever, and begins to achieve some sort of stability. He writes to God: "How my mind has struggled to make coherent sense. I have not been too good at it. But I have desired to do your unknowable will, taking it, and you, without symbols. Everything of intensest significance. Especially if divested of me." Although he knows that "the buttercup would come round again, by and by," in the present he has found joy.

In Bellow's fine novellette *Seize the Day,* the central character, a slob of the first order, who hates but cannot change his nature, has a kind of mystical experience which convinces him that change is possible. Henderson, in *Henderson the Rain King,* is redeemed by the fantastic rites of King Dahfu. Herzog, on the other hand, seeks salvation by way of the intellect. He is aware that his problems are not new, and he knows what other men have made of them. (He refers to Nietzsche, Whitehead, Buber, Freud, Hobbes, and many others.) He is a man of ideas, though he is also a man of powerful emotions. He is driven, just as Wilhelm and Henderson are, but he is not driven blindly, as they are.

Herzog is not an easy novel to read; in fact, it is almost as difficult as Thomas Mann's *Doctor Faustus,* which in some ways it resembles. It is a challenge to the reader—which is by no means a bad thing. If the reader gives himself to the book, it is an exciting experience, because Bellow has so successfully dramatized his hero's philosophical quest. At one point he speaks of "the daily comedy of Moses F. Herzog," and it is true that Moses, like most of Bellow's heroes, is something of a clown, but he is also a tremendously serious man. He is full of contradictions, and it is by showing him in all his complexity that Bellow gives him life. That he has many qualities and experiences in common with his creator is obvious enough, but he is a creation, an individual in his own right. A novel that is certain to be talked about and written about for a long time to come, *Herzog* re-enforces my conviction that Bellow is the leading figure in American fiction today.

Saturday Review
September 19, 1964

Afterword

Although it was published after I had given up the regular reviewing of books, *Mr. Sammler's Planet* must be mentioned at this time, for it is the finest novel Bellow has written and validates his claim to preeminence among contemporary writers of fiction. Like *Herzog,* it is a novel of ideas, but here the thinker is mature, resolute, and uncomplaining. Although he has seen too much of the world to underestimate the powers of evil, Sammler is grateful for good wherever he may find it. He understands what he can and endures what he must. Hamlet says, "The readiness is all," and Lear, "Ripeness is all." Sammler is as ready as a man can be for death, but he is mature enough to make the most of his life so long as it lasts.

BERNARD MALAMUD

Foreword

The quarter-century since the end of World War II has not been an era of great creativity, but it has been given distinction by a number of writers of fiction. One of these is Bernard Malamud, whose steady development as a novelist and as a writer of short stories has been a satisfaction to watch. I cannot say that each book he has written has been an improvement over the last, but each does represent growth in one way or another—style, form, depth of feeling, range of emotion. Certainly not in the usual sense an art-for-art's sake man, he is a dedicated craftsman. It is suitable that his most recent novel, *Pictures of Fidelman*, is a subtle study of the character of the artist. One of his funniest books, it is also one of his most profound.

1 *The Assistant*

Bernard Malamud's *The Assistant* is a somber, meticulous examination of the complexity of human motivation. It may disappoint some of the admirers of *The Natural,* for it has neither the extravagance nor the humor of that book. On the contrary, the material is familiar and the tone quiet. But it is in its own way as good and even as original as the earlier novel, and though at first my interest was tepid, I found myself more and more deeply involved.

Mr. Malamud tells the story of a Jewish grocer, a man getting on in years, one who has worked hard all his life and has been scrupulously honest, and who has been rewarded by nothing but poverty. Business has become so bad that Morris and his wife depend largely on the earnings of their daughter, Helen, who has given up her dreams of college to take a job she hates. As if his luck were not bad enough, Morris is held up by a couple of men, robbed of the little money he has in the cash register, and badly beaten.

The assistant of the title is Frank Alpine, a stranger who, with extraordinary persistence, insists on helping in the store while Morris is incapacitated. As the reader soon realizes, Frank is one of the men who held up the store, and he is moved, at least in part, by contrition. He works hard and the store prospers, but at the same time he steals small amounts of money. Although his wife is violently opposed, Morris keeps Frank on after he has himself recovered, and Frank is eager to stay, not only because he is in love with Helen but also because the store and Morris himself have come in some baffling way to be indispensable to him.

Just as Frank has begun to return the money he has stolen,

Morris gets proof of his thieving and dismisses him. Then Frank forces himself on Helen, destroying the affection she has begun to feel for him. Once more Morris is ill, and once more Frank makes great sacrifices to keep the store going, but Helen will have nothing to do with him. When Morris is able to return to the store, Frank confesses his part in the holdup, which Morris has already suspected, and again he is discharged. Morris's situation becomes more and more desperate, until he is delivered from it by death. For the third time, Frank assumes the burden of the store, and at last Helen is willing to admit that he is a changed man, although we never know for sure whether that means that she will marry him.

The possibility of change in a human being is one of the book's principal themes. Before the holdup, Frank has been an unlucky fellow, pretty much a ne'er-do-well, not really a criminal but apparently indifferent to, perhaps unaware of, moral obligations. The contrition he feels when his partner cracks Morris's skull is nothing he has expected. But Frank is not changed overnight: He will do penance by working for Morris for next to nothing, but his conscience permits him to steal money with the excuse that it is he who has made the store prosper. Yet, his sense of the debt he owes Morris is real, and it persists even after he has lost hope of winning Helen, eventually making him the honest man he has aspired to be. Helen suddenly recognizes the change:

"It's true, he's not the same man, she said to herself, I should have known by now. She had despised him for the evil he had done, without understanding the why or aftermath, or admitting there could be an end to the bad and a beginning of good."

Closely related to the change in Frank is his attitude toward Jews. Knowing nothing about their beliefs to begin with, he becomes intensely preoccupied with his idea that Judaism is a religion for people who suffer, a religion that not only enables its adherents to endure suffering but demands suffering from them. We see him sitting alone in the funeral parlor after the services for Morris: "Suffering, he thought, is like a piece of goods. I bet the Jews could make a suit of clothes out of it." Then he adds: "The other funny thing is that there are more of them around than anybody knows about." And at the end Frank becomes a Jew. This is not to say however, that Malamud accepts Frank's interpretation of Judaism or accepts Judaism as Frank interprets it. Morris's last thought is, "I gave away my life for nothing," and Helen, after listening to the rabbi's moving eulogy of her father's devotion and honesty, reflects that the rabbi has not told the whole truth about Morris. "He made himself a victim," she thinks. "He would, with a little more courage, have been more than he was."

The novel appears to be laid in the Depression, and one cannot help contrasting it with the Depression novels that were written in the 30's. Neither Morris's predicament nor Frank's is blamed, by the author or by any of the characters, on what we used to talk about as social conditions. Malamud's attention is focused on psychological, ethical and religious problems. I cannot say that one approach is right and the other wrong, but I am convinced that it would have been impossible for this kind of novel to be written in the 30's, just as I believe it would have been pointless for Mr. Malamud to write the other kind of novel in 1957. What matters is that he has a strong grasp on the problems that concern him and writes about them with admirable insight.

The New Leader
April 29, 1957

2 *The Magic Barrel*

Malamud's first novel, *The Natural*, published in 1952, was a wildly original extravaganza of baseball. In his second, *The Assistant*, which appeared last year, he wrote, with calm, deep assurance about a Jewish storekeeper. It is in the world of Jewish storekeepers and their like that most of the stories in *The Magic Barrel,* are laid. In *The Assistant,* which seems to me one of the important novels of the postwar period, Jewish experience is used as a way of approaching the deepest, broadest problems of love and fear, of communion and isolation in human life. So, too, in *The Magic Barrel*: the more faithfully Malamud renders Jewish life, the wider his meanings are.

Malamud's stories often have a legendary quality, whether his method is realistic, as in "The First Seven Years," or fantastic, as in "Angel Levine." In these particular stories there are echoes of the Bible: the allusion to Jacob and Rachel in the title of the first, the paraphrase of Job in the opening of the second. He does not merely allude to legends, however; he creates them. The title story, for instance, seems to be the kind of tale that is handed down from generation to generation in a culture that depends on oral tradition. This and certain of the other stories appear to have been brought to the exactly right shape by a process of attrition.

His stories are varied, more varied than I had realized as I encountered them in magazines. "Summer's Reading" has a deceptive simplicity that reminds me of Sherwood Anderson. "The Lady of the Lake" ends with a twist that would have amused O. Henry, though Malamud, needless to say, has not written it for the sake of the twist. Some stories are put together with textbook precision, but others pass themselves off as mere anecdotes. Although compassion is obviously Malamud's great quality, he has many resources, among them the comic inventiveness of such a story as "Behold the Key."

The question Malamud asks more often than any other is: what are the limits of human responsibility? In "The Last Mohican" he develops the theme with a rare combination of humor and pathos, whereas in "Take Pity" he approaches it by way of fantasy. More often he is quietly matter-of-fact, as in "The Bill" and "The Loan." "The Loan" will serve as an example of what Malamud can do. Here are Lieb the baker and his wife, aging and ill, and here is Kobotsky, also aging and ill, who asks Lieb for money so that he can place a stone on his wife's grave. That, in the midst of so much physical suffering, the three can undergo profound agonies of soul, Kobotsky in asking a favor, the others in deciding whether or not to grant it, becomes, in Malamud's hands, a triumph of the human spirit.

Saturday Review
May 17, 1958

3 *A New Life*

I have never seen a briefer or more accurate blurb than appears on the jacket of Bernard Malamud's *A New Life*. It reads in its entirety: "This is the story of S. Levin, thirty, a bearded man with a burdensome past, who comes from New York to a small town in the Pacific Northwest, to live a new life." In simplicity and precision it matches the opening sentence: "S. Levin, formerly a drunkard, after a long and tiring transcontinental journey, got off the train at Marathon, Cascadia, toward evening of the last Sunday in August, 1950."

The story that is introduced in this way is not easy to describe. Seymour Levin has crossed the continent to undertake his first job as a teacher of college English and to enter upon what he dearly hopes will be a new life, since he has little reason to be pleased with his old one. In a sense the theme reverses one of the popular themes of nineteenth-century fiction, the story of the young man from the provinces; Levin goes from the city to the province, and he is looking not for fame or fortune but for a chance to lead the kind of life that can be called good.

As the novel develops, it becomes a comedy of errors, for Levin is a first-class blunderer. It is also a harsh satire on the higher education as practiced in certain American colleges. But mostly it is a pathetic tale of struggle and failure and renewed struggle, for Levin discovers that there is no escaping from the past, and he learns that the good life is difficult of achievement.

We are not told anything very specific about Levin's past until we are more than halfway through the book, but a great deal is suggested. For one thing, though not much is said about it, Levin is a poor Brooklyn Jew, and, especially if we have read *The Assistant* and the stories in *The Magic Barrel,* we are familiar with his background. But, as we eventually learn, he has experienced not only the poverty and suffering Malamud has often described; his beginnings were more squalid than anything Malamud has hitherto portrayed. His father a criminal, his mother a suicide, he fell into absolute despair: "I drank, I stank. I was filthy, skin on bone. . . . For two years I lived in self-hatred, willing to part with life."

Then there was a moment of revelation, which transformed him, as he puts it, into "a man of principle," but this was followed by a period of dreadful apathy. A second revelation came when he rediscovered that "the source of freedom is the human spirit." Now he truly became a new man, secured an education, taught in a high school, aspired to the good life.

Levin's conversion is a little like that of Frank in *The Assistant,* but Frank's is the climax of the book, whereas *A New Life* shows us what happened to Levin afterwards. The appointment at Cascadia, achieved after many failures and achieved, as we learn near the end of the book, by a freakish accident, represents the fulfillment of a dream: at last, he believes, he is to be identified with the great tradition of liberal thought that has come to mean so much to him.

Disillusionment comes quickly. Not only is Cascadia not a liberal arts college; there are only one or two members of the English department who bother to pay even lip service to the liberal tradition. Most of Levin's colleagues are good at sports, handy with gadgets, reliable in the matter of turning in their grades, but utterly indifferent to the life of the intellect. One would like to believe that this is caricature, but, alas, institutions such as Cascadia exist.

Levin has been no more successful in his relations with women than in his career, and a series of unfortunate experiences marks his first months at Cascadia. Then he falls in love, at least for a time, with the wife of a colleague, and although this affair affords him some moments of satisfaction, it becomes complicated and difficult, and it works its way to a conclusion that holds little promise of happiness.

Meanwhile he has decided that he must become a man of action and do something about a situation that seems to him so deplorable, and he offers himself as a candidate for the chairmanship of the department. Nothing, of course, could be more preposterous: this Jew, this New Yorker, this beginning instructor who is already known as a troublemaker and suspected of being a radical. Yet one knows that Levin would pursue just such a course, and he pursues it with an unscrupulousness that surprises both him and the reader. Moreover, it appears that his revolution might have succeeded if he had not been exposed as an adulterer.

The tone varies from farce to pathos, but at every point Malamud knows what he is doing. What he has attempted in the book, I think, is a rather special kind of realism, disregarding all the familiar categories of fiction. This is basically a serious novel about the difficulties of leading the good life, and in the end, because he will not abandon his struggle, Levin emerges as a hero. But Malamud has taken pains not to clothe him in heroic trappings. He is a clown, grotesque in appearance, completely unsuited to the environment in which he finds himself, and inevitably many ridiculous things happen to him. Yet the reader learns to respect him.

The novel has a less immediate impact than *The Assistant*. There, in the relationship between Frank and the Bober family, the situation is sharply defined, and the story rises to a dramatic and moving climax. But *A New Life* is larger in scope, and the problem to which it is addressed is a more profound one. Levin, as I have said, is a hero, and very much a hero of our times. He has escaped from despair, only to find himself surrounded by triviality, but he has the courage to cling to what he believes.

Saturday Review
October 7, 1961

4 *The Fixer*

If I say, as I am prepared to do, that Bernard Malamud's *The Fixer,* is one of the finest novels of the postwar period, I don't see how there can be much argument. If, however, I go on to agree with the publishers that it is a "great" novel, I may be in semantic difficulties. Recently I asserted that there is greatness in John Barth's *Giles Goat-Boy,* which I believe to be true. Robert Scholes, on the other hand, writing in the *New York Times Book Review,* admitted of no qualification; he said flatly that it is "a great novel." He made a good case, too, but at the end he brought in an argument that I found disturbing. Barth's audience, he said, "must be that same audience whose capacities have been extended and prepared by Joyce, Proust, Mann, and Faulkner." He continued: "For some time we have been wondering what to do with the training given us by those giants of modern fiction, wondering whether we were really meant to expend our hard-earned responsiveness on such estimable but unexciting writers as C. P. Snow and Saul Bellow. The answer now seems clear. The difference between competence and genius can hardly be made clearer. And Barth is a comic genius of the highest order."

Who are the "we" who have been wondering? Mr. Scholes, I gather, and probably other academic critics. This calls to mind what Bellow said in his address to the recent International Congress of the P.E.N. Club. He complained that various critics in university posts had laid hold of the avant-garde heroes of an earlier generation, using their work to set a standard by which contemporary writers could be judged and condemned. In the version I read, in the *Times Book Review*, Bellow's argument wasn't completely clear, but I think I understand at least part of what he was saying. When Scholes calls Snow "estimable but unexciting," I can follow him, for Snow has deliberately adopted oldfashioned techniques, and the wonder is that he has managed to do as much with them as he has. But Bellow has constantly experimented with the form of the novel and has developed a powerful style that is peculiarly his. Bracketing Snow and Bellow tells us nothing about Barth—though something about Scholes.

What I am saying, of course, is what I have said before—that there are more kinds than one of literary merit and even greatness. I think *Giles Goat-Boy,* and *The Fixer,* are both unusually good and unusually important novels, though they have little in common except their excellence. Malamud has told a straight-forward story in language of the greatest austerity. Although he began his literary career with a novel based on myth, *The Natural,* and has often introduced elements of fantasy in his short stories, *The Fixer* is realistic in the most precise sense of that term. But the story is told so purely and with such power that it has the large meanings—what some people call the "universal" meanings—of legend.

Malamud tells about a Jewish handy man who was arrested in Kiev in 1911, was charged with having committed a ritual murder, and suffered greatly for more than two years before being tried. To begin with, before I had read the book, I wondered why Malamud should expect his readers to be concerned about what had happened to this one Jew half a century ago, in view of what had happened to six million Jews during the Second World War. It did not take me long to realize that Malamud had deliberately set himself this problem. Six million was a figure, but a man was a man. If he could tell this story well enough, he must have decided, this one unprepossessing man, this Yakov Bok, could represent not only the martyrs of Belsen and Auschwitz but all victims of man's inhumanity. We the readers could be made to feel for this one man what we could not possibly feel for the six million.

Malamud has written: "After my last novel I was sniffing for an idea in the direction of injustice on the American scene, partly for obvious reasons—this was a time of revolutionary advances in Negro rights—and partly because I became involved with this theme in a way that sets off my imagination in terms of art." He thought of civil rights workers in the South, of Sacco and Vanzetti, of Dreyfus, of Caryl Chessman, and then he remembered Mendel Beiliss, about whom his father had told him, and something happened. "In *The Fixer*," he explains, "I use some of his [Mendel Beiliss's] experiences, though not, basically, the man, partly because his life came to less than he had paid for by his suffering and endurance, and because I had to have room to invent. To his trials in prison I added something of Dreyfus's and Vanzetti's, shaping the whole to suggest the quality of the afflictions of the Jews under Hitler. These I dumped on the head of poor Yakov Bok. . . . So a novel that began as an idea concerned with injustice in America today has become one set in Russia fifty years ago, dealing with anti-Semitism there. Injustice is injustice."

Yakov Bok is nobody but Yakov Bok, and he is one of the most fully rendered characters in modern literature. An odd-job man, a jack-of-all-trades, a fixer, he lives in a small Jewish community near Kiev. His wife, by whom he has had no children, has deserted him, and he finally makes a deal with her father and sets out for the city with the latter's horse and wagon. He is poor, proud, and bitter, with a fine sardonic wit. When his father-in-law tells him that, in going to the city, he is looking for trouble, he replies, "I've never had to look." When his wagon collapses, he asks, "Who invented my life?" Although he has had almost no formal education, he has read Spinoza and tried to understand him, and he calls himself a freethinker.

Even before he has reached Kiev, Yakov has encountered a violently anti-Semitic ferryman, and from the first he feels the hostility of the city. Bitter as he is, however, he has compassion for a drunken Russian dying in the snow, he rescues him even though the man wears the badge of the Jew-hating Black Hundreds. Nikola Maximovitch, though he would exterminate the Jews, is capable of crying over the death of a dog, and he wants to reward his benefactor, whom he does not know to be Jewish. Thus Yakov is given a job, which he badly needs, in a brickyard. Because he is living in a district forbidden to most Jews, he is ill at ease, but he has to have money to live on.

When he is arrested, Yakov assumes that he is to be punished for some minor offense, and it takes him a while to grasp the horrible nature of the charge against him. Only when he is confronted with the witnesses for the prosecution, mostly men and women who are using anti-Semitic prejudice to conceal their own crimes, does he realize that he is the victim of a monstrous conspiracy. And he asks, as who wouldn't, why me?

Because the prosecution's case is so weak, Yakov's trial is postponed for two years, during which time his miseries multiply. Lodged in filth, never adequately fed, bowed down with disease, given little or nothing with which to occupy his mind, systematically tortured by the guards, finally chained to the wall of his cell, he endures such suffering as the reader is loath to contemplate. But Malamud, without sensationalism, without high-pitched emotionalism, makes us feel what we would prefer not to feel. Having himself fully entered into Yakov's ordeals in an extraordinary feat of empathy, he forces us to go at least some distance with him.

One of the ways in which Malamud compels realization of Yakov's suffering is to let him compare present with the past. The life in the shtetl, which had once seemed to him poisonously narrow and dull, now takes on an idyllic aspect: "You can smell the grass and the flowers and look at the girls, if one or two happen to be passing by along the road. You can also do a day's work if there's work to do. Today there's a little carpentering job. You work up a sweat sawing wood apart and hammering it together. When it's time to eat you open up your food parcel—not bad. The thing about food is to have it when you want it. A hard-boiled egg with a pinch of salt is delicious. Also some sour cream with a cut-up potato. If you dip bread into fresh milk and suck before swallowing, it tastes like a feast. . . . After all, you're alive and free. Even if you're not so free, you think you are."

But later the miseries that made Yakov's pre-Kiev life appear a paradise come to seem a kind of happiness: "Yakov thought how it used to be before he was chained to the wall. He remembered sweeping the floor with the birch broom. He remembered reading Zhitnyak's gospels, and the Old Testament pages. . . . He thought of being able to urinate without having to call the guards; and of only two searches a day instead of a terrifying six. He thought of lying down on the straw mattress any time he wanted to; but now he could not even lie down on the wooden bed except when they released him to. . . . Yakov thought he would be glad if things went back to how they had once been. He wished he had enjoyed the bit of comfort, in a way freedom, he had had then."

Throughout the days and months and years of pain and despair, Yakov faces two temptations. What anti-Semites in the government, from Czar Nicholas down, want to prove is that ritual murder is an essential part of the Jewish religion and that therefore all persecutions of the Jews are justified. More than once they promise Yakov that if he will testify that the boy was murdered by Jews for reasons of ritual, he himself will be treated leniently. Although he has never felt close to the Jewish community and has rejected the Jewish faith, he refuses to lend himself to so evil a conspiracy, even when his wife is sent to his cell with a confession for him to sign.

The other temptation is suicide. The idea inevitably occurs to him as soon as he understands the power of the forces drawn up against him. When the one Russian official who has shown a rudimentary sense of decency in his dealings with Yakov is framed because of that fact and sent to Yakov's prison where he hangs himself, the poor persecuted Jew thinks of following his example. But he realizes that suicide would also be a betrayal of millions of people. "He's half a Jew himself, yet enough of one to protect them. After all, he knows the people; and he believes in their right to be Jews and to live in the world like men. He is against those who are against them. He will protect them to the extent that he can." "I'll live," he cries out in his cell, "I'll wait. I'll come to my trial."

All that he has endured has strengthened Yakov. Always a thinker in his uneducated way, he has recognized his historic role and, though he laments its being forced on him, he accepts it. "We're all in history," he thinks, "that's sure, but some are more than some." As skeptical as ever about the existence of God, he believes that it is incumbent on men to stand for what they believe. Although in some ways more tolerant, for instance of his wife, he has not become saintly. "I'm not the same man I was. I fear less and hate more."

The climax of the novel comes in an imaginary dialogue between Yakov and the Czar. After describing his own misfortune, the latter says, "Surely it [suffering] has taught you the meaning of mercy?" Yakov replies, "Excuse me, Your Majesty, but what suffering has taught me is the uselessness of suffering, if you don't mind me saying so." He reminds the Czar of his failures as a ruler: "You had your chances and pissed them away. There's no argument against that. It's not easy to twist events by the tail but you might have done something for a better life for us all—for the future of Russia, one might say, but you didn't." While a carriage brings him closer to his trial Yakov thinks: "As for history, there are ways to reverse it. What the Czar deserves is a bullet in the gut. Better him than us." "One thing I've learned, he thought, there's no such thing as an unpolitical man, especially a Jew. You can't be one without the other, that's clear enough. You can't sit still and see yourself destroyed." There the book ends, and, when one remembers what was in Malamud's mind when it was conceived, rightly ends. Yakov has learned not merely to endure, if I may use William Faulkner's favorite word, but also to resist.

Since few Americans have heard of Mendel Beiliss, it is fortunate that Maurice Samuel's *Blood Accusation: The Strange History of the Beiliss Case* has just been published. The facts of the case are essentially these: Mendel Beiliss, a man of thirty-seven, father of five children, a worker for fifteen years in a Kiev brickyard, was arrested on July 22, 1911, was charged with the ritual murder of a Christian boy, was held in prison for more than two years before he was tried, and finally was exonerated.

Samuel, quite rightly, is concerned with the Beiliss case, not with Beiliss. He describes the reasons for the arrest, emphasizing the sad state of the Russian Empire under Czar Nicholas and tracing the history of anti-Semitism. He gives a detailed account of the trial, analyzing the strategies of both prosecution and defense, and discusses the international repercussions. The principal aim of the prosecution, which had support high in the government, was to justify persecution of the Jews. Since the jury's verdict could be interpreted as an indictment of the Jewish people, the reactionaries were not too disturbed by the fact that Beiliss, the case against whom was of the flimsiest, escaped.

Samuel is right in saying that Beiliss was of little importance; he was the accidental victim of a malignant conspiracy; during the trial he was, as Samuel says, "the forgotten man." But Yakov Bok is of the greatest importance and will not be forgotten for a long time. All of the scenes in *The Fixer,* most of which bear no relation to the facts of the Beiliss case, have been worked upon by a not merely compassionate but an anguished imagination. The style, which seems so simple, is a triumph of discipline; scarcely a word could be spared. *The Fixer* is a novel that offers a great experience, first of all a literary experience, but not merely that.

Saturday Review
September 10, 1966

5 *Pictures of Fidelman*

Bernard Malamud's new novel, *Pictures of Fidelman,* is as unexpected as it is gratifying. His fifth novel, it differs from its predecessors in almost everything but imaginative power. Whereas *The Assistant,* and *The Fixer,* for example, are tightly constructed, the new book is a series of episodes, each a dramatic entity though each makes its contribution to our understanding of the bizarre hero. Although the hero is an American Jew, the scene is Italy. Like Si Levin in *A New Life,* Fidelman is a *schlemiel,* a blunderer, an unlucky fellow, but his misfortunes are on a more extravagant scale.

On the first page we read: "Fidelman, a self-confessed failure as a painter came to Italy to prepare a critical study of Giotto, the opening chapter of which he had carried across the ocean in a new pigskin leather brief case, now gripped in his perspiring hand." We know at once that Fidelman is headed for trouble, and it promptly appears in front of the railroad station in Rome, bearing the name of Shimon Susskind ("My first hello in Rome," Fidelman thinks, "and it has to be a *schnorrer*"). Susskind is a beggar of great persuasive powers, and as time goes by Fidelman finds it hard to resist his importunities. Fidelman is serious, ambitious, and poor; he respects his obligations to himself and to the sister who financed his year in Italy out of her small savings. "Am I responsible for you then?" he asks Susskind, who replies with awful logic, "Who else?" It is a strange contest, and it comes to a strange end.

But Fidelman's adventures in Italy have barely begun. Once more determined to become a painter, he answers an advertisement for a share of a studio. The other occupant turns out to be a woman, and Fidelman, finding her sexually attractive, allows himself to be exploited by her. And if in the end he has his way with her, it is because of surprising idiosyncrasies on her part.

Whatever poor Fidelman undertakes turns out badly. When, penniless and desperate for food, he picks the pocket of an American tourist, he is saved from the police by a pair of criminals, Angelo and Scarpio, who treat him more harshly than the law would have done. Angelo, proprietor of a hotel that is really a whorehouse, makes Fidelman clean the thirty toilets daily and do other dirty jobs, and each evening the three men play cards until Fidelman has lost whatever money the whores have given him in tips. At last, in order to win his freedom, the unhappy young man promises to produce a forged Titian. There are complications, as one would expect, and the ending is a wonderful surprise.

Fidelman is bound to be a painter, no matter what the cost. At one point he carves small Madonnas to support himself while he works on what he hopes will be his masterpiece, a painting based on a photograph of his mother and himself when he was a boy. He falls in love with a prostitute, who abandons her profession to live with him, and then, when the market for his Madonnas collapses, returns to it to support him. The man for whom she was pimping when she met Fidelman naturally resents the loss of income, and he is shrewd enough to devise a crushing revenge.

When Fidelman is bemoaning his lack of success, he tends, like the rest of us, to blame circumstances. "The painter blew his nose at the open window and gazed for a reflective hour at the Tuscan hills in September haze. Otherwise, sunlight on the terraced silver-trunked olive trees, and San Miniato, sparkling, framed in the distance by black cypresses. Make an interesting impressionist oil. . . . But that's been done. Not to mention Van Gogh's tormented cypresses. That's my trouble, everything's been done or is otherwise out of style—cubism, surrealism, action painting. If I could only guess what's next."

But Fidelman's problem lies deeper than that, as he himself knows at least part of the time. "The truth is," he thinks at one point, "I am afraid to paint, like I might find out something about myself." This, however, is an insight that he usually manages to forget. For Chapter V, in which Fidelman is reduced to an absurdity, Malamud has developed a new style, impressionistic, somewhat Joycean, full of allusions to the great artists, occasionally echoing Jewish fables and legends. Again he meditates: "Ah, to sculpt a perfect hole, the volume and gravity constant. Invent space. Surround matter with hole rather than vice versa. That would have won me enduring fame and fortune." So he travels around Italy, digging these perfect holes in various combinations, and admitting spectators at ten lire each. It is all a dazzling extravaganza, with large implications.

What an extraordinary gallery of heroes Malamud has created; Roy Hobbs, the Wunderkind of baseball, in *The Natural*; Frank Alpine in *The Assistant,* a thief who becomes a kind of saint; Si Levin in *A New Life,* a blundering but resolute seeker after truth and goodness; Yakov Bok, of *The Fixer,* who grows through stark endurance into heroism; and now Fidelman. None of these characters is particularly promising, but each of them is more at the end of his story than he was at the beginning. Even Fidelman finds redemption, in ways one would never have expected. Eventually he discovers that determination, of which he has plenty, is not enough to make an artist. Learning something about both art and love, he becomes a different man.

Pictures of Fidelman is a rich, funny, and exciting book—exciting because of the inventiveness shown in each of its parts, because of its stylistic variety and virtuosity, and above all because of its wisdom concerning the nature of art and the needs of man. Some of Malamud's admirers may feel that the book is not "serious" enough to stand beside its predecessors, but if they will look back on the novels and some of the short stories—"The Jew Bird," for instance —they will recognize that for him humor and seriousness have never been incompatible.

Literary Guild Magazine
June, 1969

JAMES BALDWIN

Foreword

I reviewed James Baldwin's first novel, *Go Tell It on the Mountain*, more or less by accident, and I was delighted to discover so promising a young talent. Then came *Giovanni's Room*, which showed Baldwin to be more versatile than I had at first supposed. After that the writing became more militant. In *Another Country*, it seems to me, though not to some critics, deep passion found an appropriate rhetoric. Nothing Baldwin has written since has much importance. But it is not time yet for his funeral service.

1 *Go Tell It on the Mountain*

There is a new name to be added to the list of serious and talented young writers—that of James Baldwin. Born in Harlem in 1924, Mr. Baldwin was the son of a preacher, and, he tells us, was a preacher himself from the age of fourteen to the age of seventeen. Shortly after ceasing to preach, he turned to literature, and, in the next few years, he had two fellowships and wrote two books, neither of which was published. Now he has a book in print, *Go Tell It on the Mountain,* and a very fine book it is.

Readers of the *Partisan Review* may remember Mr. Baldwin as the author of two interesting and disturbing articles, "Everybody's Protest Novel" and "Many Thousands Gone." In these articles he discussed the dangers of indignation in fiction, the problem of stereotypes in fiction about Negroes, and the place of the Negro in American life. Re-reading them now, after reading his novel, one sees them as the statement of a personal and pressing dilemma: acknowledging the bitterness he felt as a Negro, he was putting on record his determination not to allow that bitterness to dominate his work as a novelist.

Go Tell It on the Mountain is the result of that struggle and the proof of Baldwin's victory, for there is no danger that it will be pigeonholed as a novel of protest, it neither expresses indignation nor seeks to arouse it, and we do not think of the characters as victims of injustice or as anything less than human beings.

One writes out of one thing only—one's own experience. [Baldwin has said] Everything depends on how relentlessly one forces from this experience the last drop, sweet or bitter, it can possibly give. This is the only real concern of the artist, to recreate out of the disorder of life that order which is art. The difficulty then, for me, of being a Negro writer was the fact that I was, in effect, prohibited from examining my own experience too closely by the tremendous demands and the very real dangers of my social situation.

In other words, the Negro problem was there in the foreground, and he had to get behind it to find the kind of reality that seems to him to be the artist's proper concern.

Two other talented Negro novelists, Ralph Ellison and Richard Wright, have recently written about Negroes without writing novels of protest. They have done so, however, by demonstrating that the Negro problem is at bottom merely a variant of the human problem: We are all "invisible men," we are all "outsiders." In the long run, we begin to forget that their heroes are Negroes, and that is what they want us to do. Their strategy is excellent, but Baldwin's is even subtler. His novel centers in a characteristic Harlem institution, the storefront church, and we never lose the awareness that we are reading about Negroes. The fact that his characters are Negroes is important, but increasingly we are made to feel that its importance is secondary.

What happens in the novel is that John Grimes gets religion on his fourteenth birthday, and perhaps the most remarkable thing Mr. Baldwin has done is to give this experience an intense reality. In the first part of the novel we see John in his normal range of activities. He is afraid of his father, devoted to his mother, alienated from and worried about his "bad" younger brother. He makes a birthday excursion into the sinful world of Times Square, returns to a family crisis, and helps to prepare for Saturday evening services at the Temple of the Free Baptized. In the second section, we learn about his father and mother, and then, in the third section, comes the conversion.

"In the context of the Negro problem," Mr. Baldwin has written, "neither whites nor blacks, for excellent reasons of their own, have the faintest desire to look back; but I think that the past is all that makes the present coherent, and further, that the past will remain horrible for exactly as long as we refuse to assess it honestly." In his novel, he looks steadily at that segment of the past that is relevant to his story. Through the recollections of Gabriel Grimes, John's supposed father, and those of Gabriel's sister Florence, as they take part in the Saturday-evening service, a dramatic and significant story unfolds. Their old mother, born in slavery, links them with the more remote past. They themselves are, in different ways, products of the migration northward. Gabriel's story is marked by violence and sin and the struggle for righteousness, and violence has touched the life of Elizabeth, his wife and John's mother.

The adroitness with which Mr. Baldwin sets these dramas within the framework of John's conversion is evidence of his skill as a novelist. Yet he never seems obsessed with form, as some of the other young novelists do; it is something that he knows how to make serve his purpose. Indeed, his technical skill, which is remarkable in many ways, is most remarkable for its unobtrusiveness. His narrative is assured and straightforward, and the description of John's seizure achieves its great emotional effect without any fireworks. Best of all is the dialogue, with its strong, authentic rhythms. Everything about the book bears witness to a mastery that is astonishing in so young a novelist.

The strange and fatal conflict between ideal and reality is the theme of this book, as it is of much of the world's greatest literature. The principal characters of the novel are sustained by their peculiarly dogmatic and violent interpretation of Christianity. The faith of Gabriel and Deborah and Elizabeth, and of Praying Mother Washington and Sister McCandless and Brother Elisha, is grotesque but dignified. They are the saved, set apart from the rest of the world, and their lives have meaning; but for this high privilege they pay by their adherence to a code of morality that puts a heavy burden on weak human flesh and may result, as it has resulted with Gabriel, in sins worse than those against which the saints preach.

Mr. Baldwin makes us fully aware of the meaning of religion for these people, and, because we have seen enough of Gabriel and

Elizabeth to understand the tensions of John's childhood, his conversion becomes a climax for us as well as for him. Mr. Baldwin wisely drops the story there. There are intimations that there will be other climaxes for John, but it is enough that we understand why the conversion has happened and what, for the moment, it means to him.

Mr. Baldwin has said that he wants to be "an honest man and a good writer." It is obvious that he has had a tremendous struggle against attitudes on the part of others, and emotions within himself, that might have made him a more or less dishonest propagandist; but he has achieved his goal, and he has also achieved, as a consequence of the struggle, a phenomenal maturity.

The New Leader
June 1, 1953

2 *Giovanni's Room*

Whoever has read James Baldwin's first novel, *Go Tell It on the Mountain,* or his collection of essays and sketches, *Notes of a Native Son,* knows him to be one of our gifted young writers. His most conspicuous gift is his ability to find words that astonish the reader with their boldness even as they overwhelm him with their rightness.

The theme of *Giovanni's Room* is delicate enough to make strong demands on all of Mr. Baldwin's resourcefulness and subtlety. We meet the narrator, known to us only as David, in the south of France, but most of the story is laid in Paris. It develops as the story of a young American involved both with a woman and with another man, the man being the Giovanni of the title. When a choice has to be made, David chooses the woman, Hella.

David tells the story on a single night, the night before Giovanni is to be guillotined as a murderer. He tells of his life in Giovanni's room, of deserting Giovanni for Hella and of making plans to marry her, of the effect of this on Giovanni, and of the effect of Giovanni's plight on his own relations with Hella. Mr. Baldwin writes of these matters with an unusual degree of candor and yet with such dignity and intensity that he is saved from sensationalism.

Much of the novel is laid in scenes of squalor, with a background of characters as grotesque and repulsive as any that can be found in Proust's *Cities of the Plain,* but even as one is dismayed by Mr. Baldwin's materials, one rejoices in the skill with which he renders them. Nor is there any suspicion that he is working with these materials merely for the sake of shocking the reader. On the contrary, his intent is most serious. One of the lesser characters, in many ways a distasteful one, tells David that "not many people have ever died of love." "But," he goes on, "multitudes have perished, and are perishing every hour and in the oddest places!—for the lack of it." This is Mr. Baldwin's subject, the rareness and difficulty of love, and, in his rather startling way, he does a great deal with it.

New York Times Book Review
October 14, 1956

3 *Nobody Knows My Name*

James Baldwin is the author of two fine and strikingly dissimilar novels, *Go Tell It on the Mountain* and *Giovanni's Room,* and it is good to hear that his third novel will be published before the end of the year. He is also an uncommonly interesting journalist, as was demonstrated a few years ago by a collection of his pieces, *Notes of a Native Son*. Now a second collection has appeared, *Nobody Knows My Name*. This contains pieces written during the past six years, some of them quite recently.

Not everything in the book is first-rate. For instance, Baldwin's report on the Conference of Negro-African Writers and Artists, held in Paris in 1956, is long and sometimes pedestrian. "Notes for a Hypothetical Novel," an address prepared for a conference on writing, sounds almost as if it were an unrevised transcript of an informal talk. But most of the essays are good, and several are exciting.

The book is divided into two parts, one devoted to discussions of the situation of the Negro, primarily in America, the other to literary and artistic matters. The second part, which I propose to discuss first, contains comments on Gide and Ingmar Bergman, but is chiefly notable for long essays on Richard Wright and Norman Mailer. These are interesting not only as interpretations of writers Baldwin has known well but also as statements of his views on the functions and the problems of the man of letters in contemporary society.

The article on Wright is in three sections, the first being a review of "Eight Men," written soon after Wright's death. Baldwin continues with a more personal comment. He describes his first meeting with Wright, when the latter was thirty-six and an established writer and he was a fledgling of twenty, and tells of the difficulties in their relationship. Later, in Paris, Wright was offended by an essay Baldwin had written ridiculing the novel of protest, and they were never on easy terms thereafter. Finally, Baldwin reveals his unhappiness about Wright's last years. American Negroes felt that he had lost touch with their problems during his long exile, and African Negroes lacked confidence in him. He was wandering, Baldwin feels, "in a no-man's land between the black world and the white," one of the more illustrious of the many victims, black and white, of a tragic war.

Baldwin respects Norman Mailer, and continues to like him in spite of Mailer's unflattering remarks in "Advertisements for Myself." He met Mailer in Paris six years ago. Of himself he says: "I was then (and I have not changed much) a very tight, tense, lean, abnormally ambitious, abnormally intelligent, and hungry black cat." Mailer, too, as everyone knows, is not an easy man to get along with, and one can imagine that the atmosphere was tense. "We liked each other at once, but each was frightened that the other would pull rank." Later tension relaxed, but they were never completely comfortable together. For one thing, Baldwin was distressed by Mailer's essay "The White Negro," feeling "a kind of fury that so antique a vision of the blacks should, at this late hour, and in so many borrowed heirlooms, be stepping off the A train." He also deplored Mailer's involvement with the hipsters, whom he regarded as a dreary, inferior lot.

Baldwin, however, is not primarily concerned with his relations with Mailer but is trying to explain the latter's present situation. When Mailer first talked about politics, talked about running for President, running for mayor, Baldwin did not take him seriously, but in time he came to realize that Mailer was in earnest, and he was convinced that he was making a mistake. "I do not feel," Baldwin says, "that a writer's responsibility can be discharged in this way. I do not think, if one is a writer, that one can escape it by trying to become something else. One does *not* become something else; one becomes nothing." It was a sudden sense of his predicament, Baldwin believes, that caused Mailer to break out in violence at the famous party last fall. He holds, however, that "these last sad and stormy events" can enrich Mailer's work if he can understand them.

Baldwin, obviously, has tried to learn from the experiences of both his friends. Wright's career has shown him the dangers of exile, and has pointed out some of the temptations he is going to face as an eminent Negro author. Mailer's misadventures have helped him to define the nature of the writer's responsibility. He may make his own mistakes, but he will not make theirs.

I have emphasized these two essays on literary themes, but this does not mean that I am left unmoved by the pieces in which Baldwin speaks out as an American Negro. These are eloquent, uncompromising, and, in my opinion, unanswerable. After telling how he learned in Paris that he was an American, Baldwin gives his impressions of America revisited. He begins with Harlem, and it is a horrifying picture that he presents. Moreover, he holds out no hope to the reformers: "The people in Harlem know they are living there because white people do not think they are good enough to live anywhere else. No amount of 'improvement' can sweeten this fact. Whatever money is now being earmarked to improve this, or any other ghetto, might as well be burnt. A ghetto can be improved in one way only: out of existence." As a postscript to this essay, Baldwin offers an account of the Negro demonstration at the United Nations after the killing of Lumumba, and he makes that unhappy incident all too understandable.

Two essays record his impressions of the South, which he was seeing for the first time. In one he discusses integration from the point of view of the mother of a student in an integrated school, a woman who wants her boy to have an education and is willing to make and to ask him to make great sacrifices. The other essay is a description of Atlanta, in which Baldwin shows how complex and how terribly urgent the problem is.

Finally, there is Baldwin's reply to William Faulkner. It should be said that Baldwin indicts North as well as South, leaving no footing for white complacency either side of the Mason-Dixon line. But Southern apologetics fascinate him, and he analyzes in a rigorous but not unkindly fashion the tortured maneuverings of Faulkner's conscience, the talk about the middle of the road, the plea for time.

Baldwin bases his whole argument on one simple proposition: "Negroes want to be treated like men." They want to be, and they must be, and until they are, our tensions and frustrations will grow worse and worse. Meanwhile, Baldwin speaks boldly as a Negro— that is to say, as a human being—while recognizing his responsibility to the craft he practices. Norman Mailer has written: "James Baldwin is too charming a writer to be major." If he is suggesting that Baldwin lacks conviction and determination and boldness, he could not be more wrong.

Saturday Review
July 1, 1961

4 *Another Country*

James Baldwin's *Another Country* is a novel about love and hate, and more about hate than love. In its totality and with all due allowance for occasional weaknesses in the writing, it is one of the most powerful novels of our time. The complexities of love have seldom been explored more subtly or at greater depth, and perhaps the power of hate has never been communicated with a more terrifying force.

The novel begins with Rufus Scott, a Negro, once a drummer in a jazz band, now penniless and desperate. We go back to Rufus's meeting with a poor white girl from Georgia named Leona, and we follow their relationship as, torn between love and hate, Rufus tortures and degrades Leona until she loses her mind. He is driven to destroy both her and himself, and Baldwin traces the process with relentless fury.

This episode takes less than a hundred pages, but then we are introduced to a variation of its theme. After Rufus's death, Vivaldo Moore, his best friend, falls in love with Rufus's sister Ida. She is as full of hatred of white people as Rufus, and his fate has intensified her bitterness. Her relationship with Vivaldo is not so violent as Rufus's with Leona, but it is ambivalent in the same way, and if the outcome, so far as the novel goes, is not so calamitous, we have no great cause for hope.

These are not the only varieties of love we encounter. Cass and Richard Silenski, older friends of both Rufus and Vivaldo, are at the outset a happily married couple, but Richard achieves success with a second-rate novel, and the disillusioned Cass turns away from him. And there is Eric, an actor who has been living in France. We see him first with Yves, a French boy of the streets to whom he is strongly attached. Later, after his return to New York, while waiting for Yves to join him, he becomes involved in strange ways with Cass and Vivaldo.

Baldwin does not underestimate the power of love, mysterious as its operations seem to be; but it is the power of hate that one really feels as one reads the novel. In certain of the essays in *Nobody Knows My Name* Baldwin has said directly enough that Negroes hate white people, and, if anybody needs to ask, he has explained why. It is, however, one thing to say that hatred exists and another to make it palpable, as he so magnificently does in the opening section about Rufus and again in the final account of Ida's confrontation of Vivaldo. Perhaps all Negroes do not feel as Rufus and Ida and Baldwin himself do, but if they don't, he convinces us, they ought to.

His hatred is not limited to the resentment that Negroes so legitimately feel towards the white people who have abused and exploited and scorned and despised them through the centuries. He has painted a Dantesque picture of New York—the heat, the stench, the gross inhumanity. And, rightly or wrongly, he sees New York as the symbol of contemporary American civilization. It is significant that most of his characters are outcasts—Rufus and Ida because they are Negroes, Eric because he is a homosexual, Cass out of disdain for her husband's false values, and Vivaldo because he cannot conceive of self-fulfilment except by way of alienation. The only characters who are willing to exist within the framework of contemporary society are contemptible—Richard Silenski, who welcomes a cheap success, and a cynical and empty impresario

named Ellis. American writers, Baldwin argued in an article he
wrote for the *New York Times Book Review* last winter, must accept the fact that the United States is becoming a second-rate
power. This may be true; but now I can see that, true or not, it is
what Baldwin wants to believe.

As I pointed out in my review of *Letting Go,* Philip Roth also
takes a dark view of present-day American civilization; but his
discontent seems, in comparison with Baldwin's, no more than a
kind of fractiousness, the peevish complaint of a spoiled child.
American life in Baldwin's account is a terrifying barbarism. The
very violence of the language he uses is itself an expression of
horror; all the words have appeared in print before, but they have
never been employed so ruthlessly to express disgust and to inspire
disgust. The book itself is and is meant to be an act of violence.

The novel opens with a scene of such intensity that there seems
to be nowhere for Baldwin to go, but in fact he matches it again and
again. From his very first book, *Go Tell It on the Mountain,* it has
been clear that he has a fine gift of language, but he has never
before come anywhere near the sustained power of *Another Country*. There are lapses, to be sure. He describes, for instance, a party
given by Cass and Richard Silenski, and the description is almost
completely commonplace. Sometimes, when the heat is off, he slips
into banality: " 'Ah!'—she shrugged merrily, and took a deep drag
on her cigarette—'I wasn't consulted.' " Again: "Her face, then,
made one think of a mischievous street boy. And at the same time
there gleamed in her eyes a marvelously feminine mockery." But
when two persons confront one another, whatever their sexes, whatever their color, Baldwin finds the words that will make us feel
what they are feeling.

It has to be said, of course, that Baldwin's experience of America
is limited, and limited in drastic and terrible ways. He does not
know the America I know any better than, if as well as, I know his
America. But every writer's experience is limited in one way or
another, and the question is simply what he is able to make of it.
What Baldwin has to say about contemporary civilization seems to

me only partly true, but in so far as it is true at all, it is of the utmost importance. He compels one to participate in a kind of life that is horrible and that is important because it is horrible.

The novel is an explosion, but that does not mean that it is un-controlled or artless. Baldwin seems to move haphazardly from character to character, but in fact the novel is shaped with rigorous care. Rufus, though he dies on page 88, dominates the whole book. Eric's entry on the scene comes relatively late, but it has been care-fully prepared for. The lives of the various characters are closely related, and it is Baldwin's art that makes the relationship seem so natural and uncontrived. He is not only a powerful writer; he has become a skilled craftsman. I hope that, in the controversy the book is bound to arouse, his great gifts as a novelist will not be overlooked.

Saturday Review
July 7, 1962

5 *Blues for Mister Charlie*

Early in his career Baldwin stated that Negro writers didn't have to write about the Negro problem and shouldn't allow themselves to become propagandists for the Negro, but should simply try to be as good writers as possible. In his first novel, *Go Tell It on the Mountain,* Baldwin wrote about Negroes in both North and South, and of course showed something of their predicament, but the book had no obvious "message." Its successor, *Giovanni's Room,* was laid in Europe, and its characters were white.

In his essays, however, he was more and more explicitly a spokes-man for the Negro people, and it seemed clear that he could not indefinitely keep out of his novels the problems he discussed in his nonfiction. In *Another Country* he attacked some of those problems head on, and if the novel is not propaganda in the derogatory sense of the term, if it sees the race problem in relation to other problems, it is a powerful statement of a particular point of view. It was followed by an extraordinary essay, *The Fire Next Time,* in which Baldwin tried directly to show the community what Negroes are thinking and feeling.

What is a writer to do if he feels strongly about some social or political issue? Ever since the fiasco of so-called proletarian literature in the Thirties, we have been assured that it is bad for a writer to have a cause. I grant that a cause may be dangerous, but it is not necessarily fatal. John Dos Passos's *USA* was not only not spoiled by his passion for social justice; it is the strong feeling it expresses that makes it the best of his writings. In any case, to be honest, a writer must do what he must do, and to hell with the consequences. Baldwin may ruin himself as a creative writer, but I should respect him less if he were unwilling to take that chance.

Baldwin's *Blues for Mister Charlie* is a play in the modern manner, with vaguely suggestive scenery and no concern for realistic conventions. The action moves freely in both time and space, and the dialogue is often stylized. In print the play is difficult to follow at the beginning, but on the stage, if properly directed, there would probably be no trouble.

The opening is sharply dramatic:

In the darkness we hear a shot.
Lights up slowly on LYLE, staring down at the ground. He looks around him, bends slowly and picks up RICHARD's body as though it were a sack. He carries him upstage, drops him out of sight.
LYLE: And may every nigger like this nigger end like this nigger— face down in the weeds!
Exit.

Thus the play begins with the deed that is its center of interest, for all that follows shows either the causes or the consequences of this murder. The first act chiefly presents the effect on the Negro community, although it also deals with certain events that took place before Richard's death. In the second act we see something of the white community, and again there is movement backward in time. The third act sets forth the trial of Lyle Britten for the murder of Richard Henry, and is highly stylized, with scenes from the past lives of the witnesses, and with "the State" acting in effect as attorney for the defense. Only when the trial is over is the killing enacted before our eyes.

The story, rearranged in chronological order, can easily be summarized. Richard Henry, son of the Rev. Meridian Henry, was sent to New York by his father, who hoped that in that way he could be kept out of trouble. Instead, he got into a jam, became a dope addict, and was sent to an institution. Returning to his home town after his release, he refuses to accept the treatment accorded to Negroes by the Southern whites. In particular he will not humiliate himself before Lyle Britten, and Britten shoots him. Britten is brought to trial, chiefly because of the efforts of Parnell James, editor of the local newspaper and in intention a friend of the Negroes. Of course Britten is acquitted.

What Baldwin is saying is what he said in *The Fire Next Time*—that the patience of the Negro is wearing thin. One of Richard's young friends puts it this way:

We've been demonstrating—nonviolently—for more than a year now and all that's happened is that now they'll let us into that crummy library downtown which was obsolete in 1897 and where nobody goes anyway; who in this town reads books? For that we paid I don't know how many thousands of dollars in fines. Jerome is still in the hospital, and we all know that Ruthie is never again going to be the little swinging chick she used to be. Big Deal. . . . We still can't get licensed to be electricians or plumbers, we still can't walk through the park, our kids can't use the swimming pool in town. We *still* can't vote, we can't even get registered. Is it worth it?

This is the question that all the Negroes are compelled to ask themselves, even the Rev. Meridian Henry, who has hitherto been the champion of Christian conciliation. Meridian's friend Parnell James, the only white in town to show sympathy for the Negroes, equivocates at Britten's trial, and the minister, increasingly doubtful about justice, talks of having the Bible and a gun in his pulpit. Meridian says to Parnell, "Where's the hope? If Mister Charlie can't change. . . ." Parnell asks, "Who's Mister Charlie?" and Meridian answers, "You're Mister Charlie. *All* white men are Mister Charlie." And, indeed, where is the hope for any of us, white or black, if Mister Charlie can't change?

Is the play propaganda? I suppose that it is, to the extent that Baldwin hopes to have a specific effect on an audience of Mister Charlies—to make them change, to make them see that the present crisis makes change imperative. But it is not propaganda if one means by that distortion of the truth for a political purpose. Is it a major piece of literature? I doubt it, though I believe that it should be very moving on the stage. Its weaknesses, however, do not seem to arise out of Baldwin's preoccupation with a cause but out of the limitations of his medium, or, perhaps, his unfamiliarity with it. He has made a good try, and I wish him and his play well.

Saturday Review
May 2, 1964

6 *Tell Me How Long the Train's Been Gone*

In the past few years James Baldwin has published two collections of essays, including that extraordinary polemic *The Fire Next Time,* and a play, *Blues for Mister Charlie,* but *Tell Me How Long the Train's Been Gone* is his first novel since *Another Country* appeared in 1962. Like that book, but for different reasons, it raises perplexing questions about Baldwin's future.

It is the story, told in the first person, of a successful Negro actor named Leo Proudhammer. Hospitalized after a heart attack on stage, he recalls and reflects upon episodes from his past. Although the narrative moves freely in time, doubling back and forth, it covers Leo's life from childhood to the beginning of his success in the theater. The major themes are acting, sex, and race.

In Leo's account of his early life in Harlem the principal figures, naturally, are members of his family: his sullen and often drunken father, his courageous mother, and his rebellious older brother, Caleb. Everything inside and outside his home contributes to his awareness of the inferior position of his race. After the brothers have been picked up by the police and have escaped a beating only because Leo is a child, he asks Caleb whether all white people are the same. The older brother replies, "I never met a good one." Out of pity he adds, "But that's not saying that you won't. Don't look so frightened."

Leo does find at least one good white person, but she has done her best to resign from the white race. Barbara King, daughter of rich Kentuckians, has come to New York to become an actress, and has taken with gusto to all the freedoms available in Greenwich Village. Thanks to her brashness, she and Leo are taken on as apprentices by the Actor's Means Workshop, conducted by a pair of pompous charlatans. In spite of their disillusionment, Leo and Barbara continue to long for success on the stage, which both eventually achieve, she a good deal sooner than he.

Although she has been living with another man at the workshop, Barbara really loves Leo, and for a time they are lovers. He, however, is incapable of such devotion as hers, and their relationship becomes no more than friendly. Bisexual, Leo has a series of affairs with both men and women. At the end he is attached to Black Christopher, an ardent Negro revolutionary, perhaps as a substitute for Caleb, who got religion during World War II, became a preacher, and ceased to be a rebel. Christopher is a rebel if he is anything, and, though he is the younger of the two, he treats Leo as his disciple.

What surprised me about the book from the first page on was its style. Most critics have agreed that, whenever he wanted to, Baldwin could write extremely well. Most of them have also admitted that sometimes, especially in *Another Country,* his prose has been painfully overwrought and turgid. Stanley Edgar Hyman, for one, said that any writer who could fall as low as Baldwin sometimes did was unworthy of serious critical consideration. I, on the other hand, believed and believe that the explosive force of the novel outweighs stylistic faults and that there are many wonderful passages.

The style of *Tell Me How Long* is not particularly good; for the most part it is simply flat and commonplace. There is scarcely a sentence in it that couldn't have been written by any moderately competent hack. Here, for instance, is a description of the heroine:

I remembered Barbara. For a time, we had both been artists' models at the Art Students' League on 57th Street. Barbara lasted much longer than I. She was rather more round-faced then, with very high color, and with very long, brown, curly hair, which she wore in bangs and pigtails. She had a marvelous laugh—she looked very much like what she was, a refugee schoolgirl from Kentucky. She had a very boyish figure, small breasts and not much of a behind—she was still in her teens—and wonderful long legs. She almost always wore pants, which got her in some trouble in some quarters, sometimes, but every once in a while she would put up her hair and put on lipstick and wear a dress. And it was astonishing what a difference this made. She became extraordinarily pretty, vulnerable, glowing. Then she looked like the rather proud daughter of proud Kentucky landowners.

In part because of the insipidity of the prose, the novel as a whole is rather shadowy and dim. The account of the Harlem boyhood is moving at times, but Baldwin has described Harlem more effectively in some of his essays. Of the Harlem characters the only one who truly lives is Caleb, who is convincing both as young rebel and as middle-aged preacher. Leo, on the other hand, especially after he has become a popular actor, is not easy to believe in.

I wonder why Baldwin chose to write about Leo if he could make no more of him than he has done. The lesson of the novel seems to be that Negroes hate white people and have good reason for doing so, but Baldwin has preached on this text before and much more eloquently. All that is new is an emphasis on violence. In the last scene Leo and Christopher are driving around San Francisco after the former's release from the hospital. Christopher says, "Look, I'm a young cat. I've already been under the feet of horses, and I've already been beaten by chains. Well, You want me to keep going under the feet of horses?" When Leo says he doesn't, Christopher draws the moral: "Then I think you got to agree that we need us some guns. Right?" Although he does agree, Leo demurs a little: "But we're outnumbered. You know." And Christopher replies, "Shit. So were the early Christians."

The early Christians didn't want to kill off the Romans; they wanted to convert them, and used nonviolence as a way of doing so. But, even apart from that detail, the ending is weak. That white people in America have committed terrible crimes against American Negroes seems to me undeniable, and I can't blame Negroes for hating our guts. But I can't see hatred as a political program. It seems clear by now that the more fanatical Negro leaders have hurt their people more than they have hurt white people, and what we have seen is, I'm afraid, only the beginning. Put it in terms of the book: where is Leo going now? what will he do? what can come out of the sterility of hate? Perhaps Baldwin knows, at least subconsciously, the weakness of his position, and that is why the novel lacks strength.

Saturday Review
June 1, 1968

Afterword

Baldwin's next book, according to word from his publisher, will be a collection of essays. To hear that is rather a relief, for he still can be effective as a polemicist whereas his future as a novelist is doubtful. This is not to say that he is finished as a writer of fiction. He is still young, as authors go, and he may at any time find ways of reorganizing his powers. If not, he will not be the first casualty of the racist war.

JOHN UPDIKE

1 *The Poorhouse Fair*

John Updike's *The Poorhouse Fair* is deliberately and even self-consciously offbeat. Updike has taken an unusual and, on the surface, an unattractive subject, and he has written about it in a way that is often hard to follow.

I respect his unorthodoxy, the scrupulousness of his writing, the ingenious ways he has of presenting his characters, but I feel that he has tried to make the little novel carry more weight than it is able to bear. Gradually one realizes that this story of poorhouse conflicts is supposed to be a parable of the welfare state, with Connor, the superintendent—perfect he is called here—cast in the role of benevolent dictator. Furthermore, for no good reason that I can see, Updike has chosen to set the story in the future—say about 1980—and he alludes vaguely to the progress of the welfare state outside the poorhouse's doors. If he had let the little story alone, it might have been more impressive.

Updike, who is some distance short of thirty, has published stories and poems in *The New Yorker* and they indicate, as do many parts of the novel, that he is a talented young writer. If he has fallen short of success this time, I feel that another time he may make it.

We can't expect masterpieces every day, and so we have to be grateful when we are given even a moderate degree of pleasure and some cause for hope.

Saturday Review
January 17, 1959

2 *Rabbit, Run*

John Updike in *Rabbit, Run* has told the story of an irresponsible
and troubled young man, Harry Angstrom, commonly called Rabbit. In high school he was a basketball player, famous in his own
county. Now, at twenty-six, he works in a department store and has
a wife and a child, with another child on the way.

The novel is a record of his flights. One day, on the most sudden
of impulses, he sets off in his car, heading vaguely south. As suddenly he comes back, but not to his wife. Instead he takes up with
a part-time prostitute, but he abandons her when he learns that his
wife is in labor. He and Janice are not re-united for long, however,
and when he leaves this time, she gets drunk and allows the baby to
drown in the bathtub. He runs away again after the baby's funeral,
seeks refuge with Ruth, the semi-prostitute, then runs once more.

Updike shows us Rabbit in all his weakness. He can be abysmally selfish, not only with his women but with all those who try
to help him. In his sexual activities, about which Updike is uncommonly explicit even for these times, he shows little consideration
for his partners. To the consequences of his deeds he gives no
thought. The only solution he can discover for any of his problems
is flight.

On the other hand, Rabbit has qualities that are not contemptible. For one thing, he has an idea of excellence, associated in his
mind with his erstwhile prowess in basketball. He tells Ruth: "I
was great. It's the fact. I mean, I'm not good for anything now but
I really was good at that." To Jack Eccles, a clergyman who is
trying to patch up the marriage, he says: "I once played a game
real well. I really did. And after you're first-rate at something, no
matter what, it kind of takes the kick out of being second-rate. And

that little thing Janice and I had going, boy, it was really second-rate."

He has an inner life of considerable intensity. After his fashion he is religious; Mr. Eccles calls him a mystic. At any rate he has a feeling for what he believes to be "rightness" in a situation, and he is convinced that his impulses are somehow inspired. "He is a good man," Eccles says to Rabbit's mother-in-law, who is by no means ready to accept this evaluation. When Rabbit asks Ruth why she likes him, she replies, " 'Cause you haven't given up. 'Cause in your stupid way you're still fighting." "I'm lovable," he tells her later on, and some persons find him so.

As epigraph Updike uses a quotation from Pascal: "The motions of Grace, the hardness of the heart, external circumstances." It is a summary of the novel. The hardness of the heart is what one sees first and sees again and again. But then there are the external circumstances, particularly the fact that society has no use for Rabbit's one talent, his way with a basketball. Finally, and most important, there are the motions of Grace. Updike does not make too much of them; they are, he lets us see, uncertain and questionable; but Rabbit is not merely a selfish wretch nor is he merely a victim of circumstances. One may say that he is deluded: when, for instance, at the end of the book, he feels that he is entering upon a new life, the reader has every right to be skeptical. The fact, however, that he can still think of a new life, after what he has been through, may be evidence of Grace.

Although Updike is only twenty-eight, *Rabbit, Run* is his fourth book, for he had published a volume of verse and a collection of short stories, some of them very fine, before the appearance last year of *The Poorhouse Fair*. The novel was highly, even extravagantly, praised by many critics. The quality of the writing and the characterization deserved praise, but I felt that Updike had been mistaken in trying to make the book a kind of political parable. There is no such extraneous element in *Rabbit, Run*.

The Poorhouse Fair was admirably written, but the style of the present novel, while just as controlled, is more flexible. Updike can be perfectly straightforward, particularly in dialogue, but he lets himself go whenever occasion demands. Here, for example, is a piece of description that is conventional in conception but distinctive in execution:

Sun and moon, sun and moon, time goes. In Mrs. Smith's acres, crocuses break the crust. Daffodils and narcissi unpack their trumpets. The reviving grass harbors violets, and the lawn is suddenly coarse with dandelions and broad-leaved weeds. Invisible rivulets running brokenly make the low land of the estate sing. The flowerbeds, bordered with bricks buried diagonally, are pierced by dull red spikes that will be peonies, and the earth itself, scumbled, stone-flecked, horny, raggedly patched with damp and dry, looks like the eldest and smells like the newest thing under Heaven.

Here is the drunken Janice with her baby:

She lifts the living thing into the air and hugs it against her sopping chest. Water pours off them onto the bathroom tiles. The little weightless body flops against her neck and a quick look of relief at the baby's face gives a fantastic clotted impression. A contorted memory of how they give artificial respiration pumps Janice's cold wet arms in frantic rhythmic hugs; under her clenched lids great scarlet prayers arise, wordless, monotonous, and she seems to be clasping the knees of a vast third person whose name, Father, Father, beats against her head like physical blows. Though her wild heart bathes the universe in red, no spark kindles in the space between her arms; for all of her pouring prayers she doesn't feel the faintest tremor of answer in the darkness against her. Her sense of the third person with them widens enormously, and she knows, knows, while knocks sound at the door, that the worst thing that has ever happened to any woman in the world has happened to her.

In recent months I have discussed a number of novels about irresponsible young men, and sometimes I have complained that the author has failed to convince me that I should take an interest in the character he has created. I make no such complaint about *Rabbit, Run.* Updike seizes upon qualities in Harry Angstrom that are of large significance, and, with his stylistic resources, he makes them real to us. There is something in this man—call it "the motions of Grace" if you choose—that demands our respect. Although compassion is one of his gifts, Updike is not merely compassionate; he has so deep a sense of human fallibility that he treasures the goodness, slight as it is, that he finds in Rabbit.

From now on Updike has to be regarded as one of our important young novelists, a powerful writer with his own vision of the world. In *The Poorhouse Fair* that vision sometimes seemed blurred, but here it is clear and compelling. It is a vision of good struggling in a morass of evil, and Updike has as sure a hold on one quality as on the other.

Saturday Review
November 5, 1960

3 *Pigeon Feathers*

John Updike began publishing stories in *The New Yorker* in 1954, when he was twenty-two years old, and from the start it was clear that he was a gifted and interesting writer. His first collection of stories, *The Same Door,* deserved praise, but it has been far outdistanced by his new collection, *Pigeon Feathers;* for he has been growing steadily in stylistic power, in architectural skill, and in depth of feeling. Seventeen of the nineteen stories in the present volume appeared in *The New Yorker,* but most of them go well beyond anything that can be regarded as a *New Yorker* formula. (So, it must in fairness be said, do many other stories that appear in that magazine.) Updike is not merely talented; he is bold, resourceful, and intensely serious.

His seriousness is not immediately apparent because he so often chooses to work with materials that seem slight and commonplace. Take such a story as "The Persistence of Desire": a young man, happily married, accidentally encounters a girl he had known and desired when they were both in high school, finds her attractive, and arranges to see her. That is all, and yet Updike manages to say a great deal about love and especially youth.

Take "Wife-wooing" and "Should Wizard Hit Mommy?" These are little stories about domestic life that might easily have been either completely flat or unbearably mawkish. Updike turns them into illuminating comments on the relations between husbands and wives and between parents and children. He is a most redoubtable explorer of the mysteries of the commonplace.

He could not achieve his particular effect without his astonishing gift of language, especially figurative language. "Lifeguard," for instance, is a brilliant virtuoso performance, really a single metaphor sustained by richly textured prose. Here is a passage from another story that suggests how beautifully he can create a mood:

The sky beneath the shreds of snow was stone-colored. The murk inside the high classroom gave the air a solidity that limited the overhead radiance to its own vessels: six globes of dull incandescence floated on the top of a thin sea. The feeling the gloom gave him was not gloomy but joyous: he felt they were all sealed in, safe; the colors of cloth were dyed deeper, the sound of whispers was made more distinct, the smells of tablet paper and wet shoes and varnish and face powder pierced him with a vivid sense of possession. These were his classmates sealed in, his, the plain as well as the lovely, his enemies as well as his friends, his.

Many of the stories are autobiographical and are closely related, whether the hero is called Jack or Clyde, Allan or William, David or Robert. We see this hero as son, as husband, and as father. We see him as a high school boy in Pennsylvania, as a student in England, as a householder in Massachusetts.

Updike, however, is not merely making use of autobiographical materials; he is engaging in an ardent pursuit of the past. As epigraph he quotes a fine passage from Franz Kafka's *A Report to an Academy,* in which Kafka confesses that "the strong wind that blew after me out of my past" is now "only a gentle puff of air that plays around my heels." One of Updike's characters asks, "What is the past, after all, but a vast sheet of darkness in which a few moments, pricked apparently at random, shine?"

Updike's aim is to preserve certain of these moments, not out of nostalgia but because they give meaning to life. His Jamesian eagerness to let no experience be wasted is heightened by his sense of impermanence. The title story tells vividly of a boy's horror of death and his consequent preoccupation with the problems that have always tortured men's minds. The young man who patrols the beach in "Lifeguard" spends his winters as a student, wrestling with the subtleties of the theologians, ancient and modern. "Young as I am," he reflects, "I can hear in myself the protein acids ticking; I wake at odd hours and in the shuddering darkness and silence feel my death rushing toward me like an express train." Looking at the crowd on the beach, he thinks, "No, in relation to other people oblivion is sensible and sanitary."

What Updike is up to becomes clearest in the two stories—if one can call them stories—that conclude the book. The first, entitled "The Blessed Man of Boston, My Grandmother's Thimble, and Fanning Island," is, as the name indicates, a kind of triptych. In the first part the narrator, seeing an old Chineseman after a ball game, meditates on all that could be made of his life. In the second the accidental sight of a thimble inspires a tender portrait of the narrator's grandmother. The third part begins with a quotation from Pascal: "Let us imagine a number of men in chains, and all condemned to death." What the narrator imagines is a group of Polynesians stranded on an island in the Pacific. There are no women among them, and extinction is their certain fate. He imagines the story as told by the last survivor, and he concludes:

This is the outline, but it would be the days, the evocation of the days . . . the green days. The tasks, the grass, the weather, the shades of sea and air. Just as a piece of turf torn from a meadow becomes a gloria when drawn by Dürer. Details. Details are the giant's fingers. He seizes the stick and strips the bark and shows, burning beneath, the moist white wood of joy. For I thought that this story, fully told, would become without my willing it a happy story, a story full of joy; had my powers been greater, we would know. As it is, you, like me, must take it on faith.

The awareness of the ultimate doom, the feeling for details, for the moments that shine, and joy. These are the elements also of the final story, which is, to change the figure of speech, a quartet. The four movements contrast strongly, but there is a recurrent theme— mankind's constant reassertion of its own values in the face of an apparently indifferent universe. "We in America need ceremonies," the narrator concludes, and it is with ceremonies of one sort or another that the story is concerned.

I greatly admire Updike's *Rabbit, Run,* that bitterly honest but compassionate saga of a youth who can come to no good end; but I think that some of these stories, and especially the two at the end, hold out an even larger hope for the future. We hear talk now and then of a breakthrough in fiction, the achievement of a new attitude and hence a new method; something like that seems close at hand in *Pigeon Feathers*.

Saturday Review
March 17, 1962

4 *The Centaur*

Like the preceding novels, *The Poorhouse Fair* and *Rabbit, Run,* and like some of his short stories, John Updike's *The Centaur* is laid in Pennsylvania, presumably in the neighborhood of his native

Shillington. Unlike the earlier novels, but like several stories, it has a large autobiographical element. Unlike anything he has previously written, it exists on two levels—the realistic and the mythological.

Realistically, it is the story of a fifteen-year old boy, Peter Caldwell, and his father, George Caldwell, who teaches science at the Olinger High School. We see much of the life of the school—classrooms, swimming meet, basketball game—and something of the town in which it is located. There are many fine scenes, none finer than the account of a paralyzing snowstorm. But at the center is always George Caldwell, an earnest teacher, loved and laughed at by his students, an affectionate and self-sacrificing father, a generous, harassed, eccentric man. We have three days in his life and his son's, typical days and yet critical.

Peter and his father, however, are not merely people who lived in a Pennsylvania town in 1947; they are Prometheus, the bringer of fire to mankind, and Chiron, the wise and gentle centaur, instructor to heroes, who gave up his burdensome immortality for Prometheus's sake. More than that, every character in the book is to be identified with some figure in Greek mythology. Zeus is a school principal, Hephaestus a garage operator, Apollo a country doctor, Hermes a bum. Among Peter's schoolmates are Daedalus, Io, Pandora, Hercules.

Updike tells the story in an ingenious and beautifully varied fashion. After a chapter in which we move mysteriously from Olinger to Olympus and back again, with a centaur pawing through the halls of a modern-day high school, we have a chapter of first-person narrative, Peter speaking from the perspective of the present. Peter's narrative periodically recurs, but meanwhile there is a superb account of Chiron in Arcady; the obituary of George Caldwell, written in amateur journalese; a kind of dream sequence, and a long passage in the third person. At the end Chiron and Caldwell again merge.

No one should need to be told at this point that Updike has a mastery of language to be matched in our time only by the finest poets. I have spoken of the dazzling chapter about Chiron and his pupils, but let me take, to prove my point, a description of a garage:

A deep warm darkness was lit by sparks. The floor of the grotto was waxed black by oil drippings. At the far side of the long workbench, two shapeless men in goggles caressed a great downward-drooping fan of flame broken into dry drops. Another man, staring upward out of round eyesockets white in a black face, rolled by on his back and disappeared beneath the body of a car. His eyes adjusting to the gloom, Caldwell saw heaped about him over-turned fragments of automobiles, fragile and phantasmal, fenders like corpses of turtles, bristling engines like disembodied hearts. Hisses and angry thumps lived in the mottled air.

A man who can write like this is, clearly, a man capable of dealing justly with mythology, but the question is why Updike wanted to. Anglo-Saxon writers from Chaucer on have retold the Greek myths and the Norse myths and the Arthurian legends and other legends, and each writer has made of traditional material something that had special meaning for his age. But it is only the modern writer, I think, who has told a story of his own times that could be assimilated to myth or legend. Joyce's *Ulysses* is the great example, with Eliot's *The Waste Land,* so endlessly allusive, a powerful influence. One remembers a few recent American examples: Frederick Buechner retelling the story of Philomela in *A Long Day's Dying*; Bernard Malamud echoing the legend of Sir Percival in *The Natural*; J. F. Powers alluding, rather obscurely, to the Arthurian saga in *Morte D'Urban*. Updike, then, is by no means alone.

It is to be noted that he has used mythology in two ways: in the first place, he has retold the myth of Chiron, as other authors have retold other myths; but then he has gone on to find a mythological parallel for every character in the story—or, perhaps one has to say, to find a contemporary parallel for every god in the pantheon. This second device, whatever it may add to the novel, is a serious distraction. As I began the book, I recognized that some of the characters were intended to suggest gods and heroes, but I did not take this very seriously until I stumbled on the mythological index in the back. From then on, of course, I began asking myself, "Who is this, who is that?" and the questions did interfere with my appreciation of the book. Now I have gone back over it with the characters identified and I have taken pleasure in it; but Updike risks a lot when he invites his readers either to play a guessing game or to keep turning back to the index.

At best, I feel, the value of the mythological parallel is speculative. Eliot used mythological allusions effectively to underline the sterility of our era, but Updike, so far as I can see, is not disparaging our age in comparison with the age of myth. If his human beings are not particularly godlike, neither, it has to be pointed out, are his gods. At one point Aphrodite ticks them off: "a prating bluestocking, a filthy crone smelling of corn, a thieving tramp, a drunken queer, a despicable, sad, grimy, grizzled, cuckolded tinker," and describes herself as "a born whore." What Updike seems to be saying is that gods and men are pretty much of a kind, and though that is an interesting point, I don't know how much it adds to our understanding of either.

The great test of the mythological method is in Updike's treatment of the relationship of Peter and his father. Do we really know Peter any better because he is supposed to be Prometheus? It seems to me that the situation is beautifully rendered strictly in terms of the present. You could leave Chiron out of it altogether and George would still be a magnificent character. Updike's skill in moving between realism and myth is impressive, and the Chiron passages adorn the novel, but its great value rests on the author's insight into Peter and especially George as human beings. With that insight he could have made as strong an impact if he hadn't alluded to a single myth.

I have dwelt on the use of mythology because it is interesting to see what so skilful a writer can do with it, but I don't want to leave the impression that, because the mythological method is not wholly successful, the novel is a failure. It is a brilliant achievement. We expect much from Updike, and we have every right to, for he is incredibly gifted; but if this is not the towering novel for which we are hoping, it is a book to be thankful for.

Saturday Review
February 2, 1963

5 *Assorted Prose*

Precocious and prolific, John Updike, born in 1932, has just published his eighth book, *Assorted Prose*. "In the ten years that I have written for a living," he states, "I have published a certain amount of nonfictional prose; this book collects all of it that I thought anyone might like to read."

At an early age Updike began writing for *The New Yorker,* and between August 1955 and March 1957 he was one of the bright young men in that magazine's office. During that period he contributed many pieces to "The Talk of the Town" and "Notes and Comment," and he has continued to write from time to time for these departments. Early in his career he managed to achieve the right tone, and in the pieces he has preserved we hear the true *New Yorker* voice. (He calls this section "First Person Plural.")

The variety of subjects is impressive: Russia's first moon shot, a dinosaur egg, style in sports writing, the quiz show scandal, the assassination of President Kennedy. There are also obituary notes on John P. Marquand, Grandma Moses, and T. S. Eliot. Two longer pieces, one on pigeons and one on Antarctica, show how well Updike could handle a *New Yorker* research job.

Among his other apprentice works were several parodies. "My first literary idols," he notes, "were Thurber and Benchley and

Gibbs; these few feuilletons are what remains of my ambition to emulate them." In his review of Dwight Macdonald's anthology of parodies, Updike writes, "If great parodists are not great writers, great writers, conversely, are not great parodists." Whether or not Updike is, or some day may be, a great writer, he is not a great parodist. Although the parodies were pleasant enough to read as they appeared in the magazine, most of them—the principal exception is the parody of Harry Truman—scarcely seem worth republication.

Of greater interest are several longer pieces, especially "Hub Fans Bid Kid Adieu," an account of Ted Williams's final game in Boston. Updike, a true enthusiast, wrote about the great day con amore. Although I am sure that the article would delight any baseball fan, it is interesting to me as a piece of writing. It begins, "Fenway Park, in Boston, is a lyric little bandbox of a ballpark. Everything is painted green and seems in curiously sharp focus, like the inside of an old-fashioned peeping-type Easter egg." Updike proceeds by outlining Williams's career, and then describes the ceremonies that took place on this occasion and the game itself. Finally, in the eighth inning, came what everyone was waiting for— Ted Williams's last home run. "From my angle, behind third base, the ball seemed less an object in flight than the tip of a towering, motionless construct, like the Eiffel Tower or the Tappan Zee Bridge. It was in the books while it was still in the sky."

Of the more or less autobiographical pieces, the most interesting is "The Dogwood Tree," which was written for a volume called *Five Boyhoods.* Updike speaks of it disparagingly, but I find it fascinating, not merely as a vivid reminiscence but also as a commentary on his fiction. Here are the settings of *The Poorhouse Fair, Rabbit, Run, The Centaur,* and many of the short stories. The youthful John Updike, as he presents himself here, is readily identified with boys we have met in his fiction.

Then there are the book reviews. Updike is not, and does not pretend to be, a great critic, but he is a consistently interesting literary journalist. He has reviewed a variety of books for *The New*

Yorker and other magazines, and he appears to have approached each of them with the liveliest kind of curiosity. He can write an incisive note on a novel by Richard Hughes, or he can write a long and considered discussion of a theological treatise by Karl Barth. (He says in the foreword that "Barth's theology, at one point in my life, seemed alone to be supporting it.") He writes about Alan Sillitoe, J. D. Salinger, Muriel Spark, Vladimir Nabokov, and others, and he always has something to say.

The reviews are also interesting because they suggest some of Updike's values as a writer of fiction. Sillitoe's stories, he remarks, show "enviable assurance and abundance in the writer"—qualities that Updike surely possesses. He says that Sillitoe is "well-armed with intelligence, humor, and (my guess is) stamina." He describes Muriel Spark as "one of the few writers of the language on either side of the Atlantic with enough resources, daring, and stamina to be altering, as well as feeding, the fiction machine."

Updike's versatility is as obvious as his mastery of the language. But, some people ask, isn't he spreading himself too thin? Has he written anything that is worthy of his talents? Isn't it time he wrote a Great Book?

Updike himself has something to say on this general theme in his review of Salinger's *Franny and Zooey*: "When all reservations have been entered, in the correctly unctuous and apprehensive tone, about the direction he has taken, it remains to acknowledge that it is a direction and that the refusal to rest content, the willingness to risk excess on behalf of one's obsessions, is what distinguishes artists from entertainers, and what makes some artists adventurers on behalf of us all."

But, the opposition inquires, what risks has Updike taken, and is he driven by obsessions of any sort? So far as the use of language is concerned, he is extremely bold and extremely effective, but how often does one feel a sense of urgency in his fiction?

These are reasonable questions, but I should be sorry if Updike were to pay much attention to them. Certainly we want him to write a great book, but we don't want him to feel that he must do something great or be a failure. In a wise comment on James Agee, Updike says: "A fever of self-importance is upon American writing. Popular expectations of what literature should provide have risen so high that failure is the only possible success, and pained incapacity the only acceptable proof of sincerity." If, he goes on, Agee had justly estimated what he had done, instead of weeping over what he had wanted to do, he would not have taken so unhappy a view of his career. In the same way, it might be a good thing for critics to contemplate what Updike has accomplished in a decade— two excellent novels and many first-rate stories—and not to spend so much time worrying about the books he hasn't yet even attempted.

Saturday Review
May 15, 1965

6 *Of the Farm*

A man of thirty-five takes his second wife and her eleven-year-old son to visit his widowed mother on her farm in Pennsylvania, arriving late one Friday afternoon in summer and leaving the following Sunday. During the interval nothing dramatic happens except that the mother has a seizure—what she calls a "spell"— after church on Sunday. The four characters talk, and as they talk, the reader becomes aware of the complicated relationships that exist between mother and son, man and wife, wife and mother-in-law, stepfather and stepson, and so on in all possible combinations. Certain characters not on the scene are also important, particularly the deceased husband and father and the divorced wife with her three children. When the book ends, conflicts have been clarified but not resolved.

This, I think, is a fair outline of John Updike's short novel, *Of the Farm.* The farm is located on the outskirts of Olinger, a city that appears in much of Updike's fiction. The deceased father was a schoolteacher, as was the father in *The Centaur* and in various of Updike's short stories. Both the country and the characters will seem familiar to Updike's regular readers, and the writing is as felicitous as usual.

"To produce a mighty book," Herman Melville wrote, "you must choose a mighty theme." This is a hard saying. Would the themes of *Hamlet, Anna Karenina,* or *Madame Bovary,* if stated in summary form, sound like mighty themes? We can know for sure that a theme is mighty only when a great writer shows us what can be made of it.

Besides, is mightiness the sovereign literary virtue? For some time now a few critics have been clamoring for Updike to do something "big." There is an American tendency—encouraged, I am afraid, by both Hemingway and Faulkner—to believe that a literary career is like a series of world's championship battles, that the great writer goes on slaying one giant after another until he is himself slain. Wright Morris discussed this tendency in *The Territory Ahead.* "Just the other day," he wrote, "William Faulkner, in one of his now-frequent interviews, referred to Thomas Wolfe as the greatest American of them all. Why? Because he tried to do the impossible. The romantic agony could hardly be better phrased, nor failure made so credible and flattering. To fail, that is, is the true hallmark of success."

In *Of the Farm* Updike was obviously not trying to do the impossible. He chose a small, manageable theme, one that might have seemed rather slight even to Henry James, and tried to see what he could do with it. His problem might be stated this way: if you bring four persons together for forty-eight not particularly eventful hours, how much can you show the reader about them? He complicated his problem as a novelist by having the story told by one of the participants, so that he was unable to enter the mind of any of the others.

The narrator is Joey Robinson, vaguely engaged in some sort of business enterprise, though his mother had hoped he would be a poet. He doesn't tell us much about himself, but, as we see him in relation to the others, we have an impression of his good points and bad. His mother is the central character, the one of whom Updike wants us to be most aware. Always a puzzle to Joey, she baffles him again and again as the two days pass by, and the reader is surprised and amused as the contradictions in her character reveal themselves. Although she lives in a myth she has created, she can be realistic and toughminded enough when it serves her purpose, and, for all her years and her bad health, she remains a strong woman, not particularly lovable, perhaps not even admirable, but a force to be reckoned with.

Joey's affection for his mother is more than merely dutiful; nevertheless there is a long-standing antagonism between them, growing out of the years when he took his father's side against her. Try as he will to be gentle, his resentments break out. "You poisoned one marriage for me," he says the first night after his wife has gone to bed, "and I want you to leave this one alone." When he joins his wife, he lets himself go: "I'm thirty-five, and I've been through hell and I don't see why that old lady has to have such a hold over me. It's ridiculous. It's degrading."

The mother, as Joey realizes, is a pathetic figure—old and ill and alone and by no means ready to die. ("My mother was skittish in cars; it was grotesque, how much she loved her life.") But if she is pathetic, she is still capable of defiant gestures. On the second evening she explodes. "In the kitchen, my mother smashed a plate. To abolish any doubt that it had been deliberate, she smashed another, after a bleached space of amazed silence; the explosion was somewhat muddier than the first, as if the plate had struck the floor diagonally." Later Joey explains to his stepson: "I think the reason my mother smashed the dishes was to remind us that she was there. She's afraid we'll forget her. It's a fear people have when they're her age." But this is a woman who is not likely to be forgotten.

The second wife, Peggy, is not portrayed at any depth, presumably because Joey's knowledge of her is not of the deepest. He sees her as extraordinarily desirable, but he does not romanticize either her appearance or her mind, as a young lover might do. What their domestic life may be we can only surmise, but, as the old lady suggests, it is probably not altogether harmonious. As for her son Richard, his amusing combination of sophistication and inexperience underlines the ironies of the situation.

There is no denying that it is a slight book, not calculated to quicken many pulses. But one should not underestimate it: the portrait of the mother is subtle and profound; most of the scenes are skillfully constructed so as to achieve the greatest possible revelation of character; the dialogue is lively. It's a sound novel, and we should be grateful for it.

Beyond that there is room for speculation. What would happen if Updike found himself engaged with a theme that drew upon all his experience, stretched his imagination, made the highest demands on his skills? No one knows. I prefer Updike's modest success to the messes some of his more ambitious colleagues have made. But if he did find a mighty theme and mastered it, I should rejoice.

Saturday Review
November 13, 1965

7 *The Music School*

The prolific John Updike has published three books in a year and a half: a miscellaneous volume entitled *Assorted Prose*; a short novel, *Of the Farm*, and now *The Music School*, a collection of twenty stories, all of which have appeared in *The New Yorker*. His books turn up on the stands almost as frequently as those of John O'Hara, though fortunately they are not so fat.

Although, as I have said on earlier occasions, I should be happy if Updike did something stronger and deeper and more challenging than he has thus far written, something that rose above the general level of contemporary fiction as does Bellow's *Herzog* or Malamud's *The Fixer*, I believe, as I have also said, that we should not ungratefully depreciate the work he is doing. Here are twenty stories, each of them a technical success, each of them distinguished by rich and original imagery, two or three of them first-rate. That is not a bad showing.

More than half the stories deal with domestic crises of one sort or another—couples on the verge of divorce, quarreling couples being reconciled, unfaithful husbands, jealous wives. Updike makes much of this domestic theme, catching each subtle change in a deteriorating situation. Writing as a rule from the men's points of view, he almost always manages to do justice to the women, and the reader cannot doubt the reality of the pain that is felt on both sides. This reader, however, did not become deeply involved in any of the crises portrayed.

One of the best of the stories, certainly my favorite, is "The Christian Roommates," which does not concern a married couple, though the situation has some of the elements of a domestic crisis. Brought together by the vagaries of administrative procedure, two quite dissimilar boys, one absurdly conventional and the other absurdly unconventional, share a room in their freshman year at Harvard. Much is made of the abrasive effect of the unconventional boy on his earnest roommate, but in the end we perceive that the abrasion has worked both ways. In the background are seven or eight other freshmen, neighbors in the dormitory, briefly treated but realized sufficiently to give the reader a sense of a whole college generation. And when Updike tells, in a few adroit paragraphs, what happened to all of these boys in the next twenty years or so, he says something worth listening to about contemporary American life.

Another story, which impressed me because of its technique, is "Harv Is Plowing Now." It begins: "Our lives submit to archeology. For a period of life which seems longer ago than it was, I lived in a farmhouse that lacked electricity and central heating." After three pages of description that brilliantly recreate that period, the narrator returns to the theme of archeology, dramatically summarizing discoveries made in excavations at Ur. He maintains the archeological figure of speech throughout the remainder of the story, in which he reconstructs what he can of a love affair that once engrossed him. It is Updike's sharp sense of the complexity of the mind, of the layers upon layers of experience that somehow coexist, of the immensities of time and space that can be contracted into a moment, that made me greatly admire some of the stories in *Pigeon Feathers*. None of the stories in *The Music School* is a bold step forward, but most of them measure up to Updike's standard, which is not low.

Saturday Review
September 24, 1966

8 *Couples*

An article on John Updike that appeared in *Life* magazine a while ago noted that the "present national preoccupation with sex" did not seem "particularly menacing" to him. Updike was quoted as adding, "I do buy Freud's notion about the radical centrality of sex. It's somehow so, isn't it? All kinds of activity, all the getting of money, are a form of preening. Look at all those cars out there now, all moving people from one tryst to another."

Sex has been central in much of Updike's work, but never so

strongly emphasized as in his latest novel, *Couples*. It is the story of a group of people in a Massachusetts town called Tarbox. (Tarbox is south of Boston and therefore not to be confused with Updike's hometown, Ipswich, which is north of Boston.) Ten couples figure in the novel, and, so far as the book is concerned, coupling is their most important activity. It is rather a mixed group, including two building contractors, three men concerned with science, two men concerned with finance, an airplane pilot, and one man so rich he only pretends to work. Their wives, at the beginning, have no jobs, but most of them do have children. The average age is probably in the neighborhood of thirty-five.

The couples see each other frequently, at weekend parties and, in varying combinations and at the proper seasons, in sports such as swimming, tennis, touch football, and skiing. At the parties there is much drinking, some dancing, some necking, occasionally a word game or something of the sort. They seldom talk about art, literature, philosophy, or even politics. Most of them seem rather unattractive at the outset and grow more so as the novel proceeds.

As has been indicated, Updike concentrates on the sexual relations, marital and extramarital, of these twenty people. There is at least one adulterer in nine of the families, and in several there are two. We are spared none of the details, nor any of the four-letter words, and I am not sure we ought to be. Since writers can be explicit these days, perhaps they ought to be if their theme is sex. At any rate Updike could not have done what he wanted to do if he had been more reticent, for it is only by being specific that he can show the variety in sexual behavior.

Although in the first part of the novel Updike moves freely from one character to another, he comes to concentrate more and more on Piet Hanema, one of the contractors, the other being his partner, Matt Gallagher. In the course of the novel Piet has intercourse with four of the wives in addition to his own. Involved with Georgene Thorne at the start, he soon turns to Foxy Whitman, and this is the grand affair although he has two other bed-partners before the book ends.

The relationship between Piet and his creator is puzzling. "Piet," we are told on the first page, "had red hair and a close-set body; no taller than Angela, he was denser." Updike, by his pictures, is tall and slender. Moreover, Piet didn't graduate from Harvard summa cum laude; he didn't go to college at all. He doesn't write books; he builds houses. But if the hands are the hands of a contractor, the voice is often the voice of John Updike. For example, after Piet has said goodbye to a friend who is dying of cancer, we are told that "the drug-dilated eyes, eyes that had verified the chaos of particles on the floor of matter, lifted, and dragged Piet down into omniscience; he saw, plunging, how plausible it was to die, how death, far from invading earth like a meteor, occurs on the same plane as birth and marriage and the arrival of the daily mail." Again: "The world was more Platonic than he had suspected. He found he missed friends less than friendship; what he felt, remembering Foxy, was a nostalgia for adultery itself—its adventure, the acrobatics its deceptions demand, the tensions of its hidden strings, the new landscapes it makes us master." Piet, it appears, has the mind of a poet, and we had hardly been prepared for that.

The book has two epigraphs, one of them from Paul Tillich's *The Future of Religions*: "There is a tendency in the average citizen, even if he has a high standing in his profession, to consider the decisions relating to the life of the society to which he belongs as a matter of fate on which he has no influence—like the Roman subjects all over the world in the period of the Roman empire, a mood favorable for the resurgence of religion but unfavorable for the preservation of a living democracy."

The members of the Tarbox group seem to give little thought to the affairs of the nation and the world. To underline their remoteness, Updike occasionally dates a scene by referring to some happening in the world at large that plays no part whatever in the action that follows. The conspicuous example of detachment is the fact that members of the group do not cancel plans for a party on the night after President Kennedy's assassination, and, though some of the people feel vaguely guilty, the party is pretty much like all their parties.

On the other hand, there are few signs of the resurgence of religion that Tillich predicted. Aside from the Gallaghers, who are practicing Catholics, Piet is the only member of the group who is seriously concerned with religious matters. He regularly attends the Congregational Church, and sometimes the service is important for him: "On command, Piet sat and prayed. Prayer was an unsteady state of mind for him. When it worked, he seemed, for intermittent moments, to be in the farthest corner of a deep burrow, a small endearing hairy animal curled up as if to hibernate. In this condition he felt close to a massive warm secret, like the heart of lava at the earth's core. His existence for a second seemed to evade decay." He says to Foxy: "I think America now is like an unloved child smothered in candy. Like a middle-aged wife whose husband brings home a present after every trip because he's been unfaithful to her." When Foxy asks him who the husband is, he answers, "God. Obviously. God doesn't love us any more. He loves Russia. He loves Uganda. We're fat and full of pimples and always whining for more candy. We've fallen from grace." In part because of his deep fear of death, Piet cares about God's grace.

Freddy Thorne, the ostentatiously cynical dentist, says, "People are the only things people have left since God packed up. By people I mean sex." But so far as the group is concerned—what one of its ex-members sardonically refers to as "the magic circle"—sex seems to be a poor substitute for religion. Perhaps it is Piet's strength that, important as sex is in his life, he enjoys sex as sex, not as a substitute for anything.

Couples is the longest book Updike has written, but it isn't the major novel many of us have been hoping for. For one thing, Piet, as I have suggested, is not quite real; the umbilical cord has not been severed. For another thing, the book is not different from what Updike has written before but simply more—more couples, more coupling, more trouble. However—and this is as much a

cliché as saying it isn't the book we were hoping for—it is full of
good things. I've written that or something like it about every book
Updike has published, and it's always true. As almost everybody
but Norman Podhoretz agrees, Updike writes like an angel.
Although quantitatively, so to speak, *Couples* reminds me of the
work of Updike's fellow-Pennsylvanian John O'Hara, there is no
comparison in quality. Updike's style can carry the burden of
details with which the book is filled. He uses even the four-letter
words with distinction.

Saturday Review
April 6, 1968

Afterword

In reading over my reviews of John Updike's books, I am amused
to observe that I began and ended on the same note. His first novel,
The Poorhouse Fair, which I reviewed with several other first novels,
seemed to me exceptionally good in some ways and not so good in
others. I wrote in conclusion: "We can't expect masterpieces every
day, and so we have to be grateful when we are given even a
moderate degree of pleasure and some cause for hope."

As the years and the books have gone by, I have said something
of the same sort again and again. Not a few critics have felt that
Updike was capable of producing a great novel, and they have
refused to settle for anything less. I know how they feel, and sometimes I have expressed the same kind of impatience. With most of
the short stories and with so modest a novel as *Of the Farm,* it is
easy to recognize his originality and his perfection within his limits.
The really ambitious novels, such as *The Centaur* and *Couples,*

raise the issue more sharply, making us see what tremendous resources he has. They are so good we are sure that they might be better. But, as I have frequently said and will continue to say, it is more sensible to praise him for what he has done than to condemn him for not doing what we think he could and should have done.

FLANNERY O'CONNOR

Foreword

Of all the young writers of promise in the postwar period, none seems to me more extraordinary than Flannery O'Connor. There is something doubly ironic in speaking of her promise, first because she died in her fortieth year and, second, because her achievement by that age was so great. I read *Wise Blood* soon after it was published, was baffled by it, and put it aside. After I had been bowled over by her first collection of short stories, *A Good Man Is Hard to Find,* I went back to *Wise Blood* and began to understand what an extraordinary book it was in its enigmatic way.

I reviewed *A Good Man* jointly with Eudora Welty's *The Bride of the Innisfallen,* and I have given the review as it originally appeared because the juxtaposition seems to me an interesting one. I have great admiration for Miss Welty's work, and I left her out of this volume only because so many of her good stories belong to the period before the Second World War. I am glad to pay homage to her briefly in connection with a more extended discussion of a younger Southern writer.

In looking the reviews over, I notice that at different points I have described Miss O'Connor as compassionate and as lacking in compassion. I should like to believe that I was right the first time, but I am afraid that, by and large, compassion was not among Miss O'Connor's many virtues. She was more concerned with understanding the truth about people than in feeling sorry for them. She did not pity herself, though she had what would seem to be reason to, and she was not inclined to pity others.

1 *A Good Man Is Hard to Find*

This is a belated tribute to two collections of short stories, both by Southern women. They are Eudora Welty's *The Bride of the Innisfallen* and Flannery O'Connor's *A Good Man Is Hard to Find*.

Miss Welty is a Southern writer, not in the sense of belonging to a school or being a professional regionalist but simply in the sense of writing about an area of the South. As deeply rooted in her native state as her fellow-Mississippian, William Faulkner, she has succeeded, just as he has, in transcending her region.

This is not to say that the South hasn't given Miss Welty a great deal. In one of the stories in the present volume, "Kin," the narrator, after a long absence in the North, is visiting her aunt and cousin in the small Mississippi town in which she was born. "Aunt Ethel and Kate, and everybody I knew here," she reflects, "lived as if they had never heard of anywhere else, even Jackson." A degree of isolation, a degree of stability, the maintenance of family ties, the preservation of family and community and regional lore— all these provide a setting in which Miss Welty's talents operate with wonderful effectiveness.

Yet these talents can also operate without the setting, as three of these stories demonstrate. One of the three is a poetic retelling of the story of Circe and Ulysses, quite unlike anything the author has done before, though she has always had a fondness for legends. The other two seem almost calculated to prove her independence of the static qualities of Southern society, for they deal with situations that are in their nature ephemeral. "Going to Naples" describes an Atlantic crossing on an Italian vessel, while the title story is devoted to the passengers in a compartment on the boat train from London to Fishguard. Yet in portraying the transient relationships that develop in such circumstances, Miss Welty manages, almost as well as in her best stories of the South, to suggest the depths of human personality.

Miss Welty has two great gifts. The first is her ability to create an atmosphere so real and so dense that the reader finds himself immersed in it. The second is her skill in searching out and in suggesting, usually by indirection, the subtler reaches of character. Her fondness for the oblique and the parabolic leads her at times into obscurity, and at times (as, for instance, in so essentially melodramatic a story as "The Burning") makes her seem awkward and prissy. But when subject and sensibility and method all match, as generally they do, she can provide as much pleasure as any writer now living.

Miss Welty's book gives me what I have learned to expect from her work, but Miss O'Connor's comes as a surprise: I hadn't realized she was so good. All ten of her stories are laid in Georgia, her native state, and her people are either poor or are fighting hard to maintain what advantages they have. But the book is not so much a description of a certain segment of the population as it is the expression of a mood.

Several of her characters are physically defective, with a hand missing or a leg, or they are feeble-minded; most of the others are morally or spiritually deformed. What typically happens is that characters are confronted with situations to which they are inadequate. In the title story, a painfully commonplace family stumbles into extermination. In "The Artificial Nigger," an old man cannot cope with the city and is led into a betrayal of his grandson. In "A Circle in the Fire," a woman of great self-reliance is challenged and beaten by a trio of young hoodlums. And in "The Displaced Person," another very competent woman is destroyed by being compelled to face the problem of her responsibilities to other persons.

It would be hard to exaggerate the competence with which Miss O'Connor goes about the telling of these stories. Each of them is hard and sharp and dramatic. And each of them leaves, as it is meant to do, a nasty taste in the reader's mouth. This nastiness, however, is not gratuitous on the author's part. On the contrary, it is clear that Miss O'Connor regards human life as mean and brutish and that she makes this judgment from an orthodox Christian point of view. But one does not have to believe in original sin to be affected by the stories. Miss O'Connor's vision of life is presented with such conviction and such intensity that, for the moment at any rate, it authenticates itself. If there is a young writer—Miss O'Connor is thirty—who has given evidence of greater originality and power, I cannot think who it is.

The New Leader
August 15, 1955

2 *The Violent Bear It Away*

Flannery O'Connor is a Southerner and a Catholic, and both of these facts are important. Her material, up to a point at any rate, comes from her region, and is roughly of the sort described as Southern Gothic. Her attitude towards the material derives, as she has herself pointed out, from her religious convictions. But she is a particular kind of Southerner and, if she will forgive a heretic for saying so, a particular kind of Catholic. Her work is highly individual, and the better it becomes, the clearer its individuality is.

The Violent Bear It Away is better than her first novel, *Wise Blood,* and as good as the best of her short stories, which is to say that it is first-rate. She has been working on it for a long while (a chapter appeared in *New World Writing* in 1955) and it is a firm, strong, disciplined book. From now on there can be no doubt that Miss O'Connor is one of the important American writers.

The novel has a breathtaking first sentence:

Francis Marion Tarwater's uncle had been dead for only half a day when the boy got too drunk to finish digging his grave and a Negro named Buford Munson, who had come to get a jug filled, had to finish it and drag the body from the breakfast table where it was still sitting and bury it in a decent Christian way, with the sign of its Saviour at the head of the grave and enough dirt on top to keep the dogs from digging it up.

This is Southern Gothic with a vengeance, and it gives a taste of the violence and horror to come. Like *Wise Blood,* the book is one of grotesques, but this does not mean that the characters are fantastic or incredible. On the contrary, it becomes impossible not to believe in them.

Francis Marion Tarwater, who is fourteen, has been brought up by the uncle—great-uncle really—whom he fails to bury. The old man, a fanatic, in his own opinion a prophet, a moonshiner on the side, kidnaped the boy, taught him what he wanted him to know, trained him to become his successor. The boy's only other relative is a true uncle, a schoolteacher named Rayber, and it is to him that young Tarwater now turns.

The conflict between the boy and his uncle becomes the novel's central theme. Rayber himself, when he was seven, was exposed to the old man's fanaticism, but he escaped and, as he believes, achieved enlightenment. Now he wants to save his nephew, but Tarwater is recalcitrant. At the same time, however, Tarwater is by no means sure that he wants to adopt the prophetic role for which he has been prepared. In particular he hesitates before the task that, above all else, the old man imposed upon him: the baptizing of Rayber's feeble-minded son.

Both the boy and the man are divided within themselves. Tarwater has a tough, worldly streak, represented by an inner voice that gives him practical counsel, and from the beginning he struggles against his great-uncle's design for him, even though the compulsion to obey is strong. Rayber, for his part, has been more deeply influenced by the old man than he likes to admit, and he has to wage a hard fight against his fanatical tendencies. The rationalism he so glibly expounds is no more than skin deep.

Nevertheless, Rayber is diligent in his effort to lead Tarwater out of the darkness of superstition into the light of reason, and he tries one stratagem after another. He has, however, no chance of success, for the boy rejects out of hand the teacher's way of life. If he is not to become the prophet his great-uncle wanted him to be, then he will follow the bidding of his own dark impulses. His struggle reaches its climax in a scene with the half-witted child, but the climax is indecisive, for, against his will, he baptizes the child even as he drowns him. In the end, after Tarwater's further resistance, the triumph of the old man is complete.

In the essay she contributed to *The Living Novel* Miss O'Connor wrote:

> . . . when I look at stories I have written I find that they are, for the most part, about people who are poor, who are afflicted in both mind and body, who have little—or at best a distorted—sense of spiritual purpose. . . . Yet how is this? For I am no disbeliever in spiritual purpose and no vague believer. I see from the standpoint of Christian orthodoxy. This means that for me the meaning of life is centered in our Redemption by Christ and that what I see in the world I see in its relation to that . . . My own feeling is that writers who see by the light of their Christian faith will have, in these times, the sharpest eyes for the grotesque, for the perverse, and for the unacceptable . . . The novelist with Christian concerns will find in modern life distortions which are repugnant to him, and his problem will be to make these appear as distortions to an audience which is used to seeing them as natural.

The people in *The Violent Bear It Away,* then, are not merely grotesques, and their grotesqueness is not portrayed for its own sake; they are distortions. The old man is warped by fanaticism; he is ugly, intemperate, unloving. Young Tarwater, before he too becomes a fanatic, has found no better alternative than cynicism and violent action. As for Rayber, his rationalism is superficial and preposterously inadequate. He is, indeed, as we realize after the drowning of the child, a dead soul.

Yet Miss O'Connor exposes none of these characters to the contempt of the reader. She is not attacking error but portraying poor erring men. She writes about them with great compassion, and does justice to their virtues.

Miss O'Connor tells the story with stark power, making every detail carry its full weight. The conflicts she describes are wonderfully sustained and intensified, and the characters are even more fully revealed. What happens seems, when it has happened, to have been inevitable. Miss O'Connor is thoroughly in control of her world; she knows it and she knows where she stands in relation to it. Her prose is strong, supple, at times full of beauty, never pretentious. From any point of view, *The Violent Bear It Away* is a distinguished piece of work.

Saturday Review
February 27, 1960

3 *Everything That Rises Must Converge*

Flannery O'Connor died last summer in her fortieth year, having published two novels and a collection of short stories. She left enough short stories to make another collection, which has just been published: *Everything That Rises Must Converge*.

Already a kind of Flannery O'Connor legend is taking shape. Much has been written about her since her death, and *Espirit,* published by the University of Scranton, has devoted most of an issue to praise of her work by distinguished men and women of letters. Certain themes are emphasized: her devotion to Catholicism, the toughness of character that permitted her to survive and to triumph as a writer while living on an isolated Georgia farm, the courage with which she endured a crippling and incurable disease, her constant preoccupation with her craft.

Certain of Flannery O'Connor's virtues—particularly her courage and her craftsmanship—cannot be exaggerated, but she was not, as some of her admirers seem to suggest, a candidate for sainthood. She was a devout and proud Catholic: "I am no disbeliever in spiritual purpose and no vague believer," she wrote in her essay in *The Living Novel,* and, "I see from the standpoint of Christian orthodoxy." Yet she refused to conform to the literary standards set up by many priests and laymen in the name of the Church. (See, for instance, the text of one of her lectures printed in *Greyfriar,* published by Siena College, Loudonville, New York.) She insisted on expressing her orthodoxy in her own way.

Similarly, although she was an extraordinarily independent young woman, living a kind of life that few contemporary writers would put up with, she was by no means a solitary. Friends and admirers visited her in Milledgeville, and she was cordial with them, even making small talk, when that seemed called for, in the best Southern manner. She corresponded with literary people she found congenial, and her letters were lively and often gay. (*Shenandoah* for the winter of 1965 prints a collection of letters written to Richard H. Stern that reveal sides of Flannery O'Connor few people saw.) Difficult as travel was for her, she spoke at many colleges. She was in the world as much as she wanted to be, as much as was consonant with the state of her health and her integrity as a writer.

She grew steadily in her art, and the best of the stories in *Everything That Rises* are the best things she ever wrote. They are superb, and they are terrible. She took a cold, hard look at human beings, and she set down with marvelous precision what she saw.

In the title story we have a pretentious, empty-headed woman who is struggling to dominate her son, for whom, as she frequently reminds him, she has sacrificed everything. The reader's sympathies are at first altogether with the son, but slowly, ruthlessly, Miss O'Connor strips him bare. He is weak, selfish, confused, afraid of the freedom he pretends to desire. The unhappy resolution of the situation comes by way of a Negro woman, who is herself arrogant, bitter, and violent.

Miss O'Connor shows us a number of these pompous, self-satisfied, middle-class women. In "Revelation" she holds up for our appalled gaze a peculiarly outrageous specimen, and then contrives a situation in which the woman sees herself as we see her. In "Greenleaf" a hard-working, narrow-minded woman, who thinks of herself as the epitome of virtue, is pitted against a shiftless farmer, and loses the struggle.

The weak intellectual also appears in several stories. ("Intellectual" was not a flattering term in her vocabulary; in one of her letters to Stern in Chicago she speaks of his being "in that cold place among them interllekchuls.") She was particularly distrustful of the rationalistic reformer, the do-gooder. She revealed her sentiments in her portrayal of Rayber in *The Violent Bear It Away,* but her study of the type in the story called "The Lame Shall Enter First" is even more dismaying. A social worker, a widower, befriends an intelligent but badly behaved boy of the streets, even putting him ahead of his own son. Gradually the reader comes to understand the futility and wickedness of the reformer's conduct, and the twist of the screw comes when he himself is forced to understand—too late.

There is violence in most of the stories, but it rarely seems to be dragged in for its own sake. Violence is an integral part of the world Miss O'Connor is describing, an inevitable consequence of the evil she portrays. In another horrible story, "A View of the Woods," an old man and his granddaughter, who are exactly alike in their meanness, are brought into physical conflict, which becomes grotesque and terrible.

I find almost no compassion in these stories. In "Judgment Day" Miss O'Connor seems to be sorry for the old man who has been transplanted from his Georgia farm to his daughter's New York City apartment, but she is not very sorry for many of her characters. I was devastated by the fate of the reformer in "The Lame Shall Enter First," but Miss O'Connor appears to believe that he got what he deserved. I see him as a man who made mistakes but in the end was to be pitied. Miss O'Connor, I think, saw him as a man who rejected Divine Grace and could expect nothing but hellfire. (The urchin the man tries to befriend knows himself to be a child of Satan, but to the man that is all nonsense.)

I am not saying that Miss O'Connor's Catholicism was responsible for the harshness of her judgments; but the harshness, which probably had many causes, was compatible with her religion as she conceived it. The evil of unredeemed human nature was part of her dogma, and she saw plenty of evidence of it. She was not a pessimist, of course, because she believed there was a way of salvation, but I know of no pessimist who has painted a darker picture of the world we live in.

What are we who are not believers in her sense to make of this? Simply that she set down what she saw. We may have pity where she did not, but we cannot deny the testimony of her eyes. Again and again the reader is brought up short by the precision with which she communicates her insights. She appears to be a rather simple, even casual, sort of writer, but the more one analyzes her stories, the more one is impressed by her artistry. She may not have been a saint, but she was one of the best writers of short stories this era has seen.

Saturday Review
May 29, 1965

4 *Mystery and Manners*

When I visited Flannery O'Connor at her mother's home near Milledgeville, Georgia, in the spring of 1962, she was thirty-seven years old and had only two more years to live. I was surprised to find her so dependent on her crutches. I knew that she suffered from a disease, a form of lupus, that was presumably going to kill her, and that she was already far along in a horrible deteriorative process. But both her published work and the few letters she had written me were so vigorous that I really hadn't believed in her invalidism.

I soon forgot about it. She said that she spent from nine to twelve each morning writing and the rest of the day recuperating. I can believe that she needed to recuperate: three hours a day of her kind of writing would wear a strong man down, and her physical resources were limited. But recuperation did not mean withdrawal from life, at least not for long. The plantation was explosive with birth and rebirth: not fifty yards from the house a mare was licking her newborn foal; you couldn't move around the place without disturbing hens and ducks and geese on their nests; and Flannery's beloved peafowl, raucous and beautiful, were everywhere. Nor did she find human life alien to her; she was no recluse. Her mother, a woman of great energy, not only managed the plantation efficiently but also, as a member of one of Milledgeville's leading families, took her place in its social activities. Flannery not only mingled with her mother's friends but, to my surprise and amusement, talked to them as if she were any little old Southern girl.

Almost the only activity that took Flannery away from Milledgeville in the last decade of her life was her lecturing and reading from her work in colleges, mostly but not exclusively in the South.

Traveling by plane must have been difficult, but she managed it competently, and obviously enjoyed these excursions. In their collection of her occasional prose, *Mystery and Manners,* Sally and Robert Fitzgerald include versions of several of these lectures as well as some of the few articles she prepared for periodical publication. As the Fitzgeralds point out in their introduction, Flannery never gave the same lecture twice; she always worked over her notes, adding here and subtracting there. As a result there came to be several versions of each lecture, and the Fitzgeralds had to select and combine and rearrange. I had read some of these lectures in one form or another, but until they were brought together I had not realized what an impressive body of literary criticism they constituted.

To go back to the spring of 1962, my central impression of Flannery O'Connor was that here was a young woman who had come to terms with herself and her life. In the past ten or fifteen years she had made a series of difficult and important decisions. In the first place, and I think in a way it was the most important of these decisions, she had decided to be a writer, and, as the reader of the book clearly sees, her commitment could not have been more serious if she had decided to enter a nunnery. In the second place, after what seems to have been a period of doubt, she reaffirmed her loyalty to the Catholic Church. Here again what might have been a casual decision, since she had been brought up in a Catholic family, involved every part of her being. In the third place, she had chosen to spend the remainder of her life in the environs of Milledgeville, and she believed that this had saved her from the rootlessness from which, she felt, so many of her contemporaries suffered. Finally, she had faced the almost certain prospect of a deterioration of her strength leading to a premature death. She was sustained, I know, by her religious faith, but also, I am sure, by the challenge of a craft that called for the exertion of all her remaining powers.

She had a tough streak and didn't suffer fools gladly. Her tongue could be sharp when she wanted it to be. "Everywhere I go," she remarked in one lecture, "I'm asked if I think the universities stifle writers. My opinion is that they don't stifle enough of them." She was quick to demolish romantic notions about the literary life: "People are always saying that the modern novelist has no hope and that the picture he paints of the world is unbearable. The only answer to this is that people without hope do not write novels. Writing is a terrible experience, during which the hair often falls out and teeth decay."

She faced up to every problem that confronted her, including problems raised by her adherence to Catholicism. She wrote, for example: "The business of protecting souls from dangerous literature belongs properly to the Church. All fiction, even when it satisfies the requirements of art, will not turn out to be suitable for everyone's consumption, and if in some instance the Church sees fit to forbid the faithful to read the work without permission, the author, if he is a Catholic, will be thankful that the Church is willing to perform this service for him." This chills my once Protestant blood; but look at the concluding sentence: "It means that he can limit himself to the demands of art." And that is what was important to Flannery O'Connor as a writer.

As she made clear in several short stories and in *The Violent Bear It Away,* Flannery had little patience with liberal more-or-less Protestant do-goodism. In one lecture she says that she speaks of Catholic rather than Christian literature because "the word Christian is no longer reliable. It has come to mean anyone with a golden heart. And a golden heart would be a positive interference in the writing of fiction." She writes, "It is the business of fiction to embody mystery in manners, and mystery is a great embarrassment to the modern mind." To many modern minds, yes; but not to the minds out of which has come the best of contemporary fiction, for mystery is always at the heart of their work, whatever faith or lack of faith they profess. The streamlined, new and improved, computerized modern mind has little to do with art of any sort.

The first and last pieces stand apart from the others as being not quite what one would have expected from Flannery O'Connor, and yet they turn out to be perfectly characteristic. The first, on peacocks, was written for *Holiday* magazine; it is charming, mildly sardonic, and full of useful information if you ever plan to raise a peacock. The other is an introduction to a book called *A Memoir of Mary Ann,* a book prepared by the Sisters of Our Lady of Perpetual Help Free Cancer Home in Atlanta, in tribute to a child whose brief and pain-burdened life inspired those who ministered to her. Flannery could not be betrayed into sentimentality even by piety, but the piece has a tenderness that must be remembered when we think of her toughness.

Saturday Review
May 10, 1969

HERBERT GOLD

Foreword

The exigencies of literary journalism sometimes led me to review two or more books in one piece. Sometimes this worked out rather well but sometimes it didn't. I reviewed Chester Himes's *The Third Generation* along with Herbert Gold's *The Prospect Before Us* for the reason that both touched on the race problem. It was not a satisfactory combination. Himes's novel, like most of his work I have read, was interesting chiefly as a sociological document, whereas *The Prospect Before Us*—Gold's second novel and the first of his I had read—was, as I said, "a novel that was really 'written.' "

I have kept the transitional paragraphs because, I hope, they suggest the satisfaction that a literary journalist does feel every now and then. As subsequent reviews show, I have not always been so happy with Gold's work, but he has not lost his ability to touch my imagination.

1 *The Prospect Before Us*

The apparent theme of *The Third Generation* is the havoc wrought by a particular kind of color-consciousness. Lillian Taylor, a light Negro, so resents the blackness of her husband that she ruins his life and hers and the lives of their children. We are especially concerned with Charles, who is her favorite son, and we follow his headlong pursuit of death through a staggering series of accidents, diseases, vices and crimes.

The real theme, in short, is the devastating impact of a neurotic woman on the persons associated with her, and the causes of her neuroses are of secondary importance. Perhaps, indeed, her obsession with color is a symptom rather than a cause. In any case, the reader is interested in Charles as a human being, not as a Negro; and if Himes has been able to make us believe in Charles's self-destructive behavior, this would be another example of the broadening and maturing of our Negro novelists. Unfortunately, however, the novel is serious only in intent, not in execution. The writing is usually undistinguished and sometimes slovenly, and the characters come alive only in occasional episodes. Toward the end, when the novel should be most impressive, it is merely sensational.

Gold's *The Prospect Before Us,* is a novel that is really "written," and it makes me eager to read his first book, *Birth of a Hero,* which I missed. *The Prospect Before Us* is the story of Harry Bowers, an immigrant who has prospered in a world that lies just within the boundaries of respectability. As the owner of a small, profitable hotel, he is liked and looked up to in that world; in his own eyes and those of his associates he is a success. And then an organization

interested in the rights of the Negro decides to make a test in the
Green Glade Hotel, and sends a young woman, Claire Farren, to
take a room there. Bowers is perfectly aware of what is going on,
and he knows the tricks by which hotel proprietors deal with such
awkward situations; but, for reasons that are never quite clear to
him, he decides to play the game straight. It is mostly a matter of
pride. He is king on Prospect Avenue, and he thinks he can beat the
pressures that he knows will be exerted on him; and, if he can't, his
reasons for thinking well of himself are gone. Of course he can't.
Customers leave, business associates threaten and try violence, the
bank bears down. And, in the end, his kingdom is brought low
and he with it.

If we need to be reminded of the injustices and humiliations to
which Negroes are subjected in our society, *The Prospect Before
Us* does the job, and does it all the more effectively for its gentle
air of objectivity. The petty prejudices of the Green Glade's guests,
the ranting and greed of Gil Leary, President of the Prospect Avenue
Businessmen's Association, the abusive anonymous letters to Claire
Farren—these things are American civilization at its most degraded.
And Gold makes us feel them as few novelists, white or black, have
succeeded in doing. But they are not what the book is about.

The book is about the triumph-in-failure of Harry Bowers, and
in order to make us feel that, in all its truly tragic implications,
Gold must arouse in us a sense of Harry's greatness. On the surface,
he is not a prepossessing character: middle-aged and fat, with a
kind of professional cheeriness and a stock of corny jokes, with a
quick eye for a fast buck and the showy manners of a good spender.
But we come first to like and then to respect him. He is a man who
knows on what terms he wants to live his life and is willing to pay
the price for doing so. That his principles are tested by way of the
Negro problem is an accident, though perhaps no other test could
so well define his elements of greatness. What matters is the way he
stands the test.

Gold helps us to see Bowers by showing him in relation to other
persons. There is, first of all, a rather disreputable character named

Jake, who wants to be loved and, especially, to be loved by Harry Bowers—not, of course, in homosexual terms. The sense of obligation that Harry feels toward Jake and that makes him Jake's accomplice is a remarkably complicated emotional pattern. The same sense of obligation, with a more obvious motivation, dominates Harry's relations with his incompetent brother Morris, whom he has kept afloat for many years. Toward the bullying Gil Leary, Harry is at first politely and then outspokenly contemptuous. In all these relationships, Harry is shown to advantage, and yet each of them exposes a flaw in his character. With Claire Farren, on the other hand, through his sensitiveness and his capacity for love, he achieves complete understanding. Even as he commits arson, we see him as a good man—the most difficult kind of character to create in fiction—and, at the end, goodness and love and destruction go hand in hand.

One of the important elements in Gold's success is his mastery of a colloquial style. The dialogue is so perfect that it seems artless, and, when it serves his purpose, he uses the same style in his narrative. The effect is to immerse the reader in the garish world of Harry Bowers. "There's crinkly money in such a place," Gold writes of Prospect Avenue. "It's piece-meal money, warm, sweaty, perfumed by pockets and love. There's an honest dollar for Harry. He works for it, don't he? Everyone likes Harry because he sincerely loves himself, and money does not come first with him: first Harry, then the dollar. They go together like that, plump heavy-muscled Harry with his head-on belly, lean nimble money with its joyful voyaging into hands." By such touches as that he gives us Harry and builds an original and moving novel.

The New Leader
March 1, 1954

2 *The Man Who Was Not With It*

A couple of years ago, Herbert Gold published in the Hudson
Review an article called "The Lesson of Balzac's Stupidity." That
Balzac was stupid could, he said, be easily proved; look at his
boundless ambition, his fabulous arrogance. But Balzac, he went
on, was a great novelist, and he was great because of, not in spite
of, "his reasoned and open-eyed effort to do everything." "Certainly
he failed." But "We need such triumphant failures." "He did not
know as much as most slick fiction practitioners do about the construction of a story, about what is called 'motivation,' even about
how our world is really going. What Balzac did know (and the
quality of this knowledge!—he even snores with pride) is that he is
important, his people are important, and they have been born with
the power to contend as persons in the struggle for mastery of their
lives."

One would scarcely have thought of Gold as being a disciple of
Balzac, and in any of the more obvious ways he certainly isn't. But
if there is nothing Balzacian in his method, his new novel, *The
Man Who Was Not With It,* like its two predecessors, shows how
Balzacian he is in spirit. The people he writes about are not important people as the newspapers reckon importance, but they are
terribly important to him, and he makes them important to us.

Gold's first novel, *Birth of a Hero,* published less than five years
ago, was concerned with the twin themes of selfhood and relationship. Although he is married and has children, Reuben Flair is
essentially unrelated, not really a husband, not really a father. The
closest he has come to a genuine relationship is in his friendship
with a dealer in secondhand books, who is a substitute father to
him. Likewise, he has made no attempt to discover and to be him-

self. "It could not be said that he had slept for these forty-five years, but surely he had dozed."

On his forty-fifth birthday, Reuben Flair decides that he wants to become a hero—that is, to be himself. An immediate consequence of this resolution is an affair with a woman, Lydia Fortiner, whom he supposes to be a widow. This, in turn, leads to a strange relationship with Larry Fortiner, who is really Lydia's estranged husband, though she tells Reuben he is her brother. Reuben is involved now, head over heels. The complications, indeed, seem likely to end in disaster for everyone, and there are disasters, but not for Reuben Flair, who has achieved both selfhood and relationship, who ultimately has learned to be a husband and a father.

Reuben Flair learns how to contend in the struggle for mastery of his life, and Gold traces his development with great wisdom and subtlety, but in the end we are as much interested in the enigmatic Larry Fortiner as we are in Reuben. Larry is himself, thinks his own thoughts, ignores convention, lives dangerously. Lydia Fortiner says at his deathbed, "I married him because I thought that the man who lives like that has got what I wanted most in life—oh, he seemed to know how to get all he needed." Yet, Larry is afraid of love and dies believing himself unloved, unwanted, though Reuben has tried to tell him "that he was loved and wanted and that he could want in the way love wants, and that therefore he could live." Lydia wonders if Larry could have understood, and Reuben says, "I think he saw something in the end." "How terrible to die like that," she says, "knowing all at once what you've missed!" "He knew it all the time," Reuben answers.

Harry Bowers, the hero of *The Prospect Before Us,* is closer to Larry Fortiner than he is to Reuben Flair. Like Larry, he is alert, self-reliant, unconventional. Unlike Larry, however, Bowers has found a way of life that suits him. His hotel prospers, and his abilities are respected. He is on good terms with many people, has been responsible and patient in his dealings with his incompetent brother, and is decent to the bums who hang around the hotel. In his own opinion, he has nothing to complain of. But then an organization interested in the rights of Negroes decides to make a test case of the Green Glade Hotel, and Harry discovers that he has to pay a price for being Harry Bowers. At the same time, he develops a relationship with Claire Farren, the Negro girl who takes a room at his hotel, that is deeper than any relationship he has previously known. Again Gold is saying that only a person who is himself can be related to other persons and that it is only in relations with other persons that the self is fully developed and revealed.

The *Man Who Was Not With It* is another exploration of what is described in *The Prospect Before Us* as "the awful business of being a human being." Bud Williams, hero and narrator, is the most extreme example of unrelatedness Gold has created. When we meet him, he is running a con game in a carnival. "I was with it and for it" he explains. He explains further. "A business-like five-dollar habit helped me to mix the carnie hardness with the carnie softness which takes the place of the rules of courtesy in a traveling show." Motherless and to all intents and purposes fatherless, for his father has withdrawn from him after the mother's death, Bud is content to drift along with the unexacting companionship of the carnival and his cocaine.

There is in the carnival a barker named Grack, whose performances Gold portrays with great gusto. Grack, in the role of father, undertakes to break Bud's habit and, after a terrible struggle, succeeds. Bud goes back to his father's home, but he can establish no relationship with his father or his former girl or his old friends. And when he finds that his father, with the connivance of his own weaknesses, has rejected a plea from Grack, he takes off for the carnival. He says: "We who are waiting for decisions to be made by others have already lost our parents, mother, father, or someone to love . . . A will to live is the great thing a father can bequeath his son."

However, Bud has begun to change, and change is encouraged when he falls in love with Joy, daughter of the carnival's fortune-teller. On the other hand, he is dismayed to learn that Grack, who is no longer with the carnival, is taking drugs and is suspected of theft. When, on the night of his wedding, Bud finds Grack engaged in robbery, there is nothing he can do, in view of the debt he owes him and the affection he feels for him, but to try to save him. So Grack goes with Bud and Joy on their honeymoon, and the account of the trip to the Canadian border, with the detours necessitated by Grack's need for his drug, with the different kinds of tension that arise, with the conflict of loyalties that tears at Bud—this is as dramatic a passage as you can find in contemporary literature. In the course of the experience, Bud grows up.

As the reader was attracted to the puzzling character of Larry Fortiner in *Birth of a Hero,* so in this book he finds himself worrying about Grack rather than Bud. Bad as Bud's start is, one can see fairly soon that he is going to make out all right. But Grack at the outset seems to be so much more of a person than Bud that one is appalled by his disintegration. Like Larry, and like Harry Bowers, too, Grack appears to be cast in the heroic mold, to be the kind of individualist Gold admires. But there is in him, as in Larry—though not, as the story turns out, in Harry Bowers—a fatal flaw. What it is, is hard to say. Perhaps he has settled for too easy a triumph. At any rate his end, like Larry's, is pathetic, whereas Harry Bowers's is tragic.

What is wrong with Grack may be what is wrong with the carnival life that Gold so vividly describes and tries to characterize. He speaks of "the carnival, that absolute future, that American place which, descended from Rome and the gypsies, was the footloose moving image of the get-rich-quick, get-love-quick, get-ahead-quick of America. It was a world where everyone was his own mama and papa, and cash money the only promised land, and signifying (bragging, wearing Texas hats, flashing the roll) the only way-station before heaven." Bud tries to understand: "The carnie is brave, yes; he is always in a strange place and puts up with it, and for it." That is Grack, and a good man, too. But it is also true that "he carried a small, dim and locked world with him. Not only the secrecy of heroin and the privacy of morphine, no! The privacy of expecting so little—cash, kicks, calliope music—and a guarantee down in advance that only success is possible." Those who suspect that Gold has more in mind than the carnival world are probably not wrong.

Carnival jargon fills the book. In the *Prospect Before Us,* Gold displayed his mastery of a vernacular style, but he has gone much farther in the new novel. Sometimes, perhaps, too far. There are passages in the beginning that leave an uninitiated reader baffled. "Marko" and "pitch" and "mainline" and "hay-rube" are familiar or explain themselves, but "countstore" and "skillo" and "patch" and "geek," for me at any rate, took some guessing. Basically, however, Gold places no great reliance on this exotic vocabulary. What he does depend on is the rhythms, the imagery, and the quick twists of everyday speech. Miraculously, in spite of tired journalese, the glib announcements on radio and TV, the hard-worked phrases of the advertising agencies, there persists, below the literary level, a creativeness in the use of words. This kind of talk Gold has attentively listened to, and he has made it the foundation of his style. He has adapted it so successfully that, when one comes to the last sentence of the novel, one knows what it means and knows that its meaning could not have been otherwise communicated. The last sentence reads: "There's a good and with it way to be not with it, too."

Last fall, in a second article in the *Hudson Review,* Gold again called for an "active sense of the decisive value of personality." "The option which I choose to name the 'true' one," he wrote, "is the one which commits itself to a thickness of feeling, a richness of time and change, and above all a high valuation of human life. This is commitment enough for the novel because it is the largest commitment which we can make on earth." That is well said and very important. What is more important is the fact that Gold has the courage to practice what he preaches and talent enough to make his novels even more interesting than his ideas about them.

The New Leader
February 20, 1956

3 *The Optimist*

There are no writers under forty—and there are few of any age—for whom I have more admiration than I have for Herbert Gold. His first novel, *Birth of a Hero,* published while he was still in his twenties, was an extraordinarily perceptive study of love in middle age. He followed it with a dramatic and vivid novel of city life and race conflict, *The Prospect Before Us,* and then came his tale of carnival ways, the drug habit, and young love, rich in carnie talk, *The Man Who Was Not With It.* He has also written several first-rate short stories and some vigorous criticism. In less than ten years he has produced a body of work that establishes him as a central figure in today's literature.

All this being true, I find it unpleasant to have to say that I am puzzled and a little disappointed by Gold's new novel, *The Optimist.* In view of the author's unmistakable talent, there are only two possible explanations for my dissatisfaction: either I have missed something or Gold's achievement has fallen short of his intention—which can happen even with the very good writers. While recognizing that the first hypothesis may be the correct one, I have to set down my findings, which naturally support the second.

Although it is not in any literal sense autobiographical, *The Optimist* is the story of a young man who is Gold's exact contemporary and who has been shaped by some of the same forces. We meet Burr Fuller on his seventeenth birthday, when he is drawing up a list of resolutions, a list that reminds us of the one Jay Gatsby drew up back in the days when he was James Gatz. "Burr Fuller, like others," Gold tells us, "dreamed of nothing less than perfection. . . . He saw no reason why he shouldn't get everything he wanted." And again: "He believed in failure as much as he believed in the inevitability of old age. Not at all. Never. Not for him."

After this brief introduction, we see Burr as a sophomore at the University of Michigan, where he is involved with two girls, one permissive, as the current jargon phrases it, the other not. The next section, told in the first person, sets forth a series of wartime incidents, only one of them of a military nature, that leave their mark on Burr. We then leap ahead to 1956, to find that Burr is married to Laura, the girl who was not permissive, and that they have two sons. He is a lawyer in Detroit, and is just entering politics as the Democratic candidate for Congress in a strongly Republican district.

From this point on we are concerned with politics and marriage, but more with the latter than with the former. Of the campaign we are told enough to see that Burr has a considerable aptitude for the game he has chosen to play. His aptitude, indeed, distresses his old college friend Mike Murray, who believes that Burr should stand for something. Burr, however, wants to be elected now; programs can come later.

Meanwhile, Burr's marriage is falling apart. The campaign accelerates the process, for Laura resents Burr's frequent absences, but disintegration had begun much earlier. She and Burr try now and then to shore up the ruins, but their efforts are unsuccessful. At last he turns to another woman, one of the workers in his campaign, and Laura eventually takes up with the old bachelor friend of the family, Mike, who feels sorry for her. Burr's soul-searching after he has learned of Laura's infidelity provides the climax of the novel.

This is Burr Fuller's book, and everything hinges on whether or not the reader can really lay hold of this character. I find Burr elusive, and that is the basis of my dissatisfaction. In scene after scene he is perfectly real, but then he slips away from me, and, in the end, I cannot put my hands on him. In a way, I can see, this is all to Gold's credit, for he has refused to content himself and gratify us with a superficial view of Burr's character. Burr is no more elusive than I am to you or you are to me. We never really know anyone, either in life or in fiction. But in a successful novel one feels, not that the mystery of personality has been solved once and for all, but that a precious secret has been revealed. For me the moment of revelation never comes in *The Optimist*.

I have another ground for complaint. In its latter half this is the story of the disintegration of a marriage, and a powerful account it is that Gold gives. But the failure of the marriage tells us little about Burr. I think it was Gold's intention to show that Burr and Laura are both responsible for the collapse of the marriage and that behind their short-comings lie faults of the society in which they have grown up. What the reader is made to feel, however, is that, Laura being what she is, the marriage could not possibly have succeeded. When we first meet her in 1956, she is admitting to herself that "her life was poisoned by a sense of changeless, senseless discontent," and "poisoned" is exactly the right word. She is headed—why we do not know—for self-destruction, and nothing can save her. As a consequence we come to feel sorry for Burr, but we see him as a victim, as one who is acted upon instead of acting.

After Laura has told him about Mike, Burr wanders about Greektown, contemplating but quickly rejecting the idea of suicide, trying to come to terms with himself. He tries to identify the flaws in his nature that have led to failure in marriage and failure in politics, and he makes some practical decisions; but he is still the optimist, still the seeker after perfection, and the last words of the novel are, "More. More. More! More! More!" Gold is saying, I gather, that Burr's affirmativeness is in itself good, that the problem is one of direction, but I am not sure of this. Here in this last section, where the revelation should be perfected, I am as puzzled as ever. There is something Gold has seen and is trying to make me see, and I just don't get it.

After these negative remarks, it seems almost offensive to mention again the many fine scenes or to point out that Gold's mastery of the vernacular is now complete, but something must be said to make it clear that Gold is just as much as ever a first-rate novelist. If this novel is in some sense a failure, it is the kind of failure only a first-rate man could produce. In the essay he wrote for *The Living Novel* Gold said: "The mystery of personality can be defined again and again, and then redefined; that's what mysteries are for." What no one can miss in *The Optimist* is the reverence, the consecration with which he has approached that mystery. As no one knows better than he, the serious novelist must always run the risk of failure.

Saturday Review
April 25, 1959

4 *Therefore Be Bold*

In his critical writings Herbert Gold has referred to fiction as the exploration of human possibility, and his novels and short stories demonstrate what he means. In particular he has been concerned with the effect of love on personality. His first three novels, though in other ways they are strikingly different, have a common theme: in each a man learns to love and at the same time comes to terms with himself. It is hard to tell which comes first, love or self-discovery. Indeed, Gold seems to be saying that each is the prerequisite of the other: only the person who is capable of love can accept himself, and, conversely, only the person with self-knowledge and self-respect is capable of a fruitful relationship with others. Somehow a miracle has to happen, and in *Birth of a Hero, The Prospect Before Us,* and *The Man Who Was Not With It,* Gold has examined some of the ways in which the transformation takes place. In his fourth novel, *The Optimist,* on the other hand, he has shown us a man who learns neither lesson, a man who remains alienated both from himself and from others.

Therefore Be Bold continues the study of love, and this time Gold is scrutinizing the love of adolescents. It is a theme that often has been treated humorously though sometimes with morbid seriousness. Gold is serious enough but a long way from being morbid. There are comic episodes in the book, and the narrator, who is looking back over twenty years, knows as well as anyone that he and his boyhood friends were making fools of themselves in a variety of ways. But at the same time he feels both tenderness and respect, and he has a sense that anything is possible for these boys and girls.

The place is a suburb of Cleveland, and the time is the late Thirties. The narrator is Dan Berman, who appears in some of the stories in *Love and Like* and who is to be identified—who can say how closely?—with the author. Dan has two friends, Juicer Montague and Tom Moss, and it is mostly about these three that Gold writes in the first part of the novel. They remember the Depression, and they are not unaware of what Hitler is doing in Europe, but for the most part their minds, naturally enough, are on other matters. Dan and Juicer have literary interests, and can grow ecstatic about Tom Wolfe, James Branch Cabell, and Omar Khayyam. All of them are prone to indulge in large speculations about life and destiny. But what they are chiefly interested in, again quite naturally, is girls.

The first part leads up to an episode in which the three boys decide to go camping and get drunk. Each of them snitches a little from each of his father's bottles, and thus armed they go to a state park. "We drank and then discussed questions. We listened within ourselves for the jargon of courage, mystery, love, and evil, and heard the schoolboy slang of animus and puppy mewlings. Abracadabrists, submissive to poetry, we thought of women as queens. Like royal persons they had to make the first gestures toward us."

It is soon after this that Dan goes for his first walk with Eva Masters, and they talk about poetry, and in the end they kiss. Thereafter they are together a great deal, but at a party Dan sees Eva kissing another boy. Smitten with jealousy, he makes a date with Pattie Donahue. ("If you're not too busy with your dancing and going to football practice. Occupied taken up, I mean. Scrimmage, I mean.") There is also, for him and his two companions, a visit to a prostitute. But eventually he makes up with Eva.

And now, as they become more and more intimate, there is a new problem for Dan: Eva's father, sour, dyspeptic, violently anti-Semitic. Eva defies her father, and insists on taking Dan to her home.

I chose to be led, submitting my freedom to my wonder at a girl with such economical touchings who could nevertheless feed me love spread like sweet butter over her father's ill-will. Eva was not so foolish in life as that other Dan in me asks her to be in this sad vaudeville about her. Tender and frightened, very young, she held to self-knowledge in the learning, and could live with both fright and tenderness. She liked me. She loved her father. Eva admired herself—first things still came first.

Euclid Masters's assault continues, and finally, just after Dan's and Eva's intimacy has reached its climax, he forbids Dan to see her. Eva waits for Dan to take his stand, but Dan is struggling with a complex of emotions, including pity for Mr. Masters. I am not sure that Gold quite succeeds in making us understand Dan's feelings at this point, but we do know that the boy is going through an experience that will influence his whole life. For Eva, however, his behavior is a disappointment, and though she disobeys her father and goes with Dan to the class picnic, the relationship between them is coming to an end.

Gold chooses at times to be enigmatic, but his general meaning is clear. In a kind of epilogue he writes: "We have to count on surprise and discord in this life, breathe through the mouth, and expect new songs. Therefore endless! I mean that true economy, friends, is an extravagance: Be good for our own pleasure—that the why—but be bold for the children of everyone—and this the yes." In short, the book is written in praise of human possibilities.

Perhaps I have quoted enough along the way to show that Gold has fashioned for this book an original style, and the style is responsible for much of its power. He has always had a good ear, and some of the talk—conversations of Dan's parents, for instance, or the adolescents' talk at the party—is wonderful. But it is in descriptive and reflective passages that his style is most distinctive. He employs many devices, including Joycean puns and bits of verse, but what he chiefly relies on is imagery of startling boldness. Here, for example, is Chuck Hastings at the party: "In some respects he resembled a mummy—the shriveled yellow skin, the hand and head too large for a wasted body, the bottomless eye sockets of thought beyond the Nile. But his agile Adam's apple and point-making finger made him less the Styx-swimmer dog-paddling toward Coptic limbos than a high school intellectual intimidating the navel-eyed little girl." This is high-pitched, to be sure, but the point is that Gold keeps it up and keeps it up. He has been working steadily towards greater freedom and freshness in the use of words, not for the sake of shocking the reader but in order to rouse him out of lethargy, in order to compel him to see more clearly and feel more strongly. One may feel that he is not always successful and yet respond sharply to the total effect. The book vibrates with energy. It is full of the hopefulness and courage of the young, full of belief in love, full of the sense of human possibility.

Saturday Review
October 1, 1960

5 *Fathers*

After corresponding with Herbert Gold for a couple of years, I finally met him in the summer of 1956, while he was spending some time at Yaddo in Saratoga Springs. Amazingly young to be the author of three novels, he was good-looking in a slender, romantic, boyish way, and he had extraordinary poise. He had, indeed, the kind of poise that I have always associated with tenth-generation American WASPs who have attended Groton and Harvard; but he was, as I knew, the son of a Russian-Jewish immigrant who had come to this country at the age of thirteen and had earned his living from that time on, first in the roughest kind of manual labor, later as the owner and operator of a vegetable market in Cleveland. Soon afterward, when Gold wrote two fine stories about his father— "The Heart of the Artichoke" and "Aristotle and the Hired Thugs" —I was made acutely aware of the contrast between the two generations, and I realized that this contrast was an important problem for the sophisticated young man I had come to know.

Gold has said that *Fathers* "is a book I have been stretching to write all my life," and I can believe this. "I began it as a student in Paris in 1949," he says—that is, before he published his first novel —but he wasn't ready for it. Parts of what he wanted to say appeared from time to time, as in the two stories I have mentioned; but it was only a little while ago, when he was at work on another novel, that he became convinced the moment had come. Now, he must have felt, he could do justice to his father without denying his own nature or repudiating his own life.

In a preface Gold tells about a visit his father and mother paid him in San Francisco in the spring of 1966. The father, then eighty, talked about real estate deals he wanted to make, and his son naturally urged him to take it easy—"You're secure now." But Sam Gold had never believed in security. His life has been a struggle, and he wanted it to continue that way so long as it lasted. He lived in the present, not worrying about the future, not concerned with the past. Herb asked him whether his life had been worthwhile, and he replied, "I don't look back." "Are you satisfied, Dad?" "I told you already a thousand times or so, never counted, I'm not a mathematician—never satisfied. Never satisfied!"

Gold begins his story in the little village near Kamenets-Podolsk in Russia, where his father grew up, exposed to all the sufferings of Jews in that time and place. At twelve he made up his mind to go to America, but agreed to wait two months for his bar mitzvah. Not knowing English and without a friend in New York, he managed to survive, and in an astonishingly short time he had brought his sister and three brothers to the United States. Then he went back to Russia, with a gold tooth as proof of prosperity, and persuaded his parents to migrate. But the war of 1914 intervened, and the parents were killed in a pogrom.

In time Sam Gold found his way to Cleveland, set himself up in business, married, and had his first child, Herbert. He was still working terribly hard, and was beginning to prosper. He had declared his independence of Judaism as a religion when he came to America, and now he was too busy to be concerned with religious matters even if he wanted to be. The son, Herbert, seems to have had no religious training and to have come to maturity without even a perfunctory sense of Jewish tradition.

The chief difference between father and son was that the former had grown up in extreme hardship whereas the latter was growing up in comparative affluence. Herbert's parents wanted the boy to work Saturdays in the store, not because his help was economically necessary but because the experience would teach him "the value of a dollar," as his mother said, or, as his father said, "to know what's what in life." His father knew no words in which Herbert could "explain that among the people with whom he chose to bring me up, it was more important to run end in a pickup touch football game, spinning craftily about the young trees planted by the Our Street Beautiful committee, than to fill orders in sour old orange crates on Saturday afternoons." Yet in his teens the boy, rebellious because he wasn't free to play as his friends played, could not help reminding himself that at his age his father was not only earning his own living but saving money to bring his family across the Atlantic.

The story is a dramatic example of the conflict between generations that has colored American history in the past century. But there was never, as there has been in so many families, a decisive break. Once there was a physical struggle, vigorously described; but after this the old relationship was renewed and perhaps strengthened. Young Gold partly established his independence by enlisting in the army at the age of eighteen, but after his discharge he had to deal with his father's inevitable longing for a business partner and successor. By that time, however, Herb had literary ambitions—"Hart Crane was the other poet from Cleveland"—and he opposed what he wanted for himself to what his father wanted for him. The father, who had never let anyone run his life, gave up trying to run his son's.

Herbert Gold became a father, and a devoted one, even after he had been divorced from the mother of his two daughters. He became a recognized writer, too (though he doesn't speak of that), and his father was one to value success of any kind. Their relationship became the kind of amiable truce that may exist between a father and an adult son. But all the time the son was as much a mystery to the father as the father was to the son. The father was not given to probing such mysteries, but the son was. He came to understand that his father was in certain ways a great man, with a fine capacity for life, and that he owed him a larger debt than he had ever acknowledged.

As a novelist, Herbert Gold has been more affirmative than most, searching for the conditions that make a good life possible. We can see now that he came naturally by this affirmativeness, that he had had before him the example of a man who never doubted, and doubted least of all at the age of eighty, that life was to be lived. What Gold became was, of course, in some ways a reaction against his father, but it was in other ways a reinterpretation of his father's character in a new age. In trying to show what sort of man this was, he has written a moving and enlightening and satisfying book, his best in some years.

Saturday Review
March 25, 1967

Afterword

As my reviews of *The Prospect Before Us* and *The Man Who Was Not With It* show, my first encounters with the work of Herbert Gold filled me with enthusiasm. That enthusiasm has wavered now and then as I read succeeding books, but Gold at his best always arouses my admiration. The last book of his I reviewed, *Fathers,* displayed his virtues to admirable effect. Now he has published a new novel, *The Great American Jackpot,* and it has received a number of acutely unfriendly reviews. It seems to me that the unfriendly reviewers missed the point. There is an interesting parallel between this book and *The Man Who Was Not With It.* The carnival has its equivalent in nothing less than the city of San Francisco, and the con man is Dr. Jarod Howe, a black professor. The young man in search of a way of life, who naturally falls under Jarod Howe's influence, is Al Dooley, who is perhaps even more confused than Bud Williams, which is not altogether surprising in "a child of affluence." The problems with which Gold concerned himself at the start have grown larger and larger in twenty years.

KURT VONNEGUT

Foreword

When I read *Player Piano,* it struck me that the city in the book was remarkably like Schenectady, and I was not surprised to learn that Vonnegut had once worked for General Electric. His experience in business and his experience in war had a strong and enduring effect on his literary imagination.

I rather lost track of Vonnegut during the period when he was making a reputation as a writer of science fiction. I have learned later, from reading such books as *The Sirens of Titan* and *Cat's Cradle,* that Vonnegut was not really a writer of science fiction at all. He used some of the conventions of science fiction to satirize many varieties of human activity, including the writing of science fiction.

I was delighted with the success of *Slaughterhouse-Five,* a masterpiece of indirection, a wonderful example of the truth that the most effective way to say a thing is sometimes not to say it. We now see clearly what Vonnegut has been up to all along, and I at least wish him well.

1 *Player Piano*

Two books that were popular several decades ago—Ignatius Donnelly's *Caesar's Column* and Jack London's *The Iron Heel*—are brought to mind by Kurt Vonnegut's novel. In it, as in them, we are taken into the future and shown an America ruled by a tiny oligarchy, and here too there is a revolt that fails.

The important difference lies in the fact that Mr. Vonnegut's oligarchs are not capitalists but engineers. In the future as he envisages it, the machines have completed their triumph, dispossessing not only the manual laborers but the white collar workers as well. Consequently the carefully selected, highly trained individuals who design and control the machines are the only people who have anything to do. Other people, the great majority, can either go into the Reconstruction and Reclamation Corps, which is devoted to boondoggling, or join the army, which has no real function in a machine-dominated world-society.

It is a little like *Brave New World* except that Mr. Vonnegut keeps his future closer to the present than Aldous Huxley succeeded in doing, and his satire therefore focuses more sharply on the contemporary situation. The machines he is talking about are not gadgets he has dreamed up; they are in existence, as he is careful to point out. Moreover, his engineers are less of supermen than Huxley's Alphas, and their group morale is maintained by methods one can find described in William H. Whyte's recent book, *Is Anybody Listening?*

The story, which is told in a skilful, lively fashion, concerns Paul

Proteus, one of the privileged engineers. Unhappy in his own role and increasingly aware that the masses are being frustrated and degraded, he joins and becomes nominal leader of a revolutionary organization, the Ghost Shirts. At first the rebellion seems to be succeeding, but then the mob gets out of hand, just as in *Caesar's Column* and *The Iron Heel,* and there is an orgy of destruction. Proteus and his companions, however, do not give up hope until they find that their revolutionary followers are busily making gadgets out of the scraps of the machines they have been destroying. That is too much, and they surrender to the oligarchy.

Player Piano is a less earnest book than either *Caesar's Column* or *The Iron Heel,* and a less serious one than *Brave New World,* but what Mr. Vonnegut lacks in fervor he more than makes up in fun. To take only one example, nothing could be more amusing than his account of the antics of the aspiring engineers when they gather on an island in the St. Lawrence for pep talks, competitive sports, formalized informality, and the careful cultivation of the big shots. Whether he is a trustworthy prophet or not, Mr. Vonnegut is a sharp-eyed satirist.

New York Times Book Review
August 17, 1952

2 *God Bless You,*
Mister Rosewater

Although Vonnegut was serious enough in his warning against automation in *Player Piano,* he found time for considerable comedy along the way, and the same blend of seriousness and comedy is found in his subsequent work. In *Cat's Cradle* (1960) his theme is the irresponsibility of those scientists who are unconcerned with the consequences of their discoveries. His villain, already in his grave when the book opens, was one of the major contributors to the development of the atom bomb. The novel presents his character through the testimony of his three children, while at the same time it shows the cataclysmic results of one of his postwar researches. In spite of the somber note on which it ends, the book is in large part a hilariously wacky comedy.

God Bless You, Mister Rosewater, or Pearls Before Swine is even wackier. Its chief target is inherited wealth, but, as in his earlier books, Vonnegut takes pot shots at many varieties of folly. He begins with the Rosewater fortune, "the fourteenth largest family fortune in America," which in 1947 "was stashed into a foundation in order that tax collectors and other predators not named Rosewater might be prevented from getting their hands on it." The presidency of the foundation is hereditary, and the president has complete charge of the spending of the income. The capital, however, is under the control of the Rosewater Corporation, which takes good care of it.

Eliot Rosewater, the first president of the foundation and the son of its founder, Senator Lister Ames Rosewater, tries giving away money to various individuals and causes without much satisfaction. Finally he settles down in the town of Rosewater, Indiana, where the family fortune originated, and devotes himself to helping anyone who wants help. On the windows of his office, a squalid and cluttered room on the main street, is a sign that says, "The Rosewater Foundation: How Can We Help You?" He soon has a large if not altogether savory clientele. Senator Rosewater, who is as conservative as Senator Goldwater, and rather more consistent, speaks of Eliot's having "the sniveling camaraderie of whores, malingerers, pimps, and thieves." Vonnegut goes on: "It was the Senator's conceit that Eliot trafficked with criminals. He was mistaken. Most of Eliot's clients weren't brave enough or clever enough for lives of crime. But Eliot, particularly when he argued with his father or his bankers or his lawyers, was almost equally mistaken about who his clients were. He would argue that the people he was trying to help were the same sorts of people who, in generations past, had cleared the forests, drained the swamps, built the bridges, people whose sons formed the backbone of the infantry in times of war—and so on. The people who leaned on Eliot regularly were a lot weaker than that—and dumber, too." Yet Eliot for once feels that he is being useful and is happy.

Attention now shifts to another Rosewater, Fred by name, an insurance salesman in a Rhode Island town, who is a distant cousin of Eliot's. Fred's wife's closest friend is Amanita (sic) Buntline, and the introduction of the Buntlines gives Vonnegut another opportunity to gibe at the idle rich. One of Mrs. Buntline's maids writes a friend: "What gets me most about these people isn't how ignorant they are, or how much they drink. It's the way they have of thinking that everything nice in the world is a gift to the poor people from them or their ancestors. The first afternoon I was here, Mrs. Buntline made me come out on the back porch and look at the sunset. So I did, and I said I liked it very much, but she kept waiting for me to say something else. I couldn't think of what else I was supposed to say, so I said what seemed like a dumb thing. 'Thank you very much,' I said. That was exactly what she was waiting for. 'You're entirely welcome.' she said."

An ambitious and unprincipled young lawyer has learned that, if Eliot is declared insane, his position as president of the foundation goes to his nearest Rosewater relative—who is, of course, poor Fred the insurance agent. Litigation begins, and the Senator calls in a science fiction writer named Trout, whom Eliot admires. "What you did to Rosewater County," Trout tells Eliot, "was far from insane. It was quite possibly the most important social experiment of our time, for it dealt on a very small scale with a problem whose queasy horrors will eventually be made world-wide by the sophistication of machines. The problem is this: How to love people who have no use." Later he says to Senator Rosewater, "It seems to me that the main lesson Eliot learned is that people can use all the uncritical love they can get."

Thus Vonnegut comes back to the problem that bothered him in *Player Piano,* the problem of a world that has been relieved from the curse of Adam, so that people no longer have to earn their bread in the sweat of their faces. One thing one may say is that the situation may be worse than he envisages, for, in the society of the near future, the persons who are expendable as producers will be essential as consumers. But of course Vonnegut is not an economist or a sociologist; he is a moralist and a humorist and a man of imagination.

Vonnegut belongs with the desperate humorists, of whom Joseph Heller, author of *Catch-22,* is the best known. Donald Barthelme, Bruce J. Friedman, and Richard Stern are of that company. John Hawkes can also be funny in the same way, though he has other virtues that are more important. Vonnegut's particular asset is the wildness of his imagination: there is nothing so ridiculous that he cannot make use of it. And, though one doesn't have to regard him as an infallible prophet, he has put his finger on an essential problem of our times.

Saturday Review
April 3, 1965

3 *Slaughterhouse-Five*

A year ago, in reporting on the Sophomore Literary Festival at Notre Dame, which I had been taking part in, I said that another participant, Kurt Vonnegut, Jr., had delivered as funny a lecture as I had ever listened to. A mild-mannered man, respectable and even genteel in appearance, he got away with a series of hilarious and subversive remarks on life and literature. The students had previously thought of him as a writer of science fiction, and had talked of him as such, but they came to realize how much more than that he is.

I felt then, and I feel now more strongly than ever after reading his new book, *Slaughterhouse-Five, or The Children's Crusade* that what he really is is a sardonic humorist and satirist in the vein of Mark Twain and Jonathan Swift. In earlier works, such as *Player Piano, Cat's Cradle,* and *God Bless You, Mister Rosewater,* he has made fun of the worship of science and technology. Now we can see that his quarrel with contemporary society began with his experiences in World War II, about which he has at last managed to write a book. "I would hate to tell you," he says, "what this lousy little book cost me in money and anxiety and time. When I got home from the Second World War twenty-three years ago, I thought it would be easy for me to write about the destruction of Dresden, since all I would have to do would be to report what I had seen. And I thought, too, that it would be a masterpiece or at least make me a lot of money, since the subject was so big."

He had a mighty theme all right, as Melville had commanded, but that only defined his problem without in any way solving it. So finally he took the advice of the ballad about the old man and his would-be murderous wife, and decided to sneak up from behind. "All this happened, more or less." he writes. "The war parts, anyway, are pretty much true. One guy I knew really *was* shot in Dresden for taking a teapot that wasn't his. Another guy I know really *did* threaten to have his personal enemies killed by hired gunmen after the war. And so on. I've changed all the names. I really *did* go back to Dresden with Guggenheim money (God love it) in 1967. It looked a lot like Dayton, Ohio, with more open spaces than Dayton has. There must be tons of human bone meal in the ground."

But most of the novel is devoted to a character named Billy Pilgrim, who is like Vonnegut in some ways but not in others. Like Vonnegut, Billy was drafted in 1944, was taken prisoner during the Battle of the Bulge, and was in a prison camp near Dresden when the city was wiped out by an Allied air raid. Unlike Vonnegut, Billy became a successful optometrist, thanks to his marrying the right woman, and was kidnapped by a flying saucer and taken to a planet called Tralfamadore. Many times in recent weeks I have been asked whether I think that Philip Roth's notorious hero, Alex Portnoy, is an autobiographical character. I think I can now suggest the correct answer: he is in exactly the same sense that Billy Pilgrim is.

Vonnegut tells us that Billy "has come unstuck in time." Not only can he take off for Tralfamadore whenever he feels like it; he travels backward and forward in his own life, stopping anywhere between birth and death. Thus his story comes to us in bits and pieces and in anything but chronological order. After his ignominious military career, he did rather well according to the standards of the society in which he lived: married a rich if obese wife, drove a special Cadillac, and fathered a son who joined the Green Berets. But he would have found his life dull if it had not been for time travel.

Vonnegut never does get around to describing the raid on Dresden, and that shows the wisdom of the strategy he was finally led to adopt. When the planes came over, Billy and a few other prisoners, together with four of their guards, took refuge in a meat locker, and they survived while 135,000 residents of the city were killed—twice the number killed in Hiroshima. In trying to tell what he and his fellow-survivors saw the next morning when they emerged from the locker, about all Billy can say it, "It was like the moon." It is by this and other kinds of indirection that Vonnegut makes his impression.

Vonnegut's satire sweeps widely, touching on education, religion, advertising, and many other subjects. This is a passage about free will that Mark Twain might have written in his late and bitter years: " 'If I hadn't spent so much time studying Earthlings,' said the Tralfamadorian, 'I wouldn't have any idea what was meant by "free will." I've visited thirty-one inhabited planets in the universe, and I have studied reports on one hundred more. Only on Earth is there any talk of free will.' " There is some amusing business about pornography: the first obscene photograph, made in France soon after the invention of the camera and quickly suppressed by the government, turns up in 1967 as the piece de resistance of a collection in a sordid store on Times Square.

But the central target is the institution of war. Most of the Americans among whom Billy is taken prisoner are young, poorly trained, and by that time completely demoralized. A British colonel, who has been in prison for four years, is appalled by their youthfulness. "My God, my God," he says. "It's the Children's Crusade" —thus providing the book with its subtitle. The terrible destruction of Dresden is, as Vonnegut sees it, an example of the way the military mind operates. (He quotes a military historian to the effect that the raid served no essential purpose.) He shows that in great matters as in small war is brutal and stupid, and he lets us look at the institution from the point of view of the Tralfamadorians. He draws practical conclusions too: "I have told my sons that they are not under any circumstances to take part in massacres, and that the news of massacres of enemies is not to fill them with satisfaction or glee. I have also told them not to work for companies which make massacre machinery, and to express contempt for people who think we need machinery like that."

Like Mark Twain, Vonnegut feels sadness as well as indignation when he looks at the damned human race. Billy Pilgrim is a compassionate man, and meditates a good deal on the life and teachings of Jesus and on institutionalized Christianity. (Billy's favorite science fiction writer, Kilgore Trout, has written his own version of the story of Jesus.) Partly as a result of what he has learned on Tralfamadore, Billy is to some extent reconciled to life as it is lived on Earth. But Vonnegut is not, and in this book he has expressed his terrible outrage.

Addressing his editor, Seymour Lawrence, Vonnegut says: "Sam —here's the book. It is so short and jumbled and jangled, Sam, because there is nothing intelligent to say about a massacre." But, as I have been trying to explain, it turns out to be quite a wonderful book. As I read it, I could hear Vonnegut's mild voice, see his dead pan as he told a ludicrous story, and gasp as I perceived the terrifying implications of some calm remark. Even though he is not to be identified with Billy Pilgrim, he lives and breathes in the book, and that is one reason why it is the best he has written.

Saturday Review
March 29, 1969

LOUIS AUCHINCLOSS

Foreword

Although I have read and reviewed most of Louis Auchincloss's work in the past twelve years, I hesitated about including him in this volume. Certainly he has not been one of the movers and shakers of the postwar period. He has written for the most part about "good" society, the well-to-do and the well bred, and he has written about them with authority.

What bothers me is not that he writes about this little world but that he seems to be aware of no other. Although he is conscious of its faults, he never questions its values in any serious way.

I finally decided to include him because he is one of the few conservative novelists of our time. The only comparable writer is James Gould Cozzens, who is still publishing books but who had established his reputation before the second World War. Moreover, though I believe that Cozzens's work will bulk larger than Auchincloss's in the long run, Auchincloss is a defter writer and has mastered the form of the novel.

1 *Venus in Sparta*

As has been said often enough, good novels about business are rare. There may be, and I think there are, some rather subtle reasons for this, but one explanation is obvious: few writers know much about business, and the persons who know business can't or don't learn how to write. One of the significant exceptions is Louis Auchincloss, who has a direct acquaintance with investment banking and who has made himself a skilful craftsman. In several novels and a couple of collections of short stories he has written authoritatively and persuasively about a small but important segment of American business.

Venus in Sparta is, as it turns out, only incidentally a novel about business, but Auchincloss's knowledge proves useful as he introduces us to his leading character, Michael Farish, at forty-five vice president and senior trust officer of the Hudson River Trust Company, with good reason to expect to occupy the presidency, as his grandfather had done in his time. Most businessmen in fiction are annoyingly nebulous or else their functions are described in massive and confusing detail. Auchincloss does not tell us much about Michael's duties, but what he does tell defines exactly the nature of his success and the reasons for it.

The crisis in Michael's life that is the book's theme is precipitated in part by an incident in his business career, the bringing to light of the not quite ethical act that led to his first success. But its major cause is a purely personal matter, his discovery of his wife's infidelity. Michael's world falls apart, and although for a time he seems to be putting it back together again, he comes to a bad end. What

Auchincloss chiefly seeks to do is to reveal the flaw in Michael's character that makes disaster inevitable.

As his associates see him, Michael is a man who has moved easily and confidently towards an unquestioned goal, and from this point of view his crisis seems mysterious and ironic. The reader, however, is led step by step to perceive how logical the crisis is. By a series of adroitly managed flashbacks, Auchincloss shows us that all through Michael's life his problem has been the necessity of proving, not so much to others as to himself, that he is a man. And again and again what he has taken as proof—his marriage, a war-time affair, his business success—has really been evasion. When at last he is gripped by the kind of unequivocal passion that he can accept as evidence of masculinity, it is too late.

Auchincloss is a deft prober, and he shows us how a sense of inadequacy and guilt can be created and how it can shape a life. To me the psychological problem to which he addresses himself in *Venus in Sparta* is less interesting than the ethical problem with which he was concerned in his preceding novel, *The Great World and Timothy Colt*. In its portrayal of a particular milieu, however, of a world in which there not only is money but has been money for several generations, the novel demonstrates that Auchincloss knows his stuff and knows how to use it to literary advantage.

Saturday Review
September 20, 1958

2 *Portrait in Brownstone*

After the violence of James Baldwin's *Another Country,* the turgidity of Philip Roth's *Letting Go,* and the complexity and intensity of Doris Lessing's *The Golden Notebook,* Louis Auchincloss's *Portrait in Brownstone* is a pleasant change. Auchincloss knows so well what he can do and goes about his job with such quiet competence that his novels are always satisfying, and *Portrait in Brownstone* is Auchincloss at his best.

Auchincloss, as has often been said, is a novelist of manners, one of the few extant. Like Edith Wharton, for whom he has strong but not uncritical admiration, he writes about people of wealth and position, about what is sometimes called "good society." No part of American society is or ever has been stable, but in good society there is at least an air of stability. Certain assumptions are shared, for a time at any rate, and there is some agreement as to what constitutes proper behavior. Against such a background the subtler human relationships can be studied with a precision that is quite impossible in more turbulent situations, and this is the great virtue of the novel of manners as written by Jane Austen and Henry James and all the rest of Auchincloss's predecessors.

Portrait in Brownstone is the story of Ida Hartley, a woman of sixty-one in the first chapter, wife of a powerful financier, mother of two grown children. The story, which is told partly by Ida and partly in the third person, goes back to the beginning of the century, when Ida was a little girl, and then moves forward to 1950. We learn about her relationship with her beautiful cousin Geraldine, about her marriage to Derrick Hartley, about the marital difficulties of her daughter Dorcas and the problems of her son Hugh. At last we catch up with the episode that opens the novel—Geraldine's suicide in 1950—and go beyond it to watch the emergence of a new Ida. As almost goes without saying, the movement in time and the shifts in point of view are skilfully managed.

The great element of stability in Ida's life is provided by her mother's family, the Denisons. Linn Tremain had grown up in Florence in the period after the Civil War and had dabbled in art, but then he returned to America and to "the downtown world of stocks and bonds for which nature had all along intended him." He courted Dagmar Denison, who lived in Brooklyn with her father and her younger brothers and sisters, and was reluctant to leave them. After he finally persuaded her to marry him, he moved her siblings, one by one, to Fifty-third Street, so that she wouldn't be lonely. The youngest of the family was Ida's mother, and Ida grew up in a world of Denisons.

Into this world comes Derrick Hartley, respectable enough—a Harvard graduate, son of a minister—but a stranger, a small-town boy moving from the outside in. After showing a mild interest in Ida, he falls wildly in love with the beautiful and lively Geraldine, and all sorts of complications ensue. But eventually he marries Ida, and eventually he succeeds Linn Tremain as head of the firm.

The portrait of Derrick is an admirable piece of work. Auchincloss knows Wall Street, and he has frequently made good use of his knowledge. He is not concerned, however, with the mysteries of finance but with the human beings to be encountered downtown. Derrick is not, in Auchincloss's eyes, a villain, but he is not a likable individual. He is a cold man, except for his romantic passion for Geraldine; arrogant, merciless, contemptuous. After ten years of marriage Ida reflects: "His self-sufficiency had had the effect of encasing my feeling for him in a cold-storage cellar where all of its strength but not all of its sweetness had been perpetuated. I no longer liked many of my thoughts about Derrick." Derrick is the kind of character one can believe in but would just as soon not meet.

Ida, on the other hand, is likable if not always admirable. She accepts, without too much difficulty, the way of life into which she was born. Strongly loyal to her family, she suffers her first great disillusionment with Derrick when he removes from the title of the firm the name of Uncle Linn Tremain, to whom he owes so much. But she is loyal to Derrick, too, and to the children she has borne him.

The great point about Ida is that she is not crushed by Derrick, although she might so easily have been. After they have been married for more than twenty years, he says: "Ida fascinates me. I've never been able to make the least dent in the wall of her preconceptions." She can act decisively and even unconventionally in the matter of her daughter's second marriage, and the strength she has held in reserve makes itself felt as Derrick's strength is waning. A relative tells her, "You have a whole arsenal of weapons that you've never even peeked into. Well, *peek!* Reach in, dearie, and fight for your life." She fights, all right, manipulating her son into the marriage she wants him to make, and preserving the position of her son-in-law. She is acute enough to know that she is adopting Derrick's role—"I had become, like him, a monster"—but she carries out the role with high efficiency, and Derrick in the end is grateful.

Auchincloss tells the story in a neat, dry style that repeatedly gives great pleasure. Of the relations between Derrick and Geraldine he observes, "The affair, like everything else in her life, including her brief conversion to the Catholic Church, turned out to be something of a disappointment. . . . It was hardly agreeable to feel like a piece of cheese which had fallen into the jaws of a patiently waiting fox or like another share of stock in the bursting Hartley portfolio."

The astringent style is appropriate to Auchincloss's attitude. Unlike J. P. Marquand, whom he somewhat resembles in choice of subject matter, he is given neither to satire nor nostalgia. (Marquand was often divided between them.) Auchincloss takes his people completely for granted. "The rich are different from us," Scott Fitzgerald is supposed to have said. They are different, Auchincloss would seem to be replying, in interesting but essentially minor ways. They are like most of the rest of us in being neither spectacularly good nor spectacularly bad.

What distinguishes the novel, as I suggested at the outset, is its subtlety. Sometimes we have to be hit over the head, as James Baldwin hits us, and I have no doubt that I shall remember *Another Country* when *Portrait in Brownstone* has grown misty in my mind; but the world is not all of one piece, and the insights of an Auchincloss have their importance for us. The questions he raises are not cataclysmic, but they are persistent.

Saturday Review
July 14, 1962

3 *Powers of Attorney*

During the past sixteen years Louis Auchincloss has published twelve books, most of them fiction. This is not a bad record in itself, and it is the more impressive because during this entire period Auchincloss has been a practicing lawyer with a Wall Street firm. Law, according to a statement by his publisher, "is still a nine to five job with him, while fiction writing is a five and after job." He makes good use of his leisure hours.

He also, it is clear, makes good use of his business hours as a source of material. He knows the people who work in downtown New York, how they make their money and how they spend it. He is, indeed, an authority on whatever survives as an upper class in America, and he is one of the few contemporary writers who can be described as a novelist of manners.

In the twelve stories that make up *Powers of Attorney,* Auchincloss has drawn directly on his legal experience. At least one character in every story is connected with the firm of Tower, Tilney & Webb. This firm, with seventy lawyers and a staff of over one hundred, occupies "two great gleaming floors in a new glass cube at 65 Wall Street, with modern paintings and a marble spiral staircase and a reception hall paneled in white and gold." Clitus Tilney, the senior partner, knows that the firm is sometimes described as a "law factory," but he does not mind, for he is convinced of the value of efficiency. He is not only "the finest security lawyer in New York"; he is a remarkably competent administrator. His influence makes itself felt in several of the stories.

Some of the stories have only a slight connection with Tower, Tilney & Webb. In "The Single Reader," for instance, a somewhat Jamesian story about a man who keeps a diary, the protagonist is one of the partners, but he could be anyone. Again, in "The Ambassador from Wall Street," the central figure is an old lady who dominates the social life of a Maine island resort. Her lawyer, who brings the story to a climax, is the Webb of Tower, Tilney & Webb, but there is no necessary connection.

On the other hand, the office is the background of several of the stories, and several hinge on details of legal strategy. In the first story, "Power in Trust," Clitus Tilney is matched against Francis Hyde, a partner whom he has always found barely tolerable and whom he now resolves to force out of the firm. It is by way of an ingenious device that Tilney wins the battle. In "The Power of Appointment" an old-timer, who distrusts himself and has all his life been afraid of making a fatal error, does blunder, but his mistake has no serious consequences, and he realizes that all the time he has been only a figurehead.

Office politics on a lower level is the theme of "The Revenges of Mrs. Abercrombie." A veteran secretary with a privileged position, Mrs. A. is demoted in the last year before her retirement. Learning that she is to be given a present at the Christmas party, she prepares a speech that criticizes by implication the firm and especially Clitus Tilney. The speech, however, becomes a fiasco when she has an attack of hiccups, and what happens thereafter changes her mind about Tilney.

Auchincloss describes his characters sharply. Here, for instance, is Waldron P. Webb, the firm's principal trial lawyer:

Litigation, indeed, was more than Webb's profession; it was his catharsis. He was one of those unhappy men who always wake up angry. He was angered by the sparrows outside his bedroom window in Bronxville, by the migraines of his long-suffering wife, by the socialism in the newspaper, the slowness of the subway, the wait for the elevator, the too casual greeting of the receptionist. It was only the great morning pile on his desk of motions, attachments, injunctions that restored his calm. Sitting back in his red plush armchair under the dark lithograph of an orating Daniel Webster, facing his secretary and two chief law clerks, he would open the day with a rattling dictation of letters and memoranda. Gradually, as he talked and telephoned, as he stamped again and again on the hydra-headed serpent of presumption that daily struck anew at his clients with the forked tongues of legal subterfuge, as he defeated motion with countermotion, question with accusation, commitment with revocation, the earlier irritations of the morning subsided, the Santa Claus began to predominate over the Scrooge, and Waldron P. Webb assumed his midday look of benevolent, if rather formidable, cheer.

This is the introduction to a comic, or at any rate ironic, story about divorce. There is much variety in the stories. "The Mavericks" is a complicated story about a casual affair and a great romance. "The Deductible Yacht," on the other hand, relates a simple tale about an income tax lawyer who is stricken by conscience. The last story tells how Clitus Tilney is offered the presidency of his alma mater, and is tempted, for he sees this as a noble way of rounding out his career. He is surprised by his wife's opposition, but in time he comes to recognize her wisdom.

Auchincloss entitled a collection of his essays *Reflections of a Jacobite,* and it is true that he is something of a conservative, in the sense that he accepts the world as he finds it, believing that, though it has its evils, any change would probably be for the worse. He has the kind of irony that often accompanies a mild conservatism. In the last story, for instance, Tilney is naively pleased by the offer of the college presidency until he learns why the offer was made. In "Deductible Yacht," the young income tax lawyer who makes a gallant gesture accomplishes absolutely nothing by it. In "The 'True Story' of Lavinia Todd," Chambers Todd decides that he does not want a divorce after his wife's account of the failure of their marriage has made her famous.

Always one has the feeling that Auchincloss knows what he is talking about. He is careful not to bury his readers under heaps of legal terminology; he never shows off; but he does use his knowledge of the law to good effect. The little world of Tower, Tilney & Webb seems real and alive, and full of what Hardy called "life's little ironies." Auchincloss is perhaps not so good a short story writer as he is a novelist, but he can tell an effective and engaging tale.

Saturday Review
August 17, 1963

4 *The Rector of Justin*

In almost all of his novels—and he has written many—Louis Auchincloss has devoted himself to the upper class, the well bred and well heeled, and he has found there an admirable field for his talents. In *The Rector of Justin,* he portrays a peculiarly upperclass institution, an Episcopal school for boys—such a school as Groton, which Auchincloss himself attended. The center of attention, however, is not an institution but a man, Francis Prescott, founder and headmaster of Justin Martyr.

Prescott, whom we first meet when he is eighty, is an uncommonly complex character, a forceful man, energetic and shrewd, completely devoted to the school, an heroic figure and to some godlike. Yet he can be described as "petty, vain, tyrannical, vindictive, even cruel," and we see evidence of all these traits in the course of the story.

To present this complex character Auchincloss has devised a complicated form. He lays down the foundation of the novel with extracts from the journal of Brian Aspinwall, who, at the age of twenty-seven, has become a teacher of English at Justin. He is rather a weak young man, but he is an honest one: "I am shy and lack force of personality, and my stature is small. I stammer when I am nervous, and my appearance is more boyish than manly." At first he is even more frightened of Dr. Prescott than he is of the boys, but in time he becomes friendly with Mrs. Prescott, to whom, in her last illness, he reads Henry James. After her death he is more intimate with the rector, admires him extravagantly, and resolves to become his Boswell.

These opening chapters are superbly done. Brian Aspinwall turns out to be much more of a person than he seemed at the outset, a man who has strong points as well as weak ones. Mrs. Prescott is beautifully drawn, a sharp-tongued old lady who knows her own mind. But, of course, the rector is the central figure. We see how he dominates the school, how difficult he can be and how helpful. As Brian learns more and more about him we realize that Prescott is quite different from the public image of him and much more interesting.

Although Brian's journal is an excellent device for introducing the rector, Brian's knowledge is limited. Auchincloss has therefore made use of other documents. One of Prescott's oldest friends, Horace Havistock, comes to visit, and Brian persuades the man to let him see something he has written about Prescott. This shows Prescott as a boy and young man, and tells how he lost his faith, found it again, and brought the school into existence.

We return to Brian, but only for long enough for him to tell us about David Griscam, chairman of the school's board of trustees and the rector's chief financial adviser. Griscam, too, it seems, has been writing about Prescott, and he offers to show Brian what he has done. He attended Justin when it was only five years old, became devoted to the rector, and has served him faithfully. He tells a neat story about a problem in student discipline that throws further light on Prescott.

Since Brian has now made up his mind to write a biography of the rector, he goes to see his youngest daughter, Cordelia Turnbull. Having been psychoanalyzed, she talks to Brian with a frankness that shocks him. She tell him about the men in her life, particularly Charley Strong, with whom she lived in Paris after the

First World War. As she describes her father's intervention in this case, we have a new view of the rector.

Two more witnesses, both dead, are called on for testimony. It appears that Charley Strong left a brief account of his impressions of the rector at Justin and later in Paris. More important is the statement of Jules Griscam, who was one of Prescott's failures. Rebelling against his father, that great benefactor of Justin, Jules turned against Dr. Prescott and openly defied him, refering to him as an "old charlatan" and speaking of his "vaudeville nature." Yet Jules, with all his rebellion, bears witness to the power of Dr. Prescott.

For the conclusion Auchincloss relies on Brian's journal. In the six years that have elapsed since the beginning of the story, Brian has left Justin, studied in a divinity school, and returned to Justin. Although he has retired, the rector lives near the school and takes a lively interest in it, putting the new headmaster in an unpleasant position. There seems a possibility that Prescott may assert his power in dangerous ways, but at last he learns humility.

Auchincloss has been remarkably successful in making us feel that Prescott is, in many ways, a great man. I don't know whether Auchincloss had some real headmaster in mind, and it doesn't matter whether he did or not, for the rector of the novel is a creation of the imagination, no matter whom he may resemble. Repeatedly Auchincloss introduces allusions to *King Lear,* and, though resemblances are not close, both Prescott and Lear are old men bereft of the power that was theirs for years. Brian says, near the end, "Wouldn't I rather see Dr. Prescott, if he must play an active role, howl like the anguished Lear in the tempest and ultimately bring ruin to all?" But this is exactly what, though tempted, the rector does not do, and that is the measure of his greatness.

I have always admired Auchincloss's craftsmanship and his prose, but most of his novels, though interesting enough, have failed to excite me. The subject of *The Rector of Justin* does not seem to promise excitement—the octogenarian headmaster of a small private school—and yet I was swept along by it, for the

revelation of Prescott's character is fascinating. Auchincloss admires
Henry James greatly—which is nothing to be held against him—and
he has learned much from his work. I am not sure that James
would have approved of the way the book is put together, with the
none too plausible introduction of various documents; but he could
not have said, as he did say about many writers, that the author
had failed to make the most of his donnée. For the method does
work, and, we do come to feel the reality, the complicated reality,
of Francis Prescott. As the rector himself comes to realize, his kind
of headmaster could not exist in the modern world, but it is good
for us to meet an heroic character from the not too distant past.

Saturday Review
July 11, 1964

5 *Pioneers and Caretakers*

Although Louis Auchincloss is a Wall Street lawyer, he finds time
not only to write books but also to read them, and, as his literary
criticism shows, he is a first-rate reader. *Pioneers and Caretakers*
is a collection of essays on nine American women writers of fiction:
Sarah Orne Jewett, Edith Wharton, Ellen Glasgow, Willa Cather,
Elizabeth Madox Roberts, Katherine Anne Porter, Jean Stafford,
Carson McCullers, and Mary McCarthy. I wish he had also included
Eudora Welty and Flannery O'Connor, but otherwise I have only a
few complaints.

The studies of Edith Wharton and Ellen Glasgow, which have
appeared in the University of Minnesota Pamphlets on American
Literature, are both substantial pieces of work. No one, I think, has
written more appreciatively or more discriminatingly about Mrs.

Wharton than Auchincloss, who greatly admires her gifts without overlooking her shortcomings. He deals as carefully and as justly with Miss Glasgow, who also had her failures as well as her triumphs. In speaking of her last novel, he says, "There are, however, moments. There are always moments, even in the least estimable of Ellen Glasgow's books." Such moments he is happy to recognize.

The earliest of the novelists he discusses is Sarah Orne Jewett, whom he treats with affection and respect, never claiming too much for her, never pretending that she was anything but what she was, but at the same time forcing us to do justice to her achievements. And with Willa Cather, who was in a sense Miss Jewett's disciple, he is equally discerning, praising *My Antonia* for the right reasons, analyzing critically the structure of the *Professor's House,* and recognizing the beauty of *My Mortal Enemy.*

Up to this point, Auchincloss's choice of subjects seems inevitable; not all critics, however, would have thought of including Elizabeth Madox Roberts. As Auchincloss says, her first book, *The Time of Man,* won immediate recognition for its author; but it was followed by several failures and partial successes, and her death in 1941 was not much noticed. Although Auchincloss praises not only *The Time of Man* but also *The Great Meadow* and *Black is My True-Love's Hair,* there are other books that he can describe only as tedious. Whatever her shortcomings, however, she deserves to be remembered, and I am glad that Auchincloss has included her in his book.

My chief quarrel with Auchincloss concerns his evaluation of Katherine Anne Porter. Although I agree with him in general about her short stories, some of which are magnificent, I cannot accept his judgment of *Ship of Fools,* which he calls "a perfect novel." He admires it in the first place on what may be called political grounds—as a description of conditions in the summer of 1931 that made the rise of Hitler inevitable. The Germans on the ship, he says, "encompass in their group the essential characteristics of their nation." But should we speak, as she does and he does, of "essential characteristics" that damn a whole people? I think not. I cannot believe that an anti-German prejudice is any more admirable than an anti-Semitic prejudice. In the second place, he admires her because she is "never guilty of the sentimentality that masquerades as compassion." She is equally innocent, I should say, of true compassion; almost without exception she hates the people she writes about. He thinks the "novel sparkles with vitality and humor," whereas I find it almost lifeless. Well, tastes differ; and if Auchincloss believes that *Ship of Fools* and its popularity are "the best news in fiction that we have heard in many a year," I can only disagree—respectfully, of course.

Having read his novels, one would expect Auchincloss to appreciate the work of Mrs. Wharton and Miss Glasgow, but I should not have predicted that he would admire Jean Stafford, Carson McCullers, and Mary McCarthy as much as he does. Although he does less with Miss Stafford's short stories than he might have, he discusses each of her three novels with careful appreciation, expressing the greatest admiration for *The Mountain Lion*. When he comes to Mrs. McCullers, he gives particular praise to *Reflections in a Golden Eye,* and he makes as good a case as can be made for her latest novel, *Clock Without Hands.*

After describing the autobiographical elements in Mary McCarthy's novels and stories and the fictional elements in her memoirs, Auchincloss concludes that no sharp distinction can be made. He has a high opinion of *Memories of a Catholic Girlhood,* though he speaks well of the novels too. He does, I am happy to say, have reservations about *The Group.* He speaks of "the tedium of some of her inventories," and says she makes some of the mistakes of John O'Hara. Although *The Group* has been by far the most popular of her books, he does not think, any more than I do, that it is her best.

In his prefatory note Auchincloss writes: "A notable thing about our women writers is that they have struck a more affirmative note than the men. Their darkness is not as dark as that of Dreiser or Lewis or Faulkner or O'Neill, which is not to say that they see

America less clearly, but that they see it more discriminatingly. They have a sharper sense of their stake in the national heritage, and they are always at work to preserve it. They never destroy; they never want the clean sweep. They are conservatives who are always trying to conserve."

That Edith Wharton, Ellen Glasgow, and Willa Cather were in some important sense conservatives seems clear enough, but I am not so sure about Katherine Anne Porter, Carson McCullers, and Mary McCarthy. As Auchincloss says, there is a nostalgic strain in their work, but so there is in the work of William Faulkner, Wright Morris, Bernard Malamud, or any other of a dozen of their male contemporaries. And what about affirmation? Is Katherine Anne Porter more affirmative than William Faulkner, or Mary McCarthy than Saul Bellow? I think not. So far as literary attitudes are concerned, there are greater differences between the older generation and the younger than between women writers and men.

But I am not sure that Auchincloss would make any strenuous effort to defend his generalization. He is interested in each of his writers for her own sake, and he deals justly with all, including those whose work is strikingly different from his own. In his quiet, unself-assertive way he is one of the best of contemporary critics.

Saturday Review
June 5, 1965

6 *The Embezzler*

In the first paragraph of Louis Auchincloss's new novel, *The Embezzler,* we read: "I have the distinction of having become a legend in my lifetime, but not a very nice one. In this year 1960,

perhaps not every school child (for what do they know of America's
past?) but surely every college man who has taken even a casual
course in current history knows of Guy Prime. I am a symbol of
financial iniquity, of betrayal of trust, of the rot in old Wall Street
before the cleaning hose of the New Deal. If I had not existed,
Franklin Roosevelt (who had a far more devious soul than mine)
would have had to create me. The Jews were not more useful to
Hitler than was my petty embezzlement to the Squire of the Hudson."

Reading this, I remembered that there was a prominent Wall
Street figure who was convicted of some sort of malfeasance and
jailed in the years of the New Deal. But when I tried to look up
this man, whose name I finally recalled, in four books about the
Thirties, he was not in the index of any of them. The evil that men
do may live after them but not always very long.

However, the paragraph neatly introduces the reader to Guy
Prime's apology for his crime. A man well into his seventies, living
in Panama with a young second wife, Prime tells about his life prior
to his downfall, and tries to explain why he embezzled several hundred thousand dollars. In a mildly amusing and somewhat ingra-
tiating tone, he talks about his family, about his first wife, Angelica,
and particularly about his best friend, Rex Geer, who was for a
time Angelica's lover and who, after Guy's disgrace and divorce
and the death of his own wife, became Angelica's second husband.

Guy's memoir ends, and we learn that after his death in 1962 it
came into the hands of Rex and Angelica Geer, as Guy had hoped
it would. Rex sits down to write his version of his early relationship
with Guy, of the steps leading to the embezzlement, and of his
affair with Angelica. Then Angelica, having read both manu-
scripts, has her say.

Letting each of several participants in an action give his account
of what happened is not a new device. Joyce Cary used it in the
Chester Nimmo trilogy, and Lawrence Durrell successfully carried
through a tricky variation of it in *The Alexandria Quartet*. Auchincloss, working on a smaller scale, handles the device adroitly. The

ways in which the three interpretations vary are entertaining, and the reader is left to determine for himself where the truth—if, indeed, it is possible to speak of the truth—lies.

It has often enough been pointed out that Auchincloss knows more about "good" society than most contemporary novelists. A member of a prominent family and a Wall Street lawyer, he is acquainted with people of wealth, power, and social prestige, and he has written a dozen novels about such people. They are good too, for as an admirer if not exactly a disciple of Henry James and Edith Wharton he has worked hard at the craft of fiction.

A few other authors have shared his preference for characters who are reasonably well placed in American society. J. P. Marquand began by poking a mild sort of fun at the good old Boston families, but almost all his novels are concerned with the achievement of success, usually of a material sort. James Gould Cozzens has never dealt with people at the top of the pyramid, but the Coateses, the Rosses, and the Winners are all substantial people, at least comfortably well off, respected members of their professions, honored residents of their communities. Even Doctor Bull, the non-conformist hero of *The Last Adam,* belongs to a good Connecticut family. John O'Hara has ranged widely in his short stories, but most of his novels portray the actions of the leading citizens of various Pennsylvania communities—the Tates, the Chapins, the Eatons, the Lockwoods.

Ernest Hemingway, on the other hand, never wrote about the rich and successful, except sardonically in *To Have and Have Not*; he was more at home in the world of bullfighters, boxers, smugglers, fishermen, and journalists. Faulkner wrote much about the old Southern aristocracy, but he showed it in decline, and he was even more concerned with the poor whites and the Negroes. Saul Bellow has almost always written about misfits—Augie March, Tommy Wilhelm, Henderson, and Herzog, Bernard Malamud has often portrayed the desperately poor, and most of Flannery O'Connor's characters are Georgia crackers. As I said a while ago and was scolded for saying, the characteristic hero of our time is a misfit.

One explanation of this situation is the fact that, with increased social mobility, more of our writers come from under-privileged and often minority groups; but that is not the whole story. To many people, myself included, an Italian boy who robs a poor Jew is a more challenging subject than an upperclass New Yorker who misappropriates funds, and a bewildered intellectual in search of wholeness of spirit belongs more truly to our times than the aged headmaster of a fashionable preparatory school.

It is also important to observe that Cozzens, O'Hara, and Auchincloss are in the tradition of nineteenth-century fiction. O'Hara, as I have often complained, gets his effects through an undisciplined amassing of details, but Cozzens and Auchincloss are fine craftsmen. They write, however, as if Proust and Joyce and Kafka had never lived. Faulkner was always experimenting, often with magnificent success, and Bellow has used a different technique in each of his books. Ellison, Malamud, Hawkes, Salinger, Flannery O'Connor, and Updike, among others, have experimented with fantasy, symbolism, deliberate distortion, and the use of the grotesque.

I have no quarrel with what has been called social realism, and I appreciate the contribution that Cozzens and Auchincloss have made to American literature. For me, however, as for many others, their limitations are serious. Who are the chief characters in *The Embezzler*? A man whose great pride is in the way he runs a country club, a woman who is interested only in her horses and dogs, and a man whose sole ambition is to make money. Try as he may, Auchincloss cannot persuade the reader to take these people at their own valuation. One has to be wary in stating this kind of judgment; certainly the plots of many of Henry James's novels can be described in such a way as to make them sound ridiculously trivial. But James had resources, both of insight and of stylistic subtlety, that Auchincloss cannot draw on.

Saturday Review
February 5, 1966

7 *Tales of Manhattan*

The thirteen stories in Louis Auchincloss's *Tales of Manhattan* are divided into three groups: "Memories of an Auctioneer," "Arnold & Degener, One Chase Manhattan Plaza," and "The Matrons." All touch in one way or another the world of wealth, power, and social distinction that Auchincloss has made peculiarly his.

The first five stories are told in the first person by Roger Jordan, who works for and is later vice president of "the ancient auction gallery of Philip Hone & Sons, at the corner of Park Avenue and Fifty-seventh Street." One is the tale of a man who spent his fortune on a castle off the coast of Maine; another deals with an eminent professor and a young charlatan; a third portrays a painter who just misses fame. All the stories show how knowledgeable Auchincloss is, and the writing is urbane and often witty. For instance, in speaking of the promotion of hitherto obscure painters, Jordan says: "Still, as the masterpieces of art, swept by the inexorable law of the income tax, drop, first one by one, then dozen by dozen, into the great sea of museums, that bourne from whence no traveler returns, it behooves us dealers to develop the public taste in the direction of lesser but more accessible artists."

Each of the stories has a surprise ending. All we think we know about the man who built the castle is suddenly reversed by his daughter. The charlatan does contribute to the reputation of the professor, though not in the way the latter had expected. The secret of the unappreciated painter turns out to be rather shocking. The fact that surprise endings are old-fashioned doesn't bother me, but I feel that four out of the five stories are obviously contrived.

The fifth story, "The Money Juggler," is both more credible and more substantial than the others. Four members of the Columbia Class of 1940—a Wall Street broker, a popular columnist, a corporation lawyer, and the auctioneer-narrator—are having lunch together. Their chief topic of conversation is "the failure and flight from justice of our classmate Lester Gordon," who had enjoyed a series of spectacular successes. None of the four had liked Gordon, either in college or afterwards, and they all take pleasure in his downfall. But as the conversation proceeds it becomes clear that each of these men, who consider themselves morally superior to Gordon, has had a share of the profits he has so unethically amassed. The theme is one that Bernard Shaw exploited in *Mrs. Warren's Profession* and *Major Barbara*—the universality of guilt. Shaw, of course, had a way of escape: change the system, adopt Socialism. Auchincloss has no remedy. The narrator says: "Is that capitalism? That the aristocrat, the intellectual, and the professional are bound to the chariot of the money juggler?" But in the end he falls back on cynicism: "What were we but four junior Gordons?"

The stories in the third section are pleasant but not particularly profound. The central characters are for the most part pathetic: the extra man, the hanger-on in good society, who has to face the fact that he is no longer in demand; the highly competent mother of four children who is taught her limitations; a woman on whom everyone imposes; a man who has made great sacrifices for his family. These are stories that Edith Wharton, whom Auchincloss admires, might have written in her later years.

By far the best group of stories is the second, all of them concerned, as are the stories in *Powers of Attorney,* with members of a mighty law firm in downtown New York. One of the partners says: "I plunged into the pool of law like a hot boy on a July day. The orderly, hierarchial atmosphere of the firm, where one knew precisely at all times what was expected of one and where one rose from tier to tier pretty much in proportion to one's efforts, seemed to me a tiny civilization in the midst of chaos, a Greek city-state on a plain surrounded by barbarians. I loved the law from the beginning and loved the practice of it. I have never believed in the sincerity of those who pretend to find it difficult to live within a code." I would not suggest that Auchincloss fully shares this exalted opinion of the profession to which he belongs. He would scarcely say, with the Lord Chancelor in *Iolanthe,* "The Law is the true embodiment of everything that's excellent." But, like James Gould Cozzens, who is not a lawyer, Auchincloss is fascinated with the law both as an attempt to apply reason to human affairs and as, for literary purposes, a background against which the irrationalities so common in human behavior can be effectively exhibited.

In the first of the four stories in this group Sylvaner Price, now the dominant partner of Arnold & Degener, is trying to give a proper official account of Guthrie Arnold, the founder; but something— perhaps, he thinks, the senior partner's ghost—keeps compelling him to tell the truth. The discrepancy between public image and reality is a recurring theme. Foster Evans learns something about himself and something about Lewis Bovee, his ideal: "Mr. Bovee at the end of his long table, dispensing compliments and offering little toasts, might have been the man with the long whip surrounded by seemingly docile tigers perched on stools. The whip was the law, and without the law he and I well knew to what a shambles life was reduced. Yes, my tragedy, or at least my bathos, is that I have been simply a lawyer. My guide and mentor was, in his own fashion, a man." Eric Temple, the heretical New Dealer, fares well even when under investigation by Senator McCarthy. Cliffie Dean, who leads a revolution against Lloyd Degener, gets what he wants and regrets it. ("Save a bees' nest from a burning bush, and you can count on them to sting you.")

In "The Money Juggler" Roger Jordan says: "Glancing from John to Townie to Hilary, I was suddenly struck by the size of their common denominator. It was in their eyes, in the opaque glitter of their distrustful eyes. They were all prosperous, all expensively and similarly clad. I would have defied John O'Hara himself to have told in that assemblage of colored shirts, which was the descendant of a colonial governor, which the popular columnist and which the Wall Street lawyer. Over their apparel, which was as beautiful as a *New Yorker* advertisement, glowed the snakes' eyes that saw the world at a snake's level: one inch above the ground." The irony is that the narrator's eyes can't be more than an inch higher. Auchincloss has a larger vision than that, but not so large as I could wish.

VLADIMIR NABOKOV

Foreword

The first writing of Vladimir Nabokov's I can remember reading were two or three short stories that appeared in *The New Yorker*. I found them amusing and often shrewd but in some ways baffling. When I came across these stories and others in *Pnin,* I was even more puzzled, but it seems to me now as I reread my review that I was trying to conceal my bewilderment. I soon learned that one of Nabokov's principal aims was to confuse and mislead his readers. One might not like this sort of mystification, but I was absolutely wrong to suppose that Nabokov didn't know what he was doing.

Now, only ten years after the publication of *Lolita,* it is hard to understand why there was so great a hullabaloo about the novel. I think I dealt sensibly with the supposed moral issues, and I had begun to grasp the fact that Nabokov was always playing games, but I missed many ramifications of the game that have since become clear to me. (The passage about chess problems that I quote in my review of *Speak, Memory* is illuminating.)

There are many of Nabokov's books that I haven't reviewed and several that I haven't read. As I confess in my review of *The Gift,* the novels written in Russian and dealing with Russians in exile require for full understanding a knowledge of Russian literature and history I do not have. I don't remember why I didn't review *Pale Fire*, but I did read it, with admiration for Nabokov's ingenuity and a considerable measure of exasperation at what seemed to me his abuse of his talents. As for his most recent novel, *Ada*, it was published as I was giving up regular reviewing, and, when I discovered how long it is, I was immensely relieved that I didn't have to read it just then. It still stands reproachfully on a shelf devoted to books I must read some day.

1 *Pnin*

Vladimir Nabokov, a member of a family distinguished in pre-revolutionary Russia, has himself achieved distinction in the country of his adoption. He has taught at a number of American colleges, has won a variety of honors, and has written half a dozen books in English, fiction and non-fiction.

Timofey Pnin, the central character of his present book, is also an exile and a teacher, but there the resemblance to the author stops, for, in the world's eyes, Pnin is a ludicrous failure. With his absurd way of speaking English, his grotesque manners, his rich assortment of idiosyncrasies, his incomprehensible enthusiasms, and his talent for doing the wrong thing, he is everybody's laughingstock. Teaching courses taken by two or three students, engaged in endless and perhaps fruitless research, he appears to be the very image of futility, and so most of his colleagues see him.

Telling Pnin's story in a series of loosely related episodes, Mr. Nabokov makes us laugh at him, then sympathize with him, then respect him. The laughter comes readily enough when, in the first episode, we see him blundering along on his way to keep a lecture engagement. The second episode is funny, too, with its account of Pnin's false teeth, but then Mr. Nabokov drops back to tell us about Pnin and his wife and how they traveled to America with the wife's lover. This ought to be hilarious, but we have begun to feel sorry for Pnin. And when we come to the story of Pnin and Victor, the child of his wife's infidelity, we are touched, even though Pnin does everything wrong, as we knew he would.

It seems appropriate that Pnin should have a low opinion of

Charlie Chaplin as a comedian, for he is surely a Chaplinesque figure, as the end of the book demonstrates. Pnin leaves Waindell College when the narrator arrives and in part because he arrives. The narrator is at first amused and then bored and even angered by a colleague's evening-long recitation of Pnin stories. The next morning he sees Pnin himself, his possessions loaded into his little car, the car hemmed in by trucks, as this Chaplin with a Russian accent makes his pathetically gallant departure.

I do not see why Mr. Nabokov chose to be quite so casual in his handling of his material—why, for instance, he introduced a long account of Victor at preparatory school. But he does get Pnin and that is what matters. When Pnin leaves the scene, all lost but honor, we are, like the narrator, ashamed of having laughed at him.

New York Times Book Review
March 10, 1957

2 *Lolita*

The problem presented by Vladimir Nabokov's *Lolita* is literary not moral. The moral issue has, of course, been raised, and it will be raised again and again in the weeks to come. It would have been raised if *Lolita* had no previous history, but the novel is borne to us on a tide of scandal. Rejected by four American publishers, it was published in 1955 by the Olympia Press of Paris. The French government, however, forbade export of the book, and immediately there was an uproar. Articles about *Lolita* have appeared in a dozen American periodicals in the past year or two, and the debate was on long before Putnam announced that it would publish the novel.

The moral issue is simple. A little while ago I had a letter from a woman who objected to the fact that I had praised John Cheever's *The Wapshot Chronicle,* which was, she charged, an immoral work. To substantiate her charge, she listed the improper words that, she said, Cheever employed. I think she included at least one that isn't in the novel at all—she admitted that she had burned her copy and couldn't check—but the important thing is that the words were all words with which my correspondent was familiar and which she could bring herself to put down on paper. Whatever she regarded as corrupting in the novel couldn't, she made clear, corrupt her.

This is the old story. The roster of novels that have created scandals is long: Flaubert's *Madame Bovary,* Zola's *Nana,* Hardy's *Tess,* and *Jude,* Dreiser's *Sister Carrie,* Joyce's *Ulysses,* and Lawrence's *Lady Chatterley's Lover*—to name but a few. The persons who have suppressed or tried to suppress these books have never argued that they themselves had been unaware of the existence of the supposedly objectionable kinds of behavior the books portrayed; on the contrary, the self-appointed censors have usually shown a comprehensive knowledge of vice. The argument is always that it is somehow injurious to the public morality to have these matters, whatever they may be, brought into the open. If we go on pretending that they do not exist, the argument runs, in essence, all will be well.

The case for the defense is also in essence always the same: there is no such thing as an inherently unsuitable subject for literary treatment; everything depends on what the writer does with it. And over the years the defense has had the better of the argument. Unworthy books have doubtless been defended, but they have quickly been forgotten and no harm done. The worthy books, on the other hand, such as those I have mentioned, survive, and in time they make the whole debate seem irrelevant. What they are grows more and more evident, and what they are "about" matters less and less.

What *Lolita* is "about" is by now pretty well known. It is about a man who is sexually attracted to girls of twelve or so, or at least to certain girls at that age, the type he calls "nymphets." The book purports to be the confessions of this man, Humbert Humbert, written while he is awaiting trial for murder, and, although there are some preliminary scenes in his native Europe, most of it portrays his relations with an American girl, Dolores Haze, known to him as Lolita. At first Humbert marries Mrs. Haze, a widow, in order to be near Lolita, but he is delivered from the marriage—and from the temptation to commit murder—by his wife's death, and he and the girl embark upon a transcontinental pilgrimage during which he yields himself fully to his obsession. After some time, however, he loses Lolita to another man of the same tastes, and he spends some years in tracking down his rival, whom in the end he kills.

That such persons as Humbert exist we know from the textbooks, but in the textbooks we see them from outside. They are cases; they are not at all like us. Humbert, on the other hand, we come to know quickly and thoroughly from the inside. Indeed, it is astonishing how readily Nabokov persuades the reader to identify himself with this obsessed man. We don't like him, but we cannot comfort ourselves with the thought that he is wholly alien to us.

At the same time no one can say that Nabokov has made vice attractive, has encouraged us to regard Humbert's aberration as a trivial matter. On the contrary, we never forget that he is condemned by his obsession to a bleak and terrible existence. This is human bondage in its most extreme form. The transcontinental trip, although there are episodes of pure comedy and although Humbert looks back with longing on his moments of ecstasy, is in its total effect the kind of nightmare that one would pray to be spared.

Nor are we allowed to ignore the fact that the experience is hell for Lolita as well as for Humbert. Lolita is such an unattractive little girl that, after the first sense of horror at the abnormality of the relationship wears off, we are likely to feel that what happens to her doesn't matter. It is Humbert, in one of his more analytical moods, who reminds us that it does. "Nothing," he reflects at the end, "could make Lolita forget the foul lust I had inflicted upon her. Unless it can be proven to me—to me as I am now, today, with my heart and my beard, and my putrefaction—that in the infinite run it does not matter a jot that a North American girl-child named Dolores Haze had been deprived of her childhood by a maniac, unless this can be proven (and if it can, then life is a joke), I see nothing for the treatment of my misery but the melancholy and very local palliative of articulate art."

But if horror is the book's dominant note, it is far from being the only note that is struck. Although Nabokov was born in Russia and had written a dozen books in Russian before he attempted to write in English, he is a stylist of the greatest virtuosity. Hard as it may be to believe this, *Lolita* is in large part an extremely funny book, and the humor is of many kinds. For one thing, Humbert's obsession repeatedly forces him to become an impostor, and he is always aware of the comic aspects of the roles he plays. For another, he is erudite, and Nabokov permits him to indulge in Joycean games with words. Then there is a broad vein of satire, particularly in the description of the tourist's America. Nabokov's humor takes astonishing forms: Humbert's slaying of his rival, for instance, is portrayed in such fantastic terms that the scene becomes slapstick comedy of the most macabre kind.

Humor is the last quality one would expect to find in a book on *Lolita's* theme, but, finding it, one might suppose that Nabokov was simply kidding, that Humbert's obsession wasn't taken seriously and didn't really count. Not at all. The scenes in which Humbert's passion is made explicit, although restrained in language, are fully and horribly convincing. This is the core of the book, and make no mistake about it.

One has to ask whether the book means more than it seems to mean. Some of its defenders have no doubt that it does. Harry Levin, for instance, has said that it is "a symbol of the aging European intellectual coming to America, falling in love with it but finding it, sadly, a little immature." Nabokov, however, pooh-poohs this interpretation. "For me," he says, "a work of fiction exists only insofar as it affords me what I shall bluntly call aesthetic bliss, that is a sense of being somehow, somewhere, connected with other states of being where art (curiosity, tenderness, kindness, ecstasy) is the norm." What this seems to me to mean is that, given the original idea—and he seems pretty vague about how it was given him—he was interested simply in seeing how much he was able to make of it.

As I have been trying to say, he has made a good deal. Whatever else may be true, *Lolita* is a brilliant tour de force. Is it also a novel of enduring importance? Nabokov's admirers are convinced that it is, but I cannot feel that they have succeeded in saying why. I am not sure that the book won't come to be regarded primarily as a literary curiosity, so skilfully done that it is vastly more interesting than the average run of fiction and yet not one of the memorable novels.

I remind myself that some such judgment of *Ulysses* was formed by many early readers who were impressed by the brilliance of Joyce's stylistic achievement. Perhaps the future will be as interested in Humbert Humbert and Dolores Haze as we are in Leopold Bloom and Stephen Dedalus. Whether that happens or not—and my guess is that it won't—I am sure that the future will exonerate *Lolita* from the charge of pornography as completely as we have exonerated *Ulysses*.

Saturday Review
August 16, 1958

3 *The Gift*

Whatever else he may be, and he is much else, Vladimir Nabokov is a sly fox, always up to tricks. Ever since coming to America, he has delighted in mystifying his readers—in *The Real Life of Sebastian Knight*, in *Pnin*, in *Lolita*, and especially in *Pale Fire*. This last is not, in my opinion, what Mary McCarthy called it—"one of the very great works of art of this century"—but it is a masterpiece of mystification. Here we have a long poem, and a very respectable poem, with an even longer commentary by a madman, and behind poem and commentary one discerns a variety of possibilities. In her review in the *New Republic* Miss McCarthy sometimes seemed to be making up her own story, but perhaps that is just what the reader is supposed to do.

Nabokov has had two careers as a writer, as well as a career as an entomologist and a career as a teacher. Born in Russia in 1899, he spent the Twenties and the Thirties in Germany and France, and wrote nearly a dozen books, novels and collections of short stories, in Russian. Then, in 1940, he came to the United States, taught at a number of colleges, and began writing in English. His mastery of the language, and especially of American vernacular, is a pure marvel.

Several of the Russian books have been translated at one time or another, and now we have *The Gift*, "the last novel I wrote, or ever shall write, in Russian." The first chapter was translated by Nabokov's son, the other four by Michael Scammell, and the whole thing was carefully revised by the author. Certainly the style shows his touch.

The novel, which was finished in 1937, tells about a young Russian poet, Fyodor Godunov-Cherdyntsev, an emigré living in Berlin and supporting himself by doing translations and teaching languages. He has just published a volume of poetry, and the first part of the book is mostly concerned with his poems and their reception, and with his relations with a variety of emigré intellectuals. There is then a long, impressive section describing Fyodor's father, an explorer and entomologist. Fyodor writes a book about Chernychevski, a nineteenth-century critic and revolutionist, and this is given in full. Meanwhile Fyodor is carrying on a rather tepid affair with a girl named Zina. When the novel ends, he is gathering his forces to write just such a book as *The Gift*.

Even then, twenty-five years ago, Nabokov was playing tricks on his readers. The novel begins in the first person, the "I" being Fyodor; but in a little while Fyodor is being referred to as "he," and the alternation of first person and third person continues through the novel. One never knows what to expect. Fyodor goes to a literary affair, and, we are told, leaves in the company of a poet named Koncheyev, with whom he discusses various literary matters. Suddenly, at the end of the chapter, the "I" pops up and says, "Whose business is it that actually we parted at the very first corner, and that I have been reciting a fictitious dialogue with myself as supplied by a self-teaching handbook of literary inspiration?"

The book is full of humor. The biography of Chernychevski, for instance, seems to be a joke, though the point is far from clear to one who knows little of Russian history and literature. There is also wit of a more comprehensible sort. Here, for instance, is an account of a literary critic:

The local Valentin Linyov, who from issue to issue used to pour out his formless, reckless, and not altogether grammatical literary impressions, was famous not only for not being able to make sense of the book he reviewed but also for not having, apparently, read it to the end. Jauntily using the author as a spring-board, carried away by his own paraphrase, extracting isolated phrases in support of his incorrect conclusions, misunderstanding the initial pages and thereafter energetically pursuing a false trail, he would make his way to the penultimate chapter in the blissful state of a passenger who still does not know (and in his case never finds out) that he has boarded the wrong train.

There is a good deal of this sort of thing that the reader can enjoy, but the book as a whole is tough going. That is not primarily because of Nabokov's tricks and mystifications, but because the book was written for an audience saturated in Russian literature. In his preface the author states:

Its heroine is not Zina but Russian Literature. The plot of Chapter One centers in Fyodor's poems. Chapter Two is a surge towards Pushkin in Fyodor's literary progress and contains his attempt to describe his father's zoological explorations. Chapter Three shifts to Gogol, but its real hub is the love poem dedicated to Zina. Fyodor's books on Chernychevski, a spiral within a sonnet, takes care of Chapter Four. The last chapter combines all the preceding themes and adumbrates the book Fyodor dreams of writing some day: *The Gift*.

It is a novel about the making of a poet and, very specifically, a Russian poet. To appreciate it fully, one would not only have to know the Russian classics a great deal more intimately than most of us do; one would have to be acquainted with minor writers as well. Except perhaps for a few scholars, no American can take from the book all that Nabokov is trying to give.

Yet the book is interesting, for Nabokov's special quality does come through. His acts of mystification are not completely arbitrary, though they sometimes seem so. At one point he speaks of "multi-level thinking": "you look at a person and you see him as clearly as if he were fashioned of glass and you were the glass blower, while at the same time without in the least impinging upon that clarity you notice some trifle on the side—such as the similarity of the telephone receiver's shadow to a huge, slightly crushed ant, and (all this simultaneously) the convergence is joined by a third thought—the memory of a sunny evening at a Russian small railway station; i.e., images having no rational connection with the conversation you are carrying on while your mind runs around the outside of your own words and the inside of those of your interlocutor." This is the kind of consciousness that Nabokov tries to reproduce in his novels, and therefore dreams and imaginary conversations and make-believe adventures are part of his material. His trickiness reflects the complexity of life and the deceitfulness of appearances.

Saturday Review
June 1, 1963

4 *Speak, Memory*

Vladimir Nabokov has prepared a new edition of his autobiography, originally published in 1951, in this country as *Conclusive Evidence,* in England as *Speak, Memory.* The present version is called *Speak, Memory: An Autobiography Revisited.* Nabokov has added from twenty-five to fifty pages, mostly concerned with his forebears, especially his father, whom he describes vividly and with affection. A few passages have been expanded, and there has been some stylistic revision, but the book has not been changed in any fundamental way.

What we have is what we had before—an extraordinary evocation of the life of the Russian upper class before World War I. The Nabokovs were people of social rank, considerable wealth, cosmopolitan culture, and liberal political views. The wealth and leisure they enjoyed were not abused but, by and large, served both conscience and intelligence. Young Nabokov received the education of a poet rather than the education of an autocrat, but he was bound to be an autocratic poet.

Most of the book describes Nabokov's life before the Bolshevik Revolution, which took place in his eighteenth year. The family escaped from Petrograd to the Crimea, but soon was forced to migrate to England and the Continent. Nabokov writes a little about his years at Cambridge University, and then briefly tells what it was like to be an exile and a writer in Western Europe from 1922 to 1940. It was in the latter year that he and his wife and their child fled to the United States, and it is with their departure that the book ends.

Although Nabokov wrote ten or a dozen books in Russian during his European exile, he barely touches on his literary career. He does say things, however, that bear directly or indirectly on problems raised by his novels and short stories. "In the course of my twenty years of exile," he observes, "I devoted a prodigious amount of time to the composing of chess problems. A certain position is elaborated on the board, and the problem to be solved is how to mate Black in a given number of moves, generally two or three. It is a beautiful, complex, and sterile art related to the ordinary form of the game only insofar as the properties of a sphere are made use of both by a juggler in weaving a new act and by a tennis player in winning a tournament."

After describing the fascination that the construction of such problems had for him, he continues, "Deceit, to the point of dia- bolism, and originality, verging upon the grotesque, were my notions of strategy." And lest the reader should fail to see that what Vladimir Nabokov says about his chess problems is applicable to his fiction, he declares: "It should be understood that competi- tion in chess problems is not really between White and Black but between the composer and the hypothetical solver (just as in a first- rate work of fiction the real clash is not between the characters but between the author and the world), so that a great part of the problem's value is due to the number of 'tries'—delusive opening moves, false scents, specious lines of play, astutely and lovingly prepared to lead the would-be solver astray."

Nabokov thus admits that each of his novels is a game in which he tries to mislead his reader and prove his superiority over him, and this is exactly what certain critics have charged. In *Escape Into Aesthetics: The Art of Vladimir Nabokov,* Page Stegner sets out to "dispel the notion that he is simply a trickster, a hoax player, and not a serious artist." Yet Stegner begins by demonstrating that Nabokov is a trickster, whatever else he may be. Even in his auto- biography he plays tricks, alluding in flattering terms to V. Sirin, a novelist in exile, without mentioning the fact that, as Stegner points out, he himself, Nabokov, wrote under the name of V. Sirin. In *The Real Life of Sebastian Knight* the narrator, V., and Sebastian, about whom V. is writing, may be, according to Stegner, "divided halves of a single identity." In analyzing *Bend Sinister*, whose narrative technique is strangely complicated, Stegner speaks of "a perverse talent that keeps the reader uneasily looking over his shoulder (as he steps out over the precipice) for the ambush he suspects lies behind." *Pnin* seems more straightforward than the earlier fiction, but its simplicity is in part a deception. *Lolita* is full of the "false scents" Nabokov has talked about—"word games," Stegner calls them—and in *Pale Fire* meaning lies below meaning, like the buried cities of Troy.

But Stegner insists that Nabokov is a serious artist and not merely a prestidigitator. The first point he makes is that Nabokov is a master stylist, with an amazing control over a language that is not his native tongue. In the second place, Stegner argues that Nabokov is an impressionist, in the tradition of James, Proust, Joyce, and Faulkner, and that the tricks he plays are calculated to make the kind of impression he wants. The third point is suggested by the title of Stegner's book. Escape from what? one asks. Speaking of Krug in *Bend Sinister*, Stegner writes: "His discovery that 'death is but a question of style' is the Nabokovian conviction repeatedly demonstrated in other books . . . that the only redemption from the horrors of existence is through the adoption and pursuit of a style."

Though he values Nabokov highly, Stegner is no idolater. He questions Mary McCarthy's statement that *Pale Fire* is "one of the very great works of art of this century," finding it rather too much like an impossibly difficult crossword puzzle. On the other hand, he regards *Lolita* as a "truly great novel," for he discovers in it the kind of "moral truth" he cannot discern in *Pale Fire*. I cannot go all the way with Stegner, but I have learned a good deal from him. As the first book by a very young critic and as the first book about a singularly difficult writer, *Escape Into Aesthetics* is a remarkable achievement.

Nabokov's Quartet spans, as the author points out, "four decades of literary life." "An Affair of Honor," the earliest story, shows that even as a young man Nabokov knew how to bring a trick off. Although the author warns against calling "The Visit to the Museum"

Kafkaesque or Freudian, it is an allegory of some sort. "The Vane Sister," the only one of the stories originally written in English, is another sort of game, and amusing enough, although one would be likely to miss the ultimate joke if the author's preface didn't offer a clue. Nabokov has written better stories than these, but they do suggest how persistently and in how many ways he has invited the reader to a contest of wits.

Saturday Review
January 7, 1967

JOSEPH HELLER

Foreword

For the first couple of hundred pages I thought *Catch-22* as funny a book as I had ever read, but then there seemed to be too many gags and the gags were too labored, and I was bored more often than I was amused. But as the years passed, it turned out that there were thousands of readers who were not bored, the great majority of them college students. At a literary conference at Notre Dame in 1967, at which Heller was a speaker, he was asked questions by an undergraduate audience that appeared to know the book by heart. He himself offered what is probably the right explanation: "This," he said, meaning the war in Vietnam, "is the war I was writing about all the time."

Nearly ten years after the publication of *Catch-22* Heller remains a man of one book. (His play, *We Bombed in New Haven,* is painful to read, and might be even worse to see.) The one book, however, is part of the history of a decade of student restlessness and revolt.

1 *Catch-22*

Catch-22 tells many stories, but its central figure is a bombardier named Yossarian. The war has come to seem to Yossarian quite crazy. "Men went mad and were rewarded with medals. All over the world, boys on every side of the bomb line were laying down their lives for what they had been told was their country; and no one seemed to mind, least of all the boys who were laying down their young lives." Yossarian minds very much: "He had decided to live forever or die in the attempt, and his only mission each time he went up was to come down alive."

The chief obstacle to Yossarian's achieving his ambition is Colonel Cathcart, who constantly raises the number of missions his men have to fly. Cathcart is a simon-pure opportunist, a man who will stop at nothing to get promoted, who is constantly courting the favor of his superiors, who does not care how many men are killed if he can get a little favorable publicity. He is as stupid as he is unscrupulous, and his immediate superiors have little advantage over him in either intelligence or morality.

Cathcart, of course, is a caricature, and there are plenty of caricatures in the book. With Milo Minderbinder, the mess officer, Heller goes beyond caricature into the realm of satiric fantasy. Milo, a stalwart advocate of private enterprise, organizes a syndicate whose black market activities range all over Europe. He steals the carbon dioxide cylinders that are used to inflate life jackets, and takes the syrettes of morphine from the first-aid kits. (He always leaves a mimeographed note saying, "What's good for M & M Enterprises is good for the country.") His greatest exploit is to hire himself out to the Germans to bomb his own airfield for cost plus 6 per cent.

Heller's satire cuts a wide swath. He takes after a variety of bureaucrats, makes fun of security checks, ridicules psychiatrists and army doctors in general. Sometimes he shoots way over the mark, but often his aim is good. There are several extremely funny passages, the humor usually rising out of the kind of mad logic that seems to Heller the essence of modern warfare. Here is a passage that exhibits the humor and incidentally explains the title:

Yossarian looked at him soberly and tried another approach. "Is Orr crazy?"

"He sure is," Doc Daneeka said.

"Can you ground him?"

"I sure can. But first he has to ask me to. That's part of the rule."

"Then why doesn't he ask you to?"

"Because he's crazy," Doc Daneeka said. "He has to be crazy to keep flying combat missions after all the close calls he's had. Sure, I can ground him. But first he has to ask me to."

"That's all he has to do to be grounded?"

"That's all. Let him ask me."

"And then you can ground him?" Yossarian asked.

"No. Then I can't ground him."

"You mean there's a catch?"

"Sure there's a catch," Doc Daneeka replied. "Catch-22. Anyone who wants to get out of combat duty isn't really crazy."

This is amusing and pointed, and so is much else, but the book as a whole is less effective than it might be. Heller has introduced so many characters, tried to deliver so many knock-out blows, and written in such a variety of styles that the reader becomes a little dizzy.

Saturday Review
October 14, 1961

REYNOLDS PRICE

Foreword

There is some doubt in my mind as to whether Reynolds Price really belongs in this particular assembly of writers. He is good, very good, but his range is limited. In his first two novels and his collection of short stories he exploited a vein that had not been overworked, writing about the small farmers of North Carolina with knowledge and warmth. Then, in *Love and Work,* he turned to some of the themes that have been popular among his contemporaries—identity, alienation, and the like. As I said in my review, he was right in trying a new direction, but the novel itself is a good deal less interesting and impressive than its predecessors. A novel of this sort, however, even if it seems a failure, may have great importance in a writer's career. Everything, obviously, depends on what happens next.

1 *A Long and Happy Life*

Reynolds Price is one young writer—he was born in 1933—who cannot complain that his first novel has been neglected. In advance of publication *A Long and Happy Life* has been heartily praised by Eudora Welty, Stephen Spender, and Lord David Cecil, among others, and *Harper's* magazine plans to publish the entire novel in a special supplement. Happily, the book deserves the attention it is being given.

It is a love story, and one of the simplest and most poignant I have ever read. Rosacoke Mustian has been in love with Wesley Beavers for six years, and she has never known, and does not know when the novel opens, what he feels about her or whether he feels anything. On the surface they are just ordinary young people: she lives on a farm in North Carolina and works in the local telephone exchange; he, recently discharged from the Navy, is selling motorcycles in Roanoke.

The novel begins with a dazzling passage:

Just with his body and from inside like a snake, leaning that black motorcycle from side to side, cutting in and out of the slow line of cars to get there first, staring due-north through goggles towards Mount Moriah and switching coon tails in everybody's face was Wesley Beavers, and laid against his back like sleep, spraddle-legged on the sheepskin seat behind him was Rosacoke Mustian who was maybe his girl and who had given up looking into the wind and trying to nod at every sad car in the line, and when he speeded up and passed the truck (lent for the afternoon by Mister Isaac Alston and driven by Sammy his man, hauling one pine box and one black boy dressed in all he could borrow, set up in a ladder-back chair with flowers banked round him and a foot on the box to steady it)—when he even passed that, Rosacoke said once into his back "Don't" and rested in humiliation, not thinking but with her hands on his hips for dear life and her white blouse blown out behind her like a banner in defeat.

When one first reads the paragraph, it seems excessive, almost flashy, but then one realizes how much Price has done, how much he has told us about Wesley and Rosacoke, how well he has suggested the setting of his tale, how beautifully adapted his style is to the movement he is describing. As one reads on, he proves to be a stylist of great resourcefulness. He effectively uses not only the vocabulary but also the syntax of common speech: "Everybody was bowed, including Baby Sister who took prayer serious to be so young." Yet he can range as far and as high as he sees fit.

The novel begins with Rosacoke at the funeral of a Negro girl, Mildred, a friend of hers who has died while bearing a fatherless child. From this touching scene, observed with the greatest precision, we move rapidly to a boisterous picnic and then there is an inconclusive conversation between Rosacoke and Wesley. By this time we know both of them well: Wesley is headstrong, wayward, self-centered, and aloof, but we suspect, as Rosacoke does, that there may be more to him than is immediately apparent. As for Rosa, she is just a country girl, bright enough in her way but remarkable in only one respect—her bottomless capacity for love. She demands little of Wesley, but she would like to know where she stands.

This, of course, is what she cannot know, and, as the story develops, we feel her agony. At last she gives in to Wesley's sexual importunity, hoping that in this way she can come to terms with him, but she finds in the end that they are further apart than ever, and she is left with nothing but pride and despair. When she discovers that she is pregnant, she cannot bring herself to let Wesley know but resolves to bear the burden alone. That her friend Mildred has died in childbirth, that her sister-in-law has borne a dead child, these are not thoughts to comfort her, but fear for herself is nothing in comparison with her loneliness.

The novel comes to its climax with the Christmas pageant in Delight Baptist Church. Although he has scarcely seemed to try, Price has made us acquainted with the little community: paralyzed Mister Isaac with his faithful colored servant and his horehound candy, the multitudinous Guptons, the members of Rosacoke's family, and all the others.

The pageant is like a thousand other pageants that take place in small towns every Christmas in every part of the country, and Price records it with tenderness and exactitude: the songs, the extemporized costumes, the cheap jewel box and the butter dish in which the Wise Men carry their gifts.

Because Willie Duke Aycock has run away to get married, Rosacoke has to take the part of Mary, watching over one of the Gupton progeny while the angels and the shepherds and the Wise Men make their appearances and sing their songs. As she sits there, Price takes us inside her mind, so that we feel with her as we rarely feel with a character in fiction. "All this time," she thinks, "I have lived on the hope he would change some day before it was too late and come home and calm down and learn how to talk to me and maybe even listen, and we would have a long life together— him and me—and be happy sometimes and get us children that would look like him and have his name and answer when we called. I just hoped that."

The ending is ambiguous, but the epigraph, which is from Dante, permits us to believe that the briar may blossom, that Rosacoke may realize some part of her dream. But that doesn't really matter. We have shared in Rosa's great ordeal, and it is an experience not soon to be forgotten.

Although he writes of simple matters, Price can make use of sophisticated literary devices. There are certain motifs that recur: the deer, Mister Isaac's spring, the pecan tree, Rosacoke's father's sunken grave. The hawk Rosacoke sees and the white heron she doesn't see are both significant. When she says she has hoped that she and Wesley "would have a long life together . . . and be happy sometimes," she is unconsciously and ironically echoing something she said about Mildred at the funeral service: "There I was just wanting to give her a pair of stockings and wish her a long and happy life and she was already gone." Indeed, the last scene, the scene of the pageant, is full of echoes, and one realizes how carefully conceived this apparently artless narrative is. All the author's skills, however, are tools in the service of his insight, which is phenomenal. To have created Rosacoke Mustian is an achievement that the most mature novelist might envy.

Saturday Review
March 10, 1962

2 *The Names and Faces*
of Heroes

Last year's most impressive first novel was Reynolds Price's *A Long and Happy Life.* Now Price has published a collection of short stories, *The Names and Faces of Heroes,* and if not all the stories reach the high level of the novel, the volume is a considerable satisfaction. In the novel Price made it clear that he was not afraid of pathos and that he ranked compassion high among the virtues. In the stories he shows that he is willing to run many risks, including the risk of being thought sentimental.

The first story, "A Chain of Love," written before *A Long and Happy Life,* introduces the heroine of that novel, Rosacoke Mustian. Here is Rosacoke, already in love with Wesley Beavers, but not so deeply involved as in the novel. She and her brother accompany their grandfather to a hospital in Raleigh, and for a week simply camp out in his room. (We have to take Price's word for the possibility of this happening.) There is some humor in the situation, and Price exploits it, but the crux of the story is the compassion Rosacoke feels for a stranger who is dying in another room. (Judging from evidence in other stories, I take it the stranger is to be identified with Price's father, who died a few years ago.) Rosacoke is not realized so fully as in the novel, but this is truly she.

The final and title story, obviously autobiographical, describes a nine-year-old boy and his father riding home from a religious service. Told by the boy, the story skilfully explores some of the problems of boyhood, but at the same time we are allowed to see the father more and more clearly. What emerges is a strong and poignant feeling for the tender relationship that exists between father and son.

Two other stories deal with childhood, "Michael Egerton" attacks a familiar theme, the grief of a boy whose parents have separated, and treats it freshly, "Troubled Sleep" goes deeper into the melancholy of childhood. Here are the boyish speculations and anxieties, the thoughts of death, the disturbing dreams.

Two stories portray aged Negroes, "The Warrior Princess Ozimba" begins: "She was the oldest thing any of us knew anything about, and she had never been near a tennis court, but somewhere around the Fourth of July every year, one of us (it was my father for a long time but for the past two years, just me) rode out to her place and took her a pair of blue tennis shoes." Although the portrayal of the old woman is excellent, the poignance of the story comes from the narrator's memories of his dead father.

"Uncle Grant" is perhaps a character study rather than a story, although where is one to draw the line? At any rate it is told in the first person, and the narrator is named Reynolds Price. It is an account of an uncommonly self-reliant, self-respecting individual, living out his long and arduous life, and it is told with affection and sincere regard. If a hard-boiled reader might find the ending

close to sentimentality, this, as I have said, is a risk Price is willing
to run.

All the stories are laid in the North Carolina county in which
Price was born and spent his boyhood. He is not, he has said, aim-
ing to found another Yoknapatawpha County, but he finds in his
native region materials of which he can make imaginative use.
There is, for example, a story, "The Anniversary," in which an old
woman decorates the grave of a man whom, long ago, she lost in
more senses than one. "It was to have been a small wedding," she
says, "and it was a small burial."

Saturday Review
June 29, 1963

3 *A Generous Man*

I have seldom read a first novel that had such sustained lyric power
as Reynolds Price's *A Long and Happy Life*: not pretty, pseudo-
poetic prose but a vigorous, joyful outburst of song. In his second
novel, *A Generous Man,* Price displays the same gift, but he employs it in a more varied fashion. The first novel was a love story,
simple and poignant; this describes the complicated experiences
that contribute to a young man's coming-of-age.

The young man—a mere boy in age, fifteen—is Milo Mustian,
the older brother of Rosacoke, heroine of *A Long and Happy Life.*
The time is several years before that of the first novel and Rosacoke
is only eleven, but she already shows something of the capacity for
love that is to distinguish her later life. Milo, quite a different sort
of person, is a cocky youth, and never cockier than on the morning
with which the novel opens. At breakfast he gives his family—

mother, grandfather, brother, and two sisters—a bawdy account of the previous night's adventures at the county fair, but he does not tell them—though Rosacoke guesses it—that for the first time he has had a woman.

Emma, Mrs. Mustian, has other matters on her mind, for her second son, Rato, who is less than bright, is in despair over the sickness of his dog, Phillip. So the whole family climbs into a truck, and proceeds to the nearest town to visit the veterinarian, who proves to be an unhappy clown. Milo encounters Lois, his girl of the night before, and the Mustians take her back to the fairground, where she helps her aunt with a snake show, of which the feature is a twenty-foot python name Death. The dog, at least partly recovered, takes off after Death, and Rato pursues them both; though Milo and others do their best, snake, dog, and boy vanish.

The next day a posse is organized under the direction of Sheriff Rooster Pomeroy, a philosophical and loquacious man who has made the mistake of marrying a young wife. The gathering of the posse is a little like the gathering of the searching party in Eudora Welty's "The Wide Net"—partly serious, but mostly a lark. A still figures in the story, and Milo gets drunk for the first time in his life. (Drunk, he tells the members of the party what is quite true—that they are relishing the chance to get away from their wives and talk man talk and aren't really concerned with the boy, the dog, and the snake.)

From this point on, the novel drives further and further away from plausibility. There have been references to a mysterious man named Tommy Ryden, related to the Mustians, who is supposed to have been killed in the Pacific. The sheriff's young wife, identifying Milo with this Tommy, whom she once loved, gives the boy abundant opportunity to practice what he has so recently learned. Then Tommy reappears, and so does the python, and the python nearly kills Milo. Tommy turns out to be Lois's father and her supposed aunt is really her mother, and Lois inherits a small fortune. And after a while things are straightened out.

Whatever may be going on, the dialogue is a joy. At the outset

Rosacoke has gone to Milo's room on her mother's instructions to tell him to get up.

"I hadn't got to do nothing but die."

"And you may have to do that shortly," she said, "lying there naked in early October. Where do you think you are?—Africa?"

"I was near enough to Africa late last night." He buried his dark head entirely in pillows (skin dark from sun, hair gold as crowns).

"I knew it when I saw you walking off that porch. I read it on your back as clear as light—Going To The Fair. Well, if the Warren County Fair is your idea of Africa, I pity the natives."

"I'm just talking about that snake."

"What snake?" she said.

Emma called up to her. "Is he wake yet, Rosa?"

Rosa ran to the railing. "Wake and buck-naked. Slept buck-naked on October eighth."

"Naked? You come straight down here then. You're too old for that."

"I'm not but eleven and he's lying on his stomach."

Emma didn't answer. She said, "Get him dressed" and went back to Baby Sister's oatmeal.

There are many conversations as amusing and as pointed as this, and many descriptive and narrative passages that fill the reader with admiration for the acuteness of Price's eye and the precision of his language. But there are other matters about which the reader may have doubts. Is not Milo too precocious, if not in what he does, then certainly in some of the things he says? Aren't the coincidences at the end excessive? Are we to believe that Lois can read palms with absolute accuracy?

The only possible answer to all these questions is that the novel is not intended to be realistic but is a kind of fable about youth and love. As such, it is to be judged in terms of the author's insights into his characters, and it is here that Price is most impressive. There is the relationship between Rosacoke and Milo, with Rosa's painful realization that her brother has grown away from her. There is the subtle relationship between Milo and Sheriff Pomeroy. There is the effect that Tommy Ryden has had on the women in his life. Most important, there is the maturing of Milo in these three or four crucial days, his learning about not only sex but also love, about giving as well as taking.

If Price makes Milo precocious, it may be because he wants to suggest the potentialities of youth. Towards the end Milo talks to Lois of two possibilities before him: he might become a tobacco farmer like his father and grandfather, marry some local girl, "and be whipped dry, dead but can't lie down for sixty more years"; or he might perform some great, if undefined, mission in the world. We know that he will follow the first path, but Price makes us believe that there are seeds of greatness in him. The novel is rich, original, and profound.

Saturday Review
March 26, 1966

4 *Love and Work*

Some time ago, when I had been complaining about the failure of the larger reading public to appreciate the novels of Wright Morris, a correspondent wrote me: "The trouble is that Morris writes about the kind of people who don't read books, and the people who do read books don't like books about people who don't." That sounds good, but it's wrong. In the first place, although it is true that Morris, like Sherwood Anderson, one of his masters, has often written about inarticulate people, most of his important characters have read books and some have written them. Furthermore, my correspondent's major premise is faulty: some of the American novels most admired in literary circles—*Moby Dick*,

Huckleberry Finn, The Red Badge of Courage, Light in August, and many others—present characters who, if not strictly illiterate, are not great readers.

In recent years one of the writers who have dealt effectively with sub-literary characters is Reynolds Price. Rosacoke Mustian in *A Long and Happy Life* can read, and she is able to write letters to the elusive Wesley Beavers, but she doesn't spend much time with books. Even more conspicuously heroic and even less bookish is her brother Milo in *A Generous Man.* In these two and in a number of lesser figures in both novels, Price has demonstrated how much can be done with people who not only aren't intellectuals but aren't even subscribers to a book club.

I speak of this because in *Love and Work,* Price is writing about people who do read books. Indeed, his hero Tom Eborn supports himself by teaching literature while he writes fiction and poetry. If not altogether an autobiographical character, Tom is manifestly the same kind of person as Price—as Wesley Beavers and Milo Mustian manifestly were not. Since Milo and Wesley are different from most characters in contemporary fiction, whereas Tom is not an unfamiliar figure, it might seem rather a shame that Price has taken this new tack; but I believe that, for the sake of his development, it was something he had to do.

Tom, when introduced, is thirty-four, has been married for seven years, has had a novel published and is working, not very happily, on another. His mother, who suffers from a carotid aneurysm that may end her life at any moment, lives in a town thirty miles from the university. His father died of cancer of the lung twelve years earlier.

The novel begins: "The phone's first ring pierced his study door, a klaxon vs. cheap birch veneer." The figure of speech points to Tom's apprehensiveness and his vulnerability. Having left a note for his wife, saying that he has an important piece of work to do and wishes not to be disturbed, he refuses to answer the telephone's importunate summons, and at last he hears Jane answer. Meantime he recalls the dream that had roused him early that morning, a dream in which he had been unable to bring help to injured friends. When Jane gives him an enigmatic message from his mother, he abandons his work in order to visit her.

What he was writing when the telephone rang was an essay on work. He had learned, he wrote, that only through work, through the mastery of a craft, could he achieve freedom from other human beings, "I do not mean," he continued, "that I would wish to be— or would ever become—free of the duties and debts of love toward my kin, partners, friends. What I mean is that only through my own early discovery of, cultivation of, absorption in some work—building houses, teaching school, laying roads, writing novels—could I free myself from the crippling emotional dependence upon other human beings which infects and afflicts any man who has nothing in his life upon which he can rely, nothing more permanent than other people."

It is clear that Tom is thinking of his mother's and father's dependence on one another and the former's dependence on him. In a letter written before his marriage, the father had exclaimed, "Can't we ever understand that you are mine, I am yours?" Reading the letter, Tom thinks: *"Error.* The fatal error of their lives (his parents), fatal error of Western Man!—'that you are mine, I am yours.' No one was anyone else's, ever." D. H. Lawrence once wrote, "We cannot bear connection. That is our malady." It is most certainly Tom's malady, and the novel charts its course.

Price has a remarkable gift for the rendering of states of mind. On his way home from an attempt to deal with the belongings of his mother, who has died, Tom sees an automobile accident in which a boy is killed. Afterwards: "He drove himself home as though he were glass—the brittlest pane—or as though his car were a powerful magnet which other cars resisted through hurtling luck that would fail any moment and yield his easy death. He strained not to think—of the dead boy; the woman; his name, as witness, in the hands of police; least of all, his novel that, minutes ago, had filled him, buoyed him, promised, like clear water. Instead, he focused his sight and his skills on concrete road, white and yellow lines, signs, lights, bristling junctions—each the possible site of his imminent death, his hundred-and-sixty pound contribution to the daily meat-take of summer roads (each mile thickly pasted with exploded dogs, cats reeling pink gut; the clear sky a sea of whirlpooling vultures). Cold fragility, huddled, at the mercy of objects."

We can sympathize with Tom as he is forced to ask himself whether he has not, years ago, made the wrong choice, and we can be sorry for Jane, about whom we know little except that she is the unwilling victim of his decision. Whether his painful recognition of error can bring redemption for either of them is not clear. Price seems to grant the possibility, but the tone of the novel suggests that Tom is doomed, that his awakening has come too late.

In spite of the meagerness by conventional standards of the existence led by the Mustians and the other characters in *A Long and Happy Life* and *A Generous Man,* these novels are rich with color and brightened by joy. *Love and Work,* by comparison, is spare and somber. One would not want Price to deal with the same sort of material over and over again, and the material here given him directly by his own experience, offered him a challenge that he could not ignore. I am not so excited by this novel as I was by the other two, but I recognize it as a necessary stage in his career.

Saturday Review
May 25, 1968

PHILIP ROTH

1 *Letting Go*

Rarely has a first book of any kind been more warmly received than Philip Roth's *Goodbye, Columbus,* a novella and five short stories. My paperback copy carries glowing words from Alfred Kazin, Saul Bellow, and Irving Howe. "He is acidulous, unsparing, tender," Kazin said. "At twenty-six," said Bellow, "he is skillful, witty, and energetic and performs like a virtuoso." Howe wrote: "What many writers spend a lifetime searching for—a unique voice, a secure rhythm, a distinctive subject—seem to have come to Philip Roth totally and immediately." The book won Roth the National Book Award for 1960, a Guggenheim fellowship, and a grant from the National Institute of Arts and Letters.

When a first book has had a success of this sort, it is certain that the author's second book will be given a going over. The critics who lavishly praised the first book are likely to feel that they have overextended themselves and to use the second book as an occasion for retrenchment, while the critics who didn't review it or reviewed it unfavorably are happy to have the chance to say, "Yah, yah, yah!" But it fairly often happens that the second book is not so good as the first, and even the reviewer who would like to be kind has to report the falling off. I didn't review *Goodbye, Columbus,* but I read it and liked it. *Letting Go* leaves me quite unhappy.

Letting Go is a long novel about a group of young people in the later Fifties. The central figure is Gabe Wallach, an English instructor, first at Iowa and than at Chicago, bright, well-to-do, attractive to women. At the outset a girl named Marge Howells, a rebel against Kenosha, Wisconsin, hops into his bed, and he has a difficult time pushing her out. Later there is a more serious affair with Martha Reganhart, a divorcee who has two children, and this also ends badly. Meanwhile he is deeply involved with his recently widowed father, who tries to possess him and, failing, makes a poor sort of second marriage. And then there are the Herzes, Libby and Paul.

The Herzes are almost as important in the novel as Gabe. We are told about their courtship; about their marriage, which cut them off from their families, his Jewish, hers Catholic; about the abortion; about her invalidism, about his obstinacy. It is a chronicle of disaster piled upon disaster, and there is Gabe looking on, sexually attracted by Libby but more deeply moved by pity for the unhappy pair of them.

Gabe is a privileged young man and therefore, being of the modern age, given over to feelings of guilt. He is always trying to help people and then, overcome by a realization of his inadequacies, pulling away from them. Although he is dubious about his motives, he tries to befriend the Herzes at Iowa and he gets Paul his job in Chicago. And finally he takes decisive, though by no means sensible, action on their behalf—an experience, it is intimated, that contributes to his maturity.

All this Roth reports in unrelenting detail. Each domestic squabble—and there are dozens of them—is set down as fully as if it were the Battle of the Bulge, with page after page after page of dialogue. That Roth is a careful observer and has a good ear is known to every reader of *Goodbye, Columbus,* but these are gifts that can be abused, and in the novel Roth has abused them. Line by line the writing is fine, but that does not save long stretches from being unpardonably dull and quite superfluous.

In an essay, "Writing American Fiction," that appeared in *Commentary* for March 1961, Philip Roth discussed the problems of the contemporary writer, which he found to be staggering. After commenting, not always graciously, on such novelists as Mailer, Salinger, Malamud, Bellow, Gold, and Styron, he put himself on record as favoring a fearless realism. Much modern fiction, it seems to me, demonstrates the rich possibilities of methods that are not strictly realistic, but Roth has a right to his opinion. What I quarrel with is his practice. Realism can be, must be, selective, and Roth is simply not selective enough; he goes on and on long after the reader knows all that he could conceivably need to know.

And after one has worked one's way through this mass of detail, one wonders what Roth thinks he has accomplished. In his essay he argues that contemporary reality is horrible beyond belief: "It stupefies, it sickens, it infuriates, and finally it is a kind of embarrassment to one's own meager imagination." He objects to the styles of certain writers on the ground that they are an expression of pleasure. "If," he asks, "the world is as crooked and unreal as I think it is becoming, day by day; if one feels less and less power in the face of this unreality, day by day; if the inevitable end is destruction, if not of all life, then of much that is valuable and civilized in life—then why in God's name is the writer pleased?"

If this is his vision of life, it is what he must try to set down, but I cannot feel that he has set it down convincingly in *Letting Go*. Many of his characters, to be sure, are miserable a good deal of the time, but I find in their miseries few reflections of those contemporary horrors of which Roth speaks. These are fairly ordinary young people, with a capacity for getting into trouble that is not much above normal. None of them has found a satisfying way of life, but there is nothing here that stupefies or sickens or infuriates. What the book seems to demonstrate is not that contemporary civilization is a disaster but that many people manage to mess up their lives—which isn't news.

Roth has not made the characters strikingly significant on any ground. Gabe Wallach is an amiable blunderer: "He is better, he believes, than anything he has done in life has shown him to be." Paul Herz is stronger, but he uses his strength against himself, while Libby pursues her own wretched course. Martha Reganhart seeks boldly for happiness until she is chastened into compromise. None of the characters achieves a spectacular triumph—Roth thinks writers in these days have no business being affirmative—but, on the other hand, none could possibly be regarded as tragic. They go their dull ways, and we are dragged along with them.

Let me make it clear that Roth is still a figure to be reckoned with. This is the kind of bad book that only a good writer could have written. But, after *Goodbye, Columbus,* with its vitality and sureness of touch, *Letting Go* is a disappointment.

Saturday Review
June 16, 1962

2 *When She Was Good*

The title of Philip Roth's second novel, *When She Was Good,* is intentionally misleading, for the thesis of the book is that when she —i.e., Lucy Nelson—was good, she was horrid.

In the Literary Guild *Preview* Roth gives an admirable summary of the story and a suggestive statement of his intentions. After saying that he had rewritten the manuscript eight times in the course of four years, he continues:

And yet the story I had set out to tell was the story with which I finished: A Middlewestern girl, disappointed in her long-suffering mother, infuriated with her alcoholic father, is impregnated by a boyish ex-GI, just home from his two-year confinement in the Army; rather against his will, she persuades him "to do his duty by her" and as a consequence of this decision (which had seemed to her the only one that was "moral"), she discovers herself imprisoned once again in a family situation no more loving or dignified than the one from which she had just escaped. As I remember it, what most intrigued me at the outset was the utter victimization of this girl, whose misfortune it was to have been born into a world to which she believed herself morally superior. What it took me nearly four years to discover and articulate was the exact price, in pain and deprivation, that the girl whom I called Lucy Nelson would make others pay in turn.

Roth works his way into the story slowly, beginning with an account of Lucy's grandfather, Willard Carroll, who established the family in Liberty Center. He married and had one child, Myra, who became Lucy's mother. Although Roth was born in Newark, New Jersey, he does well with the Midwestern small town background.

The key to Lucy's character, as Roth's summary suggests, is her father, Duane Nelson, commonly known as Whitey. An irresponsible fellow, he never keeps a job long, and finds consolation in liquor. From early childhood Lucy hates him, not only because he is a bad husband and father but also because he is always whining and making excuses for himself. And she scorns her mother for her weakness in forgiving him time after time. She is determined to hold herself up to the highest moral standards and to apply such standards to all with whom she is associated. When she is only fifteen, seeing her father mistreat her mother, she calls the police and has him taken to jail.

Because Lucy is ashamed of her family, she has few friends, and it is her self-imposed loneliness that makes her receptive to the attentions of Roy Bassart. Roy is a nicely drawn character—a pretty ordinary sort of American kid, weak, unsure of himself, with no particular talents, the kind that may shape up as he grows older or may not. At twenty the one thing he is certain he wants is sexual experience. Lucy has few illusions about him, and the reader knows from the outset that there is no hope for the marriage.

There is nothing unfamiliar about such a situation to one who lives in a small town and can tick off the number of shotgun marriages that have taken place this past winter. The only unusual factor is Lucy's self-righteousness, and this is unusual only in the extreme form it takes.

So far as technique is concerned, Roth leaves little room for complaint. The characters are real, and their talk once more shows what a good ear Roth has. Periodically he takes us inside Lucy's mind and lets us feel the power of her aberration:

> Eventually, must not the truth prevail? Oh, it had not been in vain then that she had sacrificed and struggled! Oh, yes, of course! If you know you are in the right, if you do not weaken or falter, if despite everything thrown up against you, despite every hardship, every pain, you oppose what you know in your heart is wrong; if you harden yourself against the opinion of others, if you are willing to endure the loneliness of pursuing what is good in a world indifferent to good; if you struggle with every fiber of your body, even as others scorn you, hate you and fear you; if you push on and on and on, no matter how great the agony, how terrible the strain—then one day the truth will finally be known—

Roth presents the disaster with great force, so that the last thirty or forty pages of the book are exciting in a way that earlier pages are not. Nevertheless the reader is likely to ask, "So what?" Roth, in the statement quoted earlier, tells us what. He does not maintain, he says, that Lucy is a typical American, but he thinks that in her character and behavior there is "much that American readers will find altogether ordinary and recognizable. For it has always seemed to me that though we are, to be sure, not a nation of Lucy Nelsons, there is a strong American inclination to respond to life *like* a Lucy Nelson—an inclination to reduce the complexities and mysteries of living to the most simple minded and childish issues of right and wrong. How deeply this perverse moralistic bent has become embedded in our national character and affected our national life is, I realize, a matter for debate; that it is even 'perverse' is not a judgment with which everyone will readily agree. What destroys Lucy (some readers may hold) has nothing whatsoever to do with the rest of us. I am of a different opinion."

Roth speaks as if he had make a great discovery, but surely the major novelists and dramatists have always known that self-righteousness and moral indignation often grow out of some serious defect of character, and in this post-Freudian era the idea is part of the "wisdom" of syndicated newspaper columns. Of course there are still persons like Lucy, and of course some other persons are taken in by them; but this does not mean that what Roth has to say about Lucy is a startling revelation.

In an article he wrote for *Commentary* some years ago Roth stated that he saw American life as terrifying and tragic. I did not find this vision expressed in *Letting Go,* which seemed to me a rather dull chronicle of commonplace marital difficulties, nor do I find it in *When She Was Good.* In my review of the earlier novel I said: "What the book seems to demonstrate is not that contemporary civilization is a disaster, but that many people manage to mess up their lives—which isn't news." It still isn't.

Saturday Review
June 17, 1967

3 *Portnoy's Complaint*

Three preliminary observations on Philip Roth's new novel, *Portnoy's Complaint,* seem to be necessary:

1. It deals explicity and even aggressively with various types of sexual activity.

2. It uses freely and rather repetitiously certain of the once-forbidden words, especially the three for which Mark Twain substituted blanks in *1601.*

3. No one *has* to read the book—or, for that matter, this review of it.

The theme is sufficiently indicated by a note from a make-believe medical dictionary defining "Portnoy's Complaint": "A disorder in which strongly-felt ethical and altruistic impulses are perpetually warring with extreme sexual longings, often of a perverse nature. Spielvogel says: 'Acts of exhibitionism, voyeurism, fetishism, auto-eroticism and oral coitus are plentiful; as a consequence of the patient's morality, however, neither fantasy nor fact issues in genuine sexual gratification, but rather in overriding feelings of shame and the dread of retribution, particularly in the form of castration.' "

Alex Portnoy tells the story as if he were talking to a psycho-analyst—a device that Roth uses effectively without making it obtrusive. Portnoy, at the time, is thirty-three, a lawyer with a reputation for humanitarian actions, and the recently appointed Assistant Commissioner for The City of New York Commission on Human Opportunity. He has the kind of career he has always wanted, and he is finding outlets for his powerful sexual impulses, but he is a mess, and it is no wonder he turns to a psychiatrist—the Dr. Spielvogel of the mythical quotation.

What Portnoy starts with, naturally, is his childhood, and we have never had so intense a description of life in a Jewish family. The first chapter is called, with the fierce irony that is one of Port-noy's recurrent moods, "The Most Unforgettable Character I've Met." It is his mother Portnoy means, and Roth presents the Jewish Mom with hot indignation and bewildered affection. When she is talking to her friends, she cannot praise Alex enough, even at the expense of his sister: "Of my sallow, overweight older sister, my mother would say (in Hannah's presence, of course: honesty was her policy too), 'The child is no genius, but then we don't ask the impossible, God bless her, she works hard, she applies herself to her limits, and so whatever she gets is all right.' Of me, the heir to her long Egyptian nose and clever babbling mouth, of me my mother would say, with characteristic restraint, 'This bonditt? He doesn't even have to open a book—A in everything. Albert Einstein the Second!' " When he doesn't do what she wants, however, she denounces him, threatens violence, parades her own miseries, and eventually brings him to tears and obedience.

After presenting several scenes that show his mother in action, Portnoy cries out: "Doctor Spielvogel, this is my life, my only life, and I am living it in the middle of a Jewish joke! I am the son in the Jewish joke—only it ain't no joke! Please, who crippled us like this? Who made us so morbid and hysterical and weak? Why, why are they screaming still, 'Watch out! Don't do it! Alex—no!' . . . Is this the Jewish suffering I used to hear so much about? Is this what has come down to me from the pogroms and the persecutions? From the mockery and abuse bestowed by the goyim over these two thousand lovely years?" He tells the story of Ronald Nimkin, a good boy who did everything his mother told him to and gave promise of becoming a concert pianist. When he hanged himself in his teens, he left a note for his mother, which said: "Mrs. Blumenthal called. Please bring your mah-jongg rules to the game tonight." Portnoy comments: "Now, how's *that* for good to the last drop?"

The other half of the story is Portnoy's sex life, about which, as I have said, Roth is explicit. On the subject of masturbation he is comic and sad and sometimes almost poetic. When Alex becomes bold enough to approach girls, he is interested only in shiksas, for he is seeking revenge both on his parents and on gentiles, and he is also gratifying his desire to be identified with the superior beings he envied in his schooldays. At last he meets the Monkey, a girl whose concupiscence matches his own—and he would have deserved at least passing mention in the Kinsey Report. But in spite of Kinsey's assumption that the more sex the better, Alex, as Dr. Spielvogel puts it, does not find "genuine sexual gratification." As he complains, he can never get away from the sense that what he is doing is sinful, and for this he blames his Jewish upbringing. But perhaps his problem lies deeper than that. Dr. Spielvogel has the last line: "So. Now vee may perhaps to begin. Yes?"

The novel is a triumph of style. Alex is, as he says, his mother's son, and Roth endows him with her kind of explosive intensity. What a family it is! The father, wrapped up in the insurance business, concerned above all with his constipation, can match his wife in crises, which, in such a household, are practically continuous. Alex does have pleasant memories, especially of times with his father, but they are not numerous, whereas the recollections of stormy scenes are constantly surging up. When, as a student at Antioch, he spends Thanksgiving with the family of his current shiksa, the life is bewilderingly alien to him. "My God! The English language is a form of communication! Conversation isn't just cross-fire where you shoot and get shot at."

Roth achieves an equal intensity when he lets Alex talk about his sexual desires and experiences. He wants lots and lots of sex, and, at least with the Monkey, he gets it. But at the same time he fears and hates his sexual drive. That is one reason why Roth lets Alex fill his narrative with the old monosyllables: They express his ambivalence. I know of no other way in which Roth could have got the effect he wanted.

Ever since the publication of his first book, *Goodbye, Columbus,* in 1959, when he was twenty-six, it has been clear that Roth was a master of the vernacular style. I felt that his gifts were at least partly wasted in his two novels, especially the second, *When She Was Good*. The trouble, I surmised, might be that Roth tried to endow the girl, Lucy, with an intensity that was not appropriate to her character as he presented it. In *Portnoy's Complaint,* on the other hand, the style is absolutely right for the character of Alex Portnoy and the experiences he talks about. The result is something very much like a masterpiece.

Saturday Review
February 22, 1969

Afterword

As I reread my reviews of Roth's books, I find myself asking several questions. Did I, for instance, undervalue *Letting Go* and *When She Was Good*? About the latter I am quite confident that I didn't. I still feel that the insight on which the book rests is neither original nor profound. *Letting Go* is a different matter: I am afraid that I may have committed the critic's commonest and probably least pardonable sin—condemning a book for not being quite other than the author intended it to be.

But my chief difficulty concerns *Portnoy's Complaint*: should I have called it "something very much like a masterpiece"? I must say that now, some time after the book was published, I think that judgment can be defended. Post-publication discussion of the book was clouded by two issues—Jewishness and sex. Most people made the mistake of identifying Portnoy with Roth. That there are resemblances between Portnoy and Roth is obvious, but there are also large differences. To attribute to Roth either Portnoy's opinions or his sexual practices is not very bright.

If *Portnoy* is in any sense a masterpiece, it is by virtue of its style. Roth, it seems to me, is the first serious writer to make full use of the new freedom in language. This story could not be told without the use of what were once known as obscenities. Most contemporary novelists use such language as a matter of realism in dialogue, and that's all right too. But it is the very foundation of Roth's way of writing in this particular book.

JOHN BARTH

1 *The Floating Opera*
2 *The End of the Road*
3 *The Sot-Weed Factor*

I have been reading for the first time John Barth's three novels, now all available in paperback editions. Born in Maryland in 1930 and educated at Johns Hopkins University, Barth has for some years been a teacher of English at Pennsylvania State University. *The Floating Opera*, published in 1956, was nominated for the National Book Award. *End of the Road* followed in 1958. Then in 1960 came *The Sot-Weed Factor*, which has had a kind of underground success, especially on college campuses.

The Floating Opera is the story, told in the first person, of Todd Andrews, a Maryland lawyer, bachelor, and eccentric. What Andrews sets out to do is to explain why he didn't commit suicide on a particular day in 1937, but he follows many bypaths, and from time to time the reader feels that he is hopelessly lost. Andrews's apparent willfulness, however, has a purpose, which is to show that persons and events are seldom what they seem. Truth is elusive, he is saying, and values are relative. The book describes, among other things, Andrews's affair with Jane Mack, an affair that is approved of by her husband, his best friend. In the end we find out why he decided to commit suicide and why he changed his mind.

The novel has both high wit and low humor. Todd's sardonic moods are rather engaging, at least at first, and he expresses his opinions in an amusing way. But I am not sure that Todd is or is intended to be an admirable figure. Barth suggests that, although much can be said for cynicism, it is not enough.

Jacob Horner, the central figure and narrator of *End of the Road* is even more ambiguous than Todd Andrews. One may regard him as either victim or villain. At least partly cured of a paralyzing neurosis by a strange, self-appointed psychiatrist, Jacob becomes a teacher of English in a small college. After finding one colleague whom he likes and admires, he proceeds to have an affair with the man's wife. The situation, developing in curiously complicated ways, ends tragically. As in *The Floating Opera,* we find Barth questioning the values by which people live and raising disturbing doubts about human motives. Nothing in life is as simple as it looks, and sex in particular is mysterious and many-sided. In both books one is aware of a lively intelligence and a fresh imagination.

It was, however, in his third book that Barth really let his imagination take off. *The Sot-Weed Factor* is a long, brilliant, bawdy, constantly surprising novel about life in Maryland about 1690. It purports to be the biography of Ebenezer Cooke, Gentleman, Poet, and Laureate of Maryland.

There was a real Ebenezer Cook—or Cooke—who wrote a satirical poem about Maryland called *The Sot-Weed Factor,* published in London in 1708. (Sot-weed is tobacco.) Although I know nothing about the historical Ebenezer, I gather that the Ebenezer of the novel is almost entirely Barth's invention. Born in Maryland, he was taken to England at an early age by his father. He and his twin sister, Anna, were tutored by a brilliant youth named Henry Burlingame. Later, after doing badly at Cambridge, Eben set himself up in London as a poet, but, having incurred the wrath of his father, he was sent to Maryland to manage the family estate. Before departing he has an interview with someone he believed to be Lord Baltimore, who appointed him Poet Laureate of the Province.

With his departure for America, Eben enters upon an extraordinary series of adventures, worthy of one of Henry Fielding's

heroes or one of Tobias Smollett's, and, in between, other characters set forth their own hazardous and harrowing experiences.
Eben encounters pirates, Indians, fugitive slaves, various conspir-
ators against the government of the province, and assorted villains
of all degrees. He is twice hoodwinked out of his father's property,
and he has to deal with several counterfeit poets laureate. Periodically his erstwhile tutor, Henry Burlingame, pops up in one disguise
or another, and although he sometimes plucks Eben out of grave
peril, he immediately plunges him into dangers just as great. Poor
Eben with great difficulty preserves his virginity, but he loses more
and more of his pristine innocence.

One of the major subplots concerns Eben's attempt to learn about
Henry's ancestry. Most of the relevant facts are discovered in an
alleged journal of Captain John Smith, one of the bawdiest and
funniest documents in contemporary literature. Other facts emerge
during Eben's stay among the Indians, until Henry is provided with
ancestors that satisfy his sardonic temperament.

Barth tells the story with a great show of erudition, which he
uses playfully. On one occasion, for instance, two minor characters
exchange insults, one finding more than a hundred synonyms for
"whore" in English, and the other responding with an equal number of equivalent French epithets. In addition to much humor of a
raucous sort, there is plenty of irony. Whereas the hero of the contemporary historical novel usually proceeds from one sexual adventure to another, Eben, though surrounded by sexual activity
of the most overt and flamboyant kind, remains a virgin. Even
more ironic is the fact that Henry Burlingame, advocate of un-
bounded sexual freedom, is impotent.

The book is to some extent a parody of the eighteenth-century
picaresque novel, although it is obvious that Barth finds the form
congenial. It is also intended to encourage distrust of written history.
(Who, after this, can believe in John Smith's narratives?) As in
the earlier books, Barth emphasizes the relativity of values, and
once more proves himself skeptical of skepticism: is Henry Burlingame's cynicism any more viable than Ebenezer Cooke's innocence?

Barth has called the book "a moral allegory cloaked in terms of colonial history," and the description will serve, though there may be some disagreement as to what the moral is. However that may be, we have a vigorous narrative, high-spirited, often hilarious, and almost always holding the reader's attention. (The book is long, but not much longer than *Tom Jones.*) The creation of the historical background is skillful and convincing, and, just as a historical novel, *The Sot-Weed Factor* is better than most. It is an extraordinary tour de force, and it is more than that; it is Barth's most resourceful attempt thus far to set forth the nature of the human predicament.

Saturday Review
July 3, 1965

4 *Giles Goat-Boy*

In a recent piece in the *New York Times Book Review* Benjamin DeMott commented on what he called the "headlessness" of Mark Twain: "In the world of large theories and thoughts he was a bundle of banal contradictions." In this respect, DeMott continues, Mark Twain was representative of our most admired writers. "Who is unaware," he asks, "that imaginative immediacy, not braininess, is the American thing, our excellence, the wonder of our books? Let it be said—by meanness or by truth—that Anderson, Dreiser, Hemingway, Faulkner, most of the heroic lot, are as men of mind puerile."

DeMott is not disparaging the writings of Mark Twain or of the other authors he names; on the contrary, he expresses hearty admiration of their virtues; but he suggests that intelligence may be a virtue too. Saul Bellow, in his speech accepting his second National Book Award and in other literary comments, has been saying something of the same sort, urging writers to try thinking for a change. Perhaps not many great writers in all literary history have had great intellects, but some have. In a time of confusion such as the present it is not surprising that most novelists and poets not only don't think but believe that thinking is futile. It is not surprising, but it may be dangerous.

John Barth's *Giles Goat-Boy* is, among other things, a philosophical novel. In the present state of our culture, I'm afraid, saying this may scare people away; so I quickly add that the book is funny, bawdy, exciting, and in general entertaining. But it remains true that Barth has made effective use of what he knows about history, politics, science, philosophy, religion, and psychology. In his first novel, *The Floating Opera*, Barth showed an impressive mastery of form, and in his third, *The Sot-Weed Factor,* he unleashed a remarkable inventiveness. The second novel, *End of the Road*, doesn't quite come off, but we can see in all three novels the workings of a lively mind. Now, in *Giles Goat-Boy,* on which he has been working for five or six years, Barth has deliberately set out to make the best possible use of his intellectual faculties.

Giles Goat-Boy is a kind of modern *Pilgrim's Progress*, though many episodes are more reminiscent of Rabelais than of Bunyan. The pilgrim is an unusual figure, a young man who spent his boyhood with a herd of goats. He begins his narrative:

George is my name; my deeds have been heard of in Tower Hall, and my childhood has been chronicled in the *Journal of Experimental Psychology*. I am he that was called in those days Billy Bocksfuss— cruel misnomer. For had I indeed a cloven foot I'd not now hobble upon a stick or need ride pick-a-back to class in humid weather. Aye, it was just for want of a proper hoof that in my fourteenth year I was the kicked instead of the kicker; that I lay crippled on the reeking peat and saw my first love tupped by a brute Angora. Mercy on that buck who butted me from one world to another; whose fell horns turned my sweetheart's fancy, drove me from the pasture, and set me gimping down the road I travel yet. This bare brow, shame of my kidship, he crowned with the shame of men: I bade farewell to my hornless goathood and struck out, a horned human student for Commencement Gate.

George's keeper was "Maximilian Spielman, the great Mathematical Psycho-Proctologist and former Minority Leader in the College Senate." In political disgrace, Max became senior goatherd and acquired not only a fondness for goats but also a high regard: "Der goats is humaner than der men, and der men is goatisher than der goats." (Max's goats are rather like Gulliver's Houyhnhnms.) George's early observations on the differences between human beings and goats, particularly in their sexual behavior, are shrewd as well as funny, and throughout the book he often adopts what he would call the caprine point of view.

After the unfortunate incident with the Angora brute, George's pilgrimage begins, and this makes it necessary for Barth to establish his allegorical framework. The world is a university, with several divisions, of which the West Campus and the East Campus are the most powerful. New Tammany College, to which George is bound, is the most important part of West Campus. The university has experienced two Campus Riots and is now in the midst of the Quiet Riot. In the Second Campus Riot the Bonifacists of Siegfrieder College slaughtered millions of Moishians. The riot ended when New Tammany College used WESCAC to destroy many Amaterus. Max, one of the scientists who created WESCAC, is still full of guilt.

As they proceed towards New Tammany College, Max and George have many adventures. Since George has made up his mind that he wants to be a human being, Max gives him instruction and he learns rapidly. (Among other things, he learns that, as it says in the Founder's Scroll, "self-knowledge is always bad news.") In time George decides that he wants to be not merely a human being but a hero. Indeed, he declares himself a candidate for Grand Tutor—other Grand Tutors having been Moishe (Moses), Enos Enoch (Jesus), Maios (Socrates), Sakhyan (Buddha), and T'ang (Confucius).

In the course of his pilgrimage George encounters various persons who play a part in his subsequent exploits. There is Anastasia, a beautiful and remarkably compliant young woman, whom he "mounts," to use his caprine terminology, as part of a ceremony taking place at a banquet given by her husband. The husband, Stoker, is a satanic figure, who manages the Powerhouse and is sometimes known as "Dean o' Flunks." Eblis Eierkopf is a former Bonifacist—he "didn't care which side he worked for as long as he could have the best laboratories"—and one of the scientists responsible for WESCAC. Reginald Hector, a former Chancellor of New Tammany College, was a leading general in Campus Riot II before he ran for office. Kennard Sear is a psychiatrist who boasts of his successful marriage, based on the principle that anything goes. Peter Greene, a rich businessman, is a master of benevolent platitudes and ruthless deeds. Later on George meets Harold Bray, his rival for the Grand Tutorship. Bray is the most ambiguous of all the characters, but none of them is merely what he seems to be at first glance.

As a candidate for Grand Tutor, George—now calling himself Giles—has to pass a series of tests, like the ordeals so common in legends and fairy tales. At first he gets along swimmingly, but suddenly there is a sharp reversal, with Bray outdoing Giles. The latter then reinterprets his instructions and makes a new start.

The villain of the piece, so to speak, is WESCAC, which is a giant computer but more than that, for it can EAT people (Electroencephalic Amplification and Transmission). In other words, it is the equivalent of the hydrogen bomb, but not merely that. Unless I am mistaken, WESCAC represents technology itself. Max Spielman, though one of the creators of WESCAC, came to fear it when he realized that it was serving its own rather than humanity's purposes. Frightened that EASCAC might overcome WESCAC, the generals gave the latter even more power, so that it became autonomous. Eierkopf invented NOCTIS (Non-Conceptual Thinking and Intuitional Syntheses) and then he and Dr. Sear developed GILES (Grandtutorial Ideal: Laboratory Eugenical Selection) of which

George Goat-Boy was the first and so far only fruit—hence his calling himself Giles.

In the course of his struggle with various persons and with WESCAC itself, Giles learns a series of lessons. Because of Max's teachings, Giles has no trouble in rejecting Eierkopf's faith in the god-like powers of science, and he is untempted by the easy optimism of Chancellor Rexford, which he contrasts with Sophocles's Tragic view of life. At this point, outraged by Rexford's conscience-less compromises and worship of consensus, he demands sharp distinctions: "It's like Stoker, or the Dean o' Flunks, or a terrible disease; if you do business with these things, they always win. Extreme in the mean is what you've got to be, and not compromise even for a second with Flundage, or let opposites get confused. An arch won't do between True and False; they've got to be cut with an edge as sharp as the Infinite Divisor, and separated." Later, however, chastened by failure, he finds a revelation in the words from the Seminar-on-the-Hill: "Passed are the flunked." "Passage was Failure, and Failure Passage; yet Passage was Passage, Failure Failure! Equally true, none was the Answer; the two were not different, neither were they the same; and true and false, and same and different—Unspeakable! Unnamable! Unimaginable!" It is no wonder that he adds, "Surely my mind must crack!" But there are answers after that, and questions after the answers.

Whatever else is true, the book, as I am sure my inadequacies have indicated, is not easy to summarize. A long book, it is full of riches of many sorts. At the beginning, for example, there is an elaborate hocus-pocus about the manuscript, involving amusing reports by various editors. When George goes to see *Taliped Decanus,* Barth provides an up-to-date translation-paraphrase-parody of *Oedipus Rex*. The satire slashes this way and that. Chancellor Hector sounds a good deal like President Eisenhower, and Chancellor Rexford not unlike President Johnson. Peter Greene carries the lingo of Madison Avenue to a ludicrous extreme: "No gosh durn good," he says. "What I mean, Truth-Beauty-and-Good-nesswise, y'know." He says of The Living Sakhyan: "Man, he's the gosh-durn most, what I mean wisewise." Dr. Sear, the permissive psychiatrist, says, "I do despise myself, of course. What other feeling is there, for a man both intelligent and honest? I can't take anybody seriously who doesn't loathe himself."

As an allegory, the book is as ambitious as Herman Melville's *Mardi* and considerably more coherent. At the center, of course, is the Quiet Riot (Cold War), with both the Student Unionists (Communists) and the Informationalists (professed believers in democracy) behaving ridiculously and risking the destruction of the entire university. Underlying this conflict is the problem of technology, the problem of whether the machine is servant or master of men. And underlying that problem are great philosophical issues concerning the nature of man and the nature of the cosmos. The literature of Greece and Rome, the world's great religions, and the embattled philosophies, past and present, are all brought into the story of the progress—if it can be called progress—of this strange pilgrim.

At the outset Max explains to Bill—later George, later Giles— why he brought him up as a goat:

Every day I looked at the human school-kids that visited the barns; they were good children, pretty children, full of passions and curiosity: I'd ask one who it was, and he'd say, "I'm Johnny So-and-So, and my daddy's a gunner in the NTC Navy, and when I grow up I'm going to be a famous scientist and EAT the Nikolayans." Then I'd ask Brickett Ranunculus, that was just a young buck then, "Who are you?" and he'd twitch one ear and go on eating his hay. There it was, Bill. On one side the Nine Symphonies and the Twelve-Term Riot; Enos Enoch and the Bonifacists! On the other side, Brickett Ranunculus eating his mash and not even knowing there's such a thing as knowledge. I'd watch you frisking with Mary's kids, that never were going to hear what true and false is, and then I'd look at the wretchedest man on the campus, that wrote *The Theory of the University* and loves every student in it, but killed ten thousand with a single Brainwave! (Max is referring to himself.) So! Well! I decided my Bill had better be a goat, for his own good, he should never have to wonder who he is!

But Bill chooses to be a man, faces the human predicament, and struggles to deal with it in a decisive way. If I say that Barth has used his intellect, it is not because I am ready to accept all his answers—I'm not even sure what some of them are—but because I think he has dared to ask himself the right questions. In his earlier work, especially *The Sot-Weed Factor*, he demonstrated that he had great stylistic resources. Now he has employed all his literary powers in a work on a grand scale, a highly ambitious attempt to show his readers man and man's fate as he understands them.

I have necessarily given only a partial account of the book. There can be endless speculation as to who represents whom and what represents what. Barth knows that, as the saying goes, one can't expect an allegory to walk on all four legs; his is sometimes a cripple and sometimes a centipede. If the book is as good as I believe, literary experts will be writing exegeses and providing footnotes for years to come. In the meantime I trust it will be read and enjoyed. Sometimes, as Giles discovers, it is difficult to distinguish between failure and success. If this isn't a great success, as at the moment I think, it is a great failure. One way or the other, there is greatness in it.

Saturday Review
August 6, 1966

5 *Lost in the Funhouse*

In an essay called, *The Literature of Exhaustion,* which appeared in the *Atlantic Monthly* a year or so ago, John Barth wrote: "I sympathize with a remark attributed to Saul Bellow, that to be technically up to date is the least important attribute of a writer, though I would have to add that this least important attribute may be nevertheless essential. In any case, to be technically out of date is likely to be a genuine defect. . . . A good many current novelists write turn-of-the-century-type novels, only in more or less mid-twentieth-century language and about contemporary people and topics; this makes them considerably less interesting (to me) than excellent writers who are also technically contemporary; Joyce and Kafka, for instance, in their time, and in ours Samuel Beckett and Jorge Luis Borges."

As all his novels show, particularly his most recent, *Giles Goat-Boy,* John Barth does not intend to be technically out of date if he can help it, and he is always trying to do something new and different. In *Lost in the Funhouse,* a collection of short stories and other pieces, a sequence of three stories points out the direction in which his mind is developing. All three are concerned with a boy named Ambrose, who probably bears a resemblance to the author.

The earliest of the stories, "Ambrose His Mark," is a little in the how-quaint-was-my-family tradition, though it is a superior example of the genre. The central figure is Ambrose's mother—he is an infant at the time—and he tells what happened when, in the vicinity of some bee hives, she exposed her breasts in order to nurse him. The story is deftly and amusingly written, but it is not, in Barth's meaning of the term, up to date.

The second story, "Water-Message," written in the third person, is also essentially conventional, although it gains an added dimension by emphasizing the self-dramatizing day dreams of Ambrose, who is now pre-adolescent.

In the third story, which gives the volume its title, the basic situation is simple enough: Ambrose, now thirteen, goes to Ocean City with his mother and father, his brother, and a girl in whom both he and the brother are interested; he takes a wrong turn in the funhouse, but nothing much happens. The whole point of the story is in the telling. The author constantly interrupts his narrative by talking about the proper way in which to tell such a story—what devices to select, what words to use. "Plush upholstery prickles uncomfortably through gabardine slacks in the July sun. The function of the beginning of a story is to introduce the principal characters, establish their initial relationships, set the scene for the main action, expose the background of the situation if necessary, plant motifs and foreshadowings where appropriate, and initiate the first complication or whatever of the 'rising action.'" Furthermore, thirteen-year-old Ambrose himself has the temperament of a writer, and he thinks about his experiences as if they were in a piece of fiction: "Strive as he might to be transported, he heard his mind take notes upon the scene: This is what they call passion. I am experiencing it." Thus Ambrose's adventures, real and imagined, are looked at from three points of view, and the theme is not what happened in the funhouse but what the mind, at various times, makes of what happened.

Like several of his contemporaries, Barth has tried to renew the art of fiction by making use of allegory, fantasy, and symbol. One of the stories in the volume, "Night-Sea Journey," is an allegory of a somber sort. Another, "Petition," makes farcical use of the idea of Siamese twins in order to say something about dual personality. There are other and wilder experiments. "'Glossolalia,'" Barth says in a note, "will make no sense unless heard in live or recorded voices, male and female, or read as if so heard; 'Echo' is intended for monophonic authorial recording, either disc or tape; 'Autobiography,' for monophonic tape and visible but silent author . . . 'Title' makes somewhat separate but equally valid senses in several media; print, monophonic recorded authorial voice, stereophonic ditto in dialogue with itself, live authorial voice, live ditto in dialogue with monophonic ditto aforementioned." I am not prepared to say how serious Barth is about all this.

The two pieces I like best are "Menelaiad" and "Anonymiad." In the essay from which I have quoted, Barth discusses Jorge Luis Borges's way of dealing with classic writers. One of the most successful experiments in *Giles Goat-Boy* is a paraphrase in modern slang of Sophocles's *Oedipus the King*. "Menelaiad" is a kind of rewriting of Book IV of the *Odyssey*. The crux of the matter is Menelaus's struggle with Proteus, about which, as Barth notes in the essay, Borges had commented. The problem is the problem of identity, and, as Barth piles confusion upon confusion, it becomes more and more difficult to grasp his meaning. Barth pretends to make things simpler by his use of quotation marks:

" ' "Nothing for it but to do as Eidothia'd bid me," ' " I say to myself I told Telemachus I sighed to Helen.

Barth finally reaches five marks—" ' " ' "In the horse's bowel" ' " ' "—but I won't go into that. We have here a kind of game, like William Gass's twenty-seven asterisks or a sentence I have quoted from Anthony Burgess's *Enderby*: "She breathed on him (though a young lady should not eat, because of the known redolence of onions, onions) onions." I am willing to give all three authors credit for a serious intent underlying the buffoonery.

My inclination is to accept Saul Bellow's view that a writer shouldn't worry too much as to whether he's up to date or not. Many a writer has been ruined by the belief that he must be original at all costs, and at this moment all the arts seem to be threatened by the frantic demand for novelty. If, however, we can't expect much from Andy Warhol and the disciples of Marshall McLuhan, we shouldn't overlook such experimental writers as Gass and Barth and Burgess, who are dedicated and highly talented. In literature as in music and painting, the serious practitioner masters the conventional forms before he engages in the innovation. Barth has proved again and again that he can equal the traditionalists at their own game, and thus he has won the right to be different. When I finished reading *Giles Goat-Boy*, I was embarrassed by the necessity for immediately forming a judgment; I needed time, I felt, to know what I thought. Now, two years later, I am sure that it is one of the most important novels of our time. *Lost in the Funhouse*, though some of its experiments don't seem to be getting anywhere, is further evidence that Barth has a first-rate imagination.

Saturday Review
September 28, 1968

Afterword

John Barth had made an impressive start as a novelist before I caught up with him, but that gave me a chance to read his first three novels one after the other, an impressive experience. With his fourth novel, *Giles Goat-Boy,* he set out to write a philosophical allegory of the most ambitious sort. A book that demands a careful, thoughtful reading, it sold rather well—presumably because of a Rabelaisian quality—but I doubt that everyone who bought it read and understood it. After the critics have analyzed it carefully, as they probably are doing right now, it may find a public that is up to it.

The modern novelist, as a general rule, refuses to repeat himself. Whether this is a sound, productive way of feeling about fiction may be argued, but to many novelists—and a certain number of critics as well—it seems perfectly clear that one can only make progress by being different. As his collection of shorter pieces, *Lost in the Funhouse,* shows, Barth is continuing to experiment. Where his experimentation may lead him is anybody's guess—to some new literary height or off the deep end—but he has some fine work already to his credit, and my hunch is that there will be a good deal more before he is finished.

NORMAN MAILER

Foreword

It sometimes sems that Mailer has left his mark on this literary era by virtue of his almost boundless energy rather than because of his talents as a writer. That energy has not only driven him from one literary experiment to another but has impelled him into such activities as producing motion pictures, leading political protests, and running for office. Many of his faults seem to result from the fact that he is always trying to do too much, but it is also true that his immersion in contemporary life is a source of strength and may turn out to be the foundation on which his reputation will rest.

As a reviewer, I caught up with Mailer in mid-career. The great success of his first novel, *The Naked and the Dead,* had thrown him off balance, as he has admitted, but, instead of trying to repeat that first success, he attempted a completely different kind of novel in *Barbary Shore* and something quite different from that in *The Deer Park*. Dissatisfied with both books, he began writing short pieces on all sorts of subjects, and he brought together a collection of these in *Advertisements for Myself*. Since then he has published more of what I once called "trivia and tripe." He also published a novel, *An American Dream,* that roused great controversy. To me much of it seems ridiculous, but at worst it is an interesting failure.

As my review of them shows, I am more impressed by the two books of personal-political journalism, *Armies of the Night* and *Miami.* Perhaps this is the genre to which he should devote himself. But whether he should or not, I am willing to bet that he won't; he will be off and away, whither bound I haven't the least idea.

1 *Advertisements for Myself*

If anyone wants to make a study of Norman Mailer, most of the relevant documents are available in *Advertisements for Myself*. The book contains short stories, extracts from two of his three published novels, articles on political and literary matters, some reviews (unfavorable) of his novels, columns written for the *Village Voice*, transcripts of interviews, letters to newspapers, some verse, a portion of a play, two extracts from a work in progress, and sundry odds and ends. Along with all this there is a running commentary in which, with a great show of candor, Mailer tells how and why he wrote the pieces and what he now thinks of them. The result is a volume to gratify the student, although the general reader will not be blamed for skipping.

What the student is likely to conclude is that the crucial fact in Mailer's life was his early success. *The Naked and the Dead*, published in 1948, when he was twenty-five, was given high praise, which it deserved in spite of large and obvious faults, and it had a vast sale. Up to then he had been simply a moderately talented young man, ambitious but no more ambitious than many another, and suddenly he was a major literary figure. What the book's reception did to him Mailer today appreciates:

Naturally, I was blasted a considerable distance away from dead center by the size of its success, and I spent the next few years trying to gobble up the experiences of a victorious man when I was still no man at all, and had no real gift for enjoying life. . . . I was prominent and empty, and I had to begin life again.

The success of *The Naked and the Dead* was followed by the failure of *Barbary Shore*. The reviewers jumped on it hard, and Mailer himself now admits that it has its shortcomings, although he obviously feels a certain tenderness towards it. What the reviewers might have recognized, but by and large didn't, is that *Barbary Shore* is an honorable failure, an attempt to do something different from *The Naked and the Dead* and more difficult.

If success had disorganized Mailer, failure did nothing to restore his balance, and, as he records, the years after *Barbary Shore* were bad years. In time, however, he hit upon a grand scheme for a series of eight novels and out of this came *The Deer Park*. The novel sold well, presumably because word got around that it was dirty, but most of the critics were against it. Reading his account in *Advertisements* of the way it was written, I wonder that it isn't worse than it is, but it is bad enough. Yet Mailer, measuring it, as writers will do, in terms of the agony it had cost him, thought of it as his masterpiece, and the fact that it was not recognized as such was a further blow to his spirit.

From his college years on, Mailer has been sympathetic to radical causes, and it has always seemed to me that he might have been a happier man if he had come to maturity in the Thirties. As matters stand, his radicalism has been unfocused, and although his interest in politics is admirable in this nonpolitical era, his political writings are not particularly cogent. Moreover, as he has become embittered as a writer, his rebelliousness has become more explicitly personal. It is not altogether surprising, therefore, that this advocate of democratic socialism and Marxian socialism and anarchism (he seems to use the three terms interchangeably) is also a proponent of Hip. Although he is still interested in the theory of surplus value, he is more interested in the effects of marijuana.

As a hipster, Mailer feels that it is his duty to shock the Squares, and it is in this mood that much of the recent material in *Advertisements* has been written. He uses four-letter words for their shock effect, just as little boys do, and he employs other devices of the very young. He goes out of his way to be rude to his elders and betters, for instance Hemingway and Faulkner. He flexes his muscles in competition with his contemporaries: there is an essay, apparently written for this volume, called "Evaluations—Quick and Expensive Comments on the Talent in the Room," which deals, mostly in offensive terms, with other American writers. ("So far as I know," Mailer smugly observes, "this is the first time any of us had talked out in public about his competitors with the same words one might use in the living room.")

So Mailer throws his weight around. He is opinionated and arrogant, and, as became apparent when he was writing a column for the *Village Voice* in 1956, he expects to be listened to whenever he opens his mouth. (He has not only preserved his columns in this volume; he has preserved the silly letters, pro and con, they evoked.) At the same time he is full of self-pity: "Fitzgerald was an indifferent caretaker of his talent, and I have been a cheap gambler with mine." In short, as he reveals himself in this volume, he is not a particularly appealing person.

But we have to remind ourselves that great works of art have been created by persons quite as unattractive as Norman Mailer. That he hopes to achieve greatness he makes clear:

> For if I have one ambition above all others, it is to write a novel which Dostoevsky and Marx; Joyce and Freud; Stendhal, Tolstoy, Proust, and Spengler; Faulkner, and even old mouldering Hemingway might come to read, for it would carry what they had to tell another part of the way.

His aspirations are admirable, and I have no doubt that, in spite of his lapses into juvenility, he is completely serious. What are his chances? The evidence to be found in this book, particularly in the two extracts from the work in progress, is inconclusive. One of the extracts is a story called "The Time of Her Time," a singularly ugly piece of writing whose only distinction is that it describes the sexual act in more detail than any piece of fiction I have read. What Mailer achieves with his physiological detail, however, is merely the coldness of a medical textbook; of sex as an approach to "the paradise of limitless energy and perception," to borrow a phrase he uses elsewhere, there is not the slightest suggestion.

On the other hand, the second extract, called "Advertisement for Myself on the Way Out," which is the prologue to the novel on which he is working, has a wild imaginativeness that engages the reader. This is the quality that made *Barbary Shore* seem hopeful in spite of its faults, that redeemed portions of *The Deer Park*. Here is a hint of the kind of apocalyptic novel that, if he could write it, would carry Mailer to the height to which he aspires. His vision of life, which so often seems dim, is at least his own, and when it comes clear, it is dazzling and horrible. I'm not at all sure he can do what he wants to do, but perhaps he can, and, in any case, I wish he would get about it instead of frittering away his time.

Saturday Review
November 7, 1959

2 *An American Dream*

Ever since the publication of his first novel, *The Naked and the Dead*, in 1948, Norman Mailer has been a figure of importance on the American literary scene. The novel had a strong impact when it was published and has lasted well; in spite of its indebtedness to Dos Passos and Hemingway and in spite of some clumsiness, it stands as the best American novel about World War II and as the most remarkable exhibition in recent times of the naturalistic technique. Since its appearance, however, Mailer's work has received rather more condemnation than approval. *Barbary Shore* was generally regarded as an interesting and—because Mailer was not content to repeat himself—an honorable failure, but a failure. Parts of *The Deer Park* were greatly admired, but as a whole it was not a success. And since that novel was published, nearly ten years ago, we have had only collections of odds and ends, of which *Advertisements for Myself* was the most notable.

However, spotty as his career has been, Mailer's name is almost always mentioned when there is talk about American literature since the war. Some people will say that this is because of his gift for getting his name before the public in nonliterary as well as literary contexts, and it is true that he has made more headlines than most of his contemporaries. But, on the other hand, he continues to be taken seriously by persons whose judgments have to be respected—for instance, Diana Trilling, who wrote an essay about him in *The Living Present*. Mailer's new novel, *An American Dream*, has stirred up talk during its appearance as a serial in *Esquire*, and one can predict that quantities of words are going to be spent on it in the weeks to come.

This, it should be pointed out, is not the big novel that, in *Advertisements for Myself*, Mailer announced he was writing. It seems, on the contrary, to be a book that he conceived and executed on the spur of the moment. At the end he dates it, "September 1963–October 1964." The jacket indicates that serial publication had begun in *Esquire* before the book was finished: "Mailer undertook to write *An American Dream* under the same conditions of serial deadline that Conrad, Dickens and Dostoevsky met in their day." (That, I think, is the extent of the resemblance between this work and the work of the aforementioned authors.)

The only way to suggest the quality of the novel is to summarize it at some length. This is how it begins: "I met Jack Kennedy in November, 1946. We were both war heroes, and both of us had just been elected to Congress. We went out one night on a double date and it turned out to be a fair evening for me. I seduced a girl who would have been bored by a diamond as big as the Ritz." The narrator is named Stephen Richard Rojack, and the girl is called Deborah Caughlin Mangaravidi Kelly. President Kennedy does not play much of a part in the novel, though he is mentioned later, but the girl does, and so does the business of being a war hero. Rojack quickly goes on to tell how he killed four Germans in Italy, an occurrence that left an enduring mark on his psyche.

Rojack, we learn, was graduated from Harvard summa cum laude, became a hero, went to Congress. Deciding he was not made for politics, he committed political suicide by supporting Henry Wallace in 1948. After that he became "a professor of existential psychology" at a university in New York City, wrote a book, and achieved success on a television program. He married Deborah seven years after he seduced her, but, at the time the novel begins, they are separated.

The novel, according to the jacket, covers a period of thirty-two hours. At the outset Rojack, suffering from what is no doubt existential nausea, contemplates suicide, but instead of killing himself, he goes to see his wife, whom he strangles. (This is the cliff-hanging climax of the first installment.) After making love, in a rather eccentric fashion, described in detail, to his wife's maid, he throws his wife's body out the window onto the East River Drive. He makes love to the maid again, though rather hurriedly this time, and descends to the street, where he is taken in charge by the police. His story, of course, is that his wife jumped.

Released by the police because of some mysterious influence, Rojack immediately goes to a joint to see a singer named Cherry, who, along with some gangsters, was involved in the traffic jam that took place when Deborah's body hit the pavement. After defying her former lover, a prizefighter, he takes her to her apartment on the East Side and, one may be sure, makes love to her.

The next day, after losing both his television job and his teaching job, he keeps an appointment with the police. Although the evidence against him seems strong, he is again released. He returns to Cherry's bed, and in due season he hears her story. She was at one time the mistress of a mysterious millionaire with underground connections, who turns out to be none other than Barney Kelly, father of Rojack's late wife. More recently she has been the mistress of a Negro singer, Shago Martin, who comes to pay a call and is thrown downstairs by Rojack.

Rojack has one more appointment, with his father-in-law, Kelly. He sees Deirdre, Deborah's daughter, presumably by her first husband, a child of whom he is fond. While he is talking with Kelly, the phone rings, "It was Jack," Kelly says. "He said to send you his regards and commiserations." After a conversation in which it appears that the situation may have international implications, Kelly reveals that Deirdre is in fact his daughter. (The novel would obviously be incomplete without a touch of incest.) There is another business of near-suicide, after which we have a report of the murder of Shago Martin, and then Rojack arrives at Cherry's apartment just in time to hear her dying words.

I hope it is clear that not for a moment can the novel be taken seriously as a portrayal of life in America—or anywhere else. This is the make-believe world of Ian Fleming and Mickey Spillane. However, Mailer has a streak of pretentiousness that keeps the book from being the good dirty fun that Fleming's books, if not Spillane's, often are.

I should like to believe that the novel is a hoax, and perhaps to some extent it is. Look at the title. What do Americans dream about? Sex and violence—as television producers and magazine publishers well know. So here, it may be argued, we have sex and violence reduced ad absurdum if not ad nauseam. In other words, the book may be a satire, an expression of moral indignation.

What I see as the great obstacle to the acceptance of this theory is the fact that in other works Mailer has spoken in favor of sex, in all forms, and in as great a quantity as possible. He also has sometimes seemed to regard violence as quite a good thing. Mrs. Trilling quotes him as having said that a murder might redeem the murderer: ". . . in the act of killing, in this terribly private moment, the brute feels a moment of tenderness, for the first time perhaps in all his experience. What has happened is that the killer is becoming a little more possible, a little bit more ready to love someone." I cannot see that the assorted murders in *An American*

Dream have this redemptive quality, although perhaps that is what Mailer meant to convey.

But if one rejects the theory that the novel is a hoax, one faces a distressing alternative. If one believes that Mailer intended *An American Dream* to be taken seriously, one has to conclude that he has gone to pieces as a writer. The least one can say for the earlier novels is that he tried hard, and in *Advertisements for Myself* he expressed the highest ambitions for his future work. *An American Dream,* however, seems to be something that he dashed off in spare moments. He accepted the challenge of *Esquire* and produced his monthly installments, ending each in the tradition of *The Perils of Pauline.* If the book is not a joke, a bad joke, it is something worse.

The absurdity of the book is not limited to the plot. Stephen Richard Rojack is a kind of superman, not only a high-powered intellectual but also a handy man in a fight. Mailer identifies himself with Rojack so closely that the poor professor is allowed to have no reality. We don't believe in him as a Congressman or as a professor or even as a lover; he exists simply as a projection of Norman Mailer's fantasies about himself. He is Mailer, as Mailer would like to be. The other characters are but dummies for Mailer-Rojack to manipulate.

The writing is the sloppiest Mailer has ever done. Here is a passage to suggest a tense moment: "I didn't realize until I reached the street that I had been holding my breath. My uneasiness was almost tangible now; I could feel some sullen air of calm, exactly that torporous calm which comes before a hurricane. It was nearly dark outside. I would be late, but I had to walk to the precinct, I had the conviction that if I entered a taxi there would be an accident." (Rojack is given to premonitions of this sort.) Here is a tender passage: "Once, in a rainstorm, I witnessed the creation of a rivulet. The water had come down, the stream had begun in a hollow of earth the size of a leaf. Then it filled and began to flow. The rivulet rolled down the hill between some stalks of grass and weed, it moved in spurts, down the fall of a ledge, down to a brook. It did not know it was not a river. That was how the tears went down Cherry's face." There are also some fancy passages about smell, Mailer having, it appears, a remarkable nose.

In the essay to which I have alluded, Mrs. Trilling wrote: "Where do we, where shall we, where can we derive our moral sanctions: from a failing tradition or from the wild, free impulses of our racial infancy, from the ego or the id? This is the ultimate pressing question of our time, separating our historical period from any that came before it. And because Mailer not only knows the full force of the question but passionately devotes himself to its answer, he transcends the follies and excesses which attend Hipsterism and claims his place in the forefront of modern writers." She also wrote: "Intense as his literary dedication unquestionably is, his religious mission is now infinitely more compelling. Just as he writes in order to preach the word of God, he acts in order to attain to God, by whatever thorny path. And when he invites us to follow his example he literally means us to join a religious crusade."

I wonder what Mrs. Trilling makes of *An American Dream*. It is possible, I suppose, to regard it as a momentary lapse and to believe that Mailer will go on to do work that will justify and even enhance his reputation. But it seems to me to represent such a failure of critical judgment that I cannot lightly dismiss it. It makes me wonder how much longer Mailer will hold "his place in the forefront of modern writers."

Saturday Review
March 20, 1965

3 *Why Are We in Vietnam?*

In his introduction to *Advertisements for Myself,* a miscellany published in 1959, Norman Mailer wrote: "Like many another vain, empty, and bullying body of our time, I have been running for President these last ten years in the privacy of my mind, and it occurs to me that I am less close now than when I began . . . The sour truth is that I am imprisoned with a perception which will settle for nothing less than making a revolution in the consciousness of our time. Whether rightly or wrongly, it is then obvious that I would go so far as to think it is my present and future work which will have the deepest influence of any work being done by an American novelist in these years."

These are lines that I reread at the present moment with wry amusement. Mailer was deliberately echoing the remark that Stephen Dedalus makes at the end of *Portrait of the Artist as a Young Man*: "I go forth . . . to forge in the smithy of my soul the uncreated conscience of my race." Stephen Dedalus, insofar as he is to be identified with James Joyce, did this. Norman Mailer hasn't done it, so far. He hasn't been able to write the kind of novel that would have the influence he desires, and that is probably why he has spent such a large part of his enormous energies in commenting on everything under the sun. He has produced two volumes of such commentaries since *Advertisements for Myself,* as well as a collection of what purport to be poems and a dramatic version of *The Deer Park*. He has also published two novels, *An American Dream* and now *Why Are We in Vietnam?* Opinions differ about both books, but I wonder whether Mailer's most bedazzled admirers would argue that either of them is likely to have a deep and enduring influence on American fiction.

I suggested that *An American Dream* was a hoax, and, in view of what is known about Mailer's boisterous sense of humor, that seems to me a reasonable and even friendly way of explaining why he published such an absurd and badly written book. Mailer, however, rejects this interpretation, preferring to describe the novel as a potboiler. *Why Are We in Vietnam?* strikes me not as a hoax but as a lark, a book that Mailer, in his perhaps perverse way, got a kick out of writing.

It is a portrait of a Texas millionaire, Rusty Jethroe, who is, I gather from the title, to be regarded as typical of other Texas millionaires, including the President of the United States. We are shown Rusty while he is on a hunt for grizzly bears in Alaska, an expedition that displays his extravagance, his domineering nature, his intense competitiveness, and his basic dishonesty.

The story is told by Rusty's son, Ranald, who usually refers to himself as D. J. D. J., who was sixteen when he accompanied his father on the bear hunt, is supposed to be eighteen at the time he sets the story down. He is in some ways a precocious youth, well acquainted with the works of James Joyce and William Burroughs, and in his own mind an authority on the psychology and psychopathology of sex.

D. J.'s style is an attempt not so much to imitate as to outdo the writing of the men he admires. If the scholars with computers ever get around to doing a word count on this book they will conclude, I am confident, that the proportion of the once forbidden Anglo-Saxon monosyllables to other and more conventional words sets a record. If I didn't hesitate to insult Mailer by imputing to him a moral purpose, I might suggest that he had set out to put an end to the literary use of four-letter words by making the reader everlastingly tired of them.

When, after wallowing through too many pages of D. J.'s adolescent reflections, we come to the hunt itself, interest picks up a little. Mailer, who at this point seems to be competing with Hemingway, writes in a knowing fashion about guns, the Alaskan terrain, and the value of helicopters to rich sportsmen. The killing of a bear by Rusty and D. J. is effectively described, and Rusty's seizure of the credit exposes his character at its lowest. It is after that that D. J. and his friend Tex run away from the expedition. D. J. tells about Tex's father, a man Dr. Kinsey should have known, and then describes, of all things, a mystical experience enjoyed by the boys under the Northern sky. (This is probably to show that he can do a Faulkner bit; cf. "The Bear.") Then D. J. and Tex, two years later, are at a big dinner party in Dallas, being given in their honor because they are leaving for Vietnam.

How much of this we are supposed to take seriously I haven't the least idea. Certainly Rusty is a heel—to use a word Mailer would scorn—and he is exposed as such in the eyes of his son, who may previously have had some lingering admiration for his old man. If such men rule the country, Mailer seems to be intimating, it is no wonder we are involved in a stupid and evil war. As for D. J., he suggests at some point that he is an uninhibited Holden Caulfield. To me he is a curious specimen of non-reality that Mailer dreamed up in the interest of what he considers good dirty fun.

Why do we—why do I—go on bothering with Norman Mailer? Not merely because he once had talent, but because he still has it. There are passages in this book that nobody else could have written —as well as passages that, I hope, nobody else would have written. It is true that there is an air of extemporization about even the good passages, but sometimes, when his Joycean puns are going well or he is taking off the idiom of business and government, Mailer is brilliant. The descriptive passages, too, though some of them are satirically purple, at times come off remarkably well. Mailer has grown a great deal in power of language since he wrote *The Naked and the Dead.*

Why, then, has he been writing trivia and tripe for the past ten years or more? The answer seems to be implied in the passage I quoted at the beginning. After the success, critical and financial, of *The Naked and the Dead,* he felt that he had been, so to speak, nominated for the presidency. He wanted to be and believed that he could be not only the best novelist of his generation but a decisive influence on generations to come. He didn't make it with *Barbary Shore* or *The Deer Park,* and he wasn't able to complete the major novel that he talked about and gave extracts from in *Advertisements for Myself.* So he has devoted himself to nonliterary matters and to fiction that can hardly be taken seriously. If he had been able and willing to do the best he could, without worrying about being President, he might have made a contribution to American letters commensurate with his abilities.

Saturday Review
September 16, 1967

4 *Armies of the Night*

In its list of ten books "of particular significance and excellence in 1968," the *New York Times Book Review* names only one novel, *The First Circle,* by Aleksandr Solzhenitsyn, which it describes as "nineteenth-century in its comprehensive, leisurely grandeur." *Holiday* magazine, on the other hand, in its quest for the worst book of the year, offers three novels as candidates: Gore Vidal's *Myra Breckenridge,* Allen Drury's *Preserve and Protect,* and Drew Pearson's *The Senator.* (*Holiday* observes: "Mr. Pearson's name appears on the book but Mr. (Gerald) Green says he wrote it, a confession that surely marks Mr. Green as the gamest author of the year.") I have read none of these, but I am willing to take *Holiday*'s word for their badness. If, however, I hadn't read James Baldwin's *Tell Me How Long the Train's Been Gone,* I should have thought the editors had lost their minds when they named it as their award winner. Alas, no!

All this, I concede, offers ammunition to my old enemies, the people who say the novel is dying if not dead. I will make an even more generous concession: Norman Mailer's *The Armies of the Night* interested me as much as any novel I have read this year. Furthermore, both that work and its companion piece of nonfiction, *Miami and the Siege of Chicago,* seem to me to have more literary merit than either *An American Dream,* or *Why Are We in Vietnam?*

Before I go on to talk about Mailer's nonfiction, I ought to point out that not all critics have as low an opinion as I of his recent fiction. In an article in a scholarly journal, *Novel: A Forum on Fiction,* for fall 1968, Robert Langbaum praises both *Dream* and *Vietnam* as examples of what he calls "hallucinated realism." He gives a coherent account of the first, which is in itself a considerable achievement, and I think he probably is close to Mailer's intention. When, however, he argues that Mailer succeeded in doing what he wanted to do, I cannot go along with him. He insists, for instance, that Rojack's walk around the parapet is "the high point of the novel, a triumph of narration." He writes: "Because we sweat it out with Rojack as wind, rain, and psychologically sensed supernatural forces (Deborah's hands, for example) threaten to dislodge him, we believe in the importance of this ordeal, that it is his Purgatory, his penance and way to salvation." I believe nothing of the sort. I believe that this is one of many unconvincing and ridiculous scenes in a preposterous book.

Even Langbaum cannot make sense of *Why Are We in Vietnam?* although he tries hard. "The wit is not cerebral," he grants; "it is the expression of physical exuberance, and employs the word 'ass' as an all-purpose intensifier." (This seems a curious non sequitur.) He admits that the obscenities are tiresome, but thinks they are "necessary for the giant qualities Mailer wants to portray." He summarizes his judgment in this fashion: "Mailer's psychological and social intelligence combines in these two novels with a wild, fantastic, unpredictable quality of mind that touches raw nerves in us because it is so alive." That Mailer has great literary gifts I affirmed in my review of *Vietnam*. That they find adequate expression in either of these novels I do not believe.

My dissatisfaction with Mailer's recent fiction tempers any regret I might otherwise feel as a result of his present abandonment of the novel. I think it is a good thing—for him and for us. Langbaum quotes a statement Mailer made in 1965: "The realistic literature had never caught up with the rate of change in American life, indeed it had fallen further behind, and the novel gave up any desire to be a creation equal to the phenomenon of the country itself: it settled for being a metaphor." Whether it is the proper function of the novel to keep abreast of change may be argued, but that it hasn't kept up is perfectly obvious. If keeping up is what Mailer wanted to do, he was right to turn to journalism.

The subtitle of *Armies of the Night*—*History as a Novel; the Novel as History*—has no more significance than Truman Capote's talk about "the non-fiction novel." What distinguishes the book from most, though by no means all, journalism is that it contains both subjective and objective reporting. Mailer was in Washington as a participant in the peace demonstration he describes, and he tells not only what happened but also what he thought and felt while it was happening. An egoist in the extreme, he has none of the usual kind of self-protective vanity, and he writes candidly about his various shortcomings. Although there is some mawkish writing and a good deal of windy theorizing, the book does give the reader a feeling for a crucial happening in American history, and I think the *Times* was right in listing it among its significant and excellent ten.

The difference between *Armies of the Night* and *Miami and the Siege of Chicago* is indicated in the fact that in the first the protagonist is called "Mailer" and in the second "the reporter." In the account of the Republican Convention Mailer is merely a journalist, a good one but no better than many others doing a job in Miami. In talking about Chicago he speaks more directly for and about himself, but most of the time there is a considerable distance between him and the events he is describing. But better this sort of competent and lively journalism than a messed-up novel such as *Why Are We in Vietnam?*

I happened to meet a college senior, one with literary hopes and ambitions, just after he had finished reading the portion of Mailer's report on the conventions that appeared in *Harper's*. "This is really it," he said excitedly. "More and more novelists are going to write this sort of thing. I see it coming." Very possibly he's right. If a personal sort of journalism can make something of aspects of contemporary life that won't lend themselves to orthodox fictional treatment, that's fine.

I am not convinced, however, that it is time to bury the novel. If there are things journalism can do and the novel can't, there are plenty of things that are beyond the grasp of journalism. The trouble with being up to date is that one gets out of date so soon. If *An American Dream* had done what Professor Langbaum thinks it did—if, that is, it had really created an American myth—it would make *Armies of the Night* look like an item on page 137 of the Sunday *Times*. If fewer good novels were published in 1968 than in 1967 or 1925 or whenever, that is of no real significance. If one good novel appears in a decade, that proves the novel is alive. And if, meanwhile, writers who haven't the talent or, as seems to be Mailer's situation, the patience to create good novels can find something else useful to do, so much the better.

Saturday Review
December 28, 1968